RAID

ON

CABANATUAN

Forrest Bryant Johnson

Registration # 204|480

Limited / First Edition

A Thousand Autumns Press

Las Vegas, Nevada

RAID ON CABANATUAN

Copyright 1978, 1988

Forrest Bryant Johnson

Printed in the United States of America.

A THOUSAND AUTUMNS PRESS

760 Hermosa Palms Ave.

Las Vegas, Nevada 89123 U.S.A.

Publishing Division

Chiaki Enterprises International

ISBN : 0-929032-01-2

Library of Congress Catalog Card Number : 88-90156

DEDICATION

In 1976, a former Filipino Guerrilla Commander Major Juan Pajota came to America to file for citizenship in the country whose Constitution he had once sworn to defend. He qualified through participation in World War II as a member of the U.S. Army, but citizenship for Filipino veterans had been blocked in Federal Court. Late in 1977, the case was resolved in favor of the veterans. Major Pajota died a few days before he could see his lifelong dream to become an American fulfilled. To Major Pajota and the other Allied soldiers who risked their lives during the Raid on Japanese POW Camp Cabanatuan, this book is most gratefully dedicated.

PREFACE

To fully comprehend the significance of the RAID ON CABANATUAN, it will be necessary to start where it all began . . . the collapse of the American Army in the Philippines in 1942. This book is not intended to be a war report although it includes detailed accounts of the fighting. Rather, it is the story of people jerked from a normal rountine and placed in a hostile enviroment called battle.

The story of a battle should be a story of individuals. When the plans of high command are reduced to a common element that element is the individual soldier who must fight for his survival as much as he fights for his unit, country, God, or Emperor. War, I propose, is a personal thing, relative to the individual warrior. As he battles on a little piece of earth to accomplish his mission, a battle also wages within a more compact area . . . his mind.

Usually, armies are created as a deterrent to preserve peace or to set about the task of destroying other armies.

The interesting fact about this story is that one army felt it necessary to divert a unit, support it, and give it a primary objective of saving rather than destroying. In the rush to shorten World War II, with the liberation pandemonium in the Phillippines in 1945, what matter of army assigns priorty to saving the lives of a few hundred men who undoubtedly were of no combat value? If battle is the story of individuals, then, is there a difference between two armies . . . one believing in the significant worth of its men and one which does not?

Or is it simply the manner in which a country measures the indiviual's worth?

RAID ON CABANATUAN

Introduction

"My men and I were the victims of shortsightedness at home, of blind trust in the respectability of scheming aggressors. The price of our unpreparedness for World War II was staggering to the imagination. The price of our unpreparedness for a World War III would be death to millions of us and the disappearance from the earth of its greatest nation."
General Jonathan M. Wainwright, 1946

In 1935 the U.S. Commonwealth known as the Phillipines invited General Douglas Mac Arthur, then Chief of Staff, to come to the islands and build a defense force. The "Field Marshal", as the Philippine government appointed him, would have ten years to complete his mission. Then the Filipinos would be ready for their promised independence.

But, MacArthur was given very little money and obsolete weapons. As an aggressive and powerful Japan escalated war in China, he demanded support from Washington. When none came, he resigned his Army commission, but continued to train 20,000 Filipino regulars and l00,000 reservists with l3,000 U.S. Servicemen.

Meanwhile Japan's need to free herself of American influential pressure had become an obsession. They were faced with the realization that their plan for Asian domination must take an all or nothing at all course. In early l94l MacArthur was invited by the U.S. to take command of a new Army. The entire Philippine Army was placed on active duty status and National Guard units began to leave for the islands to assist in the training. Members of the Philippine Army were inducted into the U.S. Army. The combined force was known as the United States Army Forces in the Far East. (U.S.A.F.F.E.)

Still MacArthur complained that U.S.A.F.F.E. lacked what was needed to repel a Japanese invasion. Washington argued that the presence of U.S. military bases in the commonwealth and the powerful Navy at Pearl Harbor was enough to discourage Japan.

Washington had defense plans for MacArthur should the Japanese attempt an invasion. The first was "War Plan Orange III", superseded in October, 1941 by "Rainbow V". Both plans called for the abandonment of Manila and a strategic withdrawal into the Bataan peninsula and the little island of Corregidor, off the tip of Bataan. Access to the valuable Manila Bay could be denied the enemy until the Pacific Fleet at Pearl Harbor arrived to relieve the defenders. Rainbow V covered a situation wherein America may be engaged with both Germany and Japan. Germany would be considered the main enemy.

The Japanese had their own plan......a sudden, co-ordinated attack on Pearl Harbor, the Philippines and Malaya, followed by assaults on Burma and the Dutch East Indies.

A few hours after the Japanese attack on Pearl Harbor, their bombers destroyed two-thirds of America's air power in the Philippines. By Christmas Day 1941, U.S.A.F.F.E., had only four P40 fighter aircraft remaining to assist in resisting the Japanese Imperial Army invasion of the Islands which began on December 10th. Manila was declared an "open city" and Rainbow V was placed into effect. It was obvious that no help would be coming from Pearl Harbor.

On Corregidor, or "The Rock" as it was called, U.S.A.F.F.E, had stored enough food to feed 10,000 men for several months. Bataan is ideally suited for a long holding action. Through the center of this twenty-five mile long peninsula, two mountain ranges were covered with thick forest. U.S.A.F.F.E. was confident. America had never deserted her troops in any war. But on Bataan, there were no mosquito nets, very little quinine and only enough food for thirty days.

The first Japanese assault on Bataan came on January 9, 1942 and resulted in a staggering defeat for the Imperial Army. U.S.A.F.F.E. was ordered to hold the enemy thirty more days and Washington promised that help was on the way.

By the end of January the men of U.S.A.F.F.E., suffering from malaria, lack of food and ammunition, were forced to withdraw to the southern half of the peninsula. They held through February but their ability to stall the Japanese much longer was doubtful.

General MacArthur following orders from President Roosevelt, evacuated Corregidor on March 17, and arrived safely in Australia. There he faced a press conference and announced, "The President of the United States ordered me to break through the Japanese lines and proceed from Corregidor to Australia for the purpose, as I understand it, of organizing the American offensive against Japan.....a primary objective of which is the relief of the Philippines. I came through and I shall return!"

General Jonathan M. Wainwright was left on Corregidor as Commander of U.S.A.F.F.E. The Army on Bataan was given to Brigadier General Edward P. King, Jr. Washington had written off U.S.A.F.F.E. as expendable. The American and Filipino soldiers on Bataan and Corregidor were doomed.

General Masaharu Homma, Commander of the Japanese Imperial Army Invasion force had projected he could defeat the U.S.A.F.F.E. in thirty days. His "time table" was now seriously disrupted. An all out assault was launched in early April, 1942 against the American positions. Many of the men of U.S.A.F.F.E., diseased, weakened by hunger and long out of ammunition fought back with bolos, knives and entrenching tools until finally overrun. Other units were forced by the Japanese advance into the last few miles at the tip of Bataan. There, they were hammered by Imperial bombs, artillery and tank fire. On April 9, 1942, U.S.A.F.F.E., on Bataan had no alternative but to surrender.

The Japanese had expected to capture only 25,000 men on Bataan. They learned their Intelligence Section was wrong. Over 72,000 American and Filipinos surrendered.

Camp O'Donnell, a former U.S.A.F.F.E. training post, some 85 miles north of the tip of Bataan had been selected as an ideal site to imprison the defenders. The Japanese were not faced with a new problem. . . . . .how to move 72,000 men to O'Donnell. A march was organized. The 72,000 would be forced to walk 80 miles out of Bataan to San Fernando in Pampanga Province, then shipped by rail cattle car to the camp.

But very few men of U.S.A.F.F.E. were in condition to march anywhere. As the movement began, so did the slaughter.

Some of the Imperial guards along the march route, specially officers educated in Western society, actually issued orders forbidding cruel treatment of prisoners, but they were definitely in the minority.

Over the next several days, 2,275 Americans and more than 13,000 Filipinos were clubbed, shot, bayonetted or hacked to death by Japanese soldiers along the route. It became known as the Bataan Death March.

Surely the brutality and callousness displayed by the Japanese Imperial Army on Bataan defies comprehension by American minds. In 1942 Japan was a self-critical country and indifference to sufferings had been deeply entrenched in custom for hundreds of years. In their crowded land, human life was cheap. Millions of uneducated people had been thoroughly indoctrinated by a small group of leaders into believing that all Orientals should be their slaves. Military victories in China and Manchuria only added to a feeling of superiority.

There was no tradition for mercy or compassion in the Japanese medieval "Code of Bushido" (the way of the warrior), only loyalty and self-sacrifice. Revenge was honorable under the Code. Surrender was a criminal act. The ability of the U.S.A.F.F.E. to hold, delay and inflict heavy casualties upon the Imperial Army only antagonized the Japanese. It was, therefore, almost impossible for the average Imperial soldier to understand the complete surrender of the American Army.

The Death March was only the beginning of the suffering for U.S.A.F.F.E. Of the 72,000 who began the march, 52,000 arrived at Camp O'Donnell . . . 9,200 Americans and about 42,800 Filipinos. Shortly, another 9,000 Filipinos, suspected of being members of U.S.A.F.F.E., were rounded up and placed into the concentration camp.

The small island of Corregidor, pounded into a barren waste land of smoldering tree stumps, buildings reduced to rubble, its big guns silenced by bombs, stood like a wounded gladiator, waiting in Manila Bay for the death blow.

On May 6, 1942, General Wainwright, in an effort to avoid more slaughter, surrendered the surviving 14,000 defenders of "The Rock". Within days, most were in Camp O'Donnell.

At the Camp, Americans were separated from Filipino soldiers. There was little food and no medicine. The Japanese also had shortages, the "captives" were told. By the time Corregidor fell . . . . in less than three weeks after the Bataan Death March, 23,000 Filipino and American prisoners either died of disease or starvation. After five weeks, the death rate among the Filipino prisoners reached 550 men a day.

By October, 1942 the Japanese decided to free the remaining Filipinos after each signed a "Statement of Allegiance" to Japan. It was a document few Filpinos considered serious. Several hundred American soldiers were sent to prison camps around Manila and Davao Penal Colony on the island of Mindanao.

The Japanese had a new death camp, also a former Filipino Army training post, prepared for the remaining 6,500 American prisoners. It was located a few miles from a major city in Nueva Ecija Province next to the Barrio of Pangatian. It would, however, be named for the big city . . . . . Cabanatuan.

When the 6,500 Americans were moved to Cabanatuan, Camp O'Donnell was closed. In its cemetery were buried 38,000 Filipinos and 2,000 Americans.

About one hundred American soldiers with the U.S.A.F.F.E. had managed to escape Bataan and did not surrender. Alone, they filtrated through the Japanese lines and journeyed to various provinces in Luzon. Half of these men would die of disease or at the hands of the Imperial Army before the end of the war. With the help of

Filipino civilians they began to organize guerilla units. Their ranks grew when Filipino soldiers were released from O'Donnell.

These Americans, who actually had no prior training in guerrilla warfare, built the nucleus of a command which gained them a well deserved place in the history of unconventional war. They maintained contact with one another when possible and soon found they had the support of the majority of Filipinos.

The Japanese had no one to blame but themselves for the guerrilla movement. Their barbarous brutality against the Filipinois had destroyed any dream the Imperial Army may have had for their "Asia for the Asiatics" program. The "Amnesty" drive came almost to a complete halt when they learned that the Filipinos were not about to be their slaves.

The Japanese encouraged the Makapili* who were bought with either favors or promises of special positions in the new government. The program was not successful. Next, Japanese soldiers rushed into areas looking for bands of guerrillas. Entire villages suspicioned of supporting guerrillas were leveled by artillery and the citizens either shot, beheaded, or sent off to labor camps. Still, the guerrilla armies grew and exercised coordinated attacks on the Japanese. By the end of 1942, Imperial Headquarters was faced with a serious guerrilla problem, recognizing that the "war in the shadows" was one they could easily lose. Their inhuman treatment of the people in the Philippines had sparked a flame which was developing into the most violent, organized system of guerrilla warfare ever experienced by any nation.

The American guerrilla officers promoted themselves to higher ranks, mostly to impress the Filipinos. And, when MacArthur finally learned of their activities, he officially recognized the rank of each. They were after all, commanding large numbers of troops and enduring hardships beyond that experienced by men of similar rank in the new Allied Army MacArthur was forming in Australia.

General MacArthur had promised to return to the Philippines. But, he and President Roosevelt had also promised the men on Bataan and Corregidor that "help was on the way." No help ever came.

Very few of the 6,500 Americans entering P.O.W. Camp Cabanatuan in late 1942 believed that anyone could save them from this new Hell.

Chapter I

"There can be no greater, more heinous or dangerous crime than the mass destruction under guise of military authority or military necessity, of helpless men incapable of further contribution to war effort...

From General Douglas MacArthur's "review" of General Homma's War Trial case; 1946.

P.O.W. Camp Cabanatuan

Nueva Ecija

Province-Luzon, The Philippines

September 1942

The day of their capture they were dragged from the headquarters building, bleeding and unconscious, and tied to posts in full view of their comrades across the road. For three days they hung there, feet several inches from the ground, refusing to die.

Everyone knew they were not dead. Occasionally a guard would pass and jab in their gut with a rifle. Each man jerked with pain, proving they were still breathing.

The seasonal rains which pounded Luzon almost everyday since the end of May ceased. The morning sun had alreadybegun to boil moisture from the rain soaked nipa and bamboo buildings and saturated earth.

Sergeant Abie Abraham scanned his sheets of paper on which he had recorded the names of dead American soldiers; then, scratching in the soft dirt beneath his barracks, buried the records. He crawled out into the hot sun and turned to face the Sierra Madre mountains.

The short Syrian-American thought for a moment... how beautiful, how tranquil the cloud shrowded peaks appeared. Quickly, he glanced in the opposite direction towards Mount Arayat as if to assure himself that nothing had changed... that he had not dreamed into a peaceful death. A devout Catholic, Sergeant Abraham made the sign of the cross, then walked slowly to the wire fence which separated his P.O.W. area from the center road of the camp. The steady breeze which always drifts across the Central Plains of Luzon cooled his gaunt face. At the fence he joined a crowd of hundreds who had gathered since daybreak, keeping a vigil for the three comrades tied to the posts.

"They are still alive?" Sergeant Abraham asked.

"Yeah." Someone answered.

The Sergeant said a silent prayer, pleading that he be spared long enough to testify against the enemy someday.

Across the road several Japanese guards, led by an N.C.O., suddenly emerged from the headquarters building. They moved swiftly to the three men at the posts and cut the ropes which held the prisoners. The thin forms crumpled to the ground and began to crawl. The guards were on them, pulling them up and tying their arms behind their backs.

"You are officers in American Army," the N.C.O. shouted in English."You caught trying to escape under fence! You intelligent! You know there is no escape! You know... anyone try to escape.... must be shot!"

Then, the long walk began towards the rear gate, the American officers being dragged by the guards. Abraham moved slowly with the multitudes along the wire, following the procession. The guards and their three prisoners approached the cemetery where, during the month of September over 1,000 Americans had been buried. It was a muddy area and the graves had all been dug by the P.O.W.'s with their bare hands. Eventually, shovels were made from wood and scraps of metal. Last night, someone had dug a shallow trench with the new tools.

The three P.O.W.'s were lined up, side by side, their backs to the trench.

"God, give them strength!", Abraham heard the man next to him whisper."Our Father, Who art in heaven..." Abraham began the prayer which was picked up by a few around him. Most simply stood silent, their shriveled hands clutching the barbed wire.

At the trench the Japanese N.C.O. held out a pack of cigarettes and offered to place one between the prisoners cracked lips. Two P.O.W.'s stared ahead, not comprehending the final gesture. The third looked up slowly, then managed to spit at the feet of the N.C.O. The N.C.O. performed a neat turn, walked a few paces to the side and drew his sword.

He raised his sword quickly above his head and barked three commands. The sound of rifle shots cut the quiet morning and rolled with a haunting echo through the valley.

Originally, there were three work camps prepared for the Americans in the Cabanatuan City area... the large camp #1 at Barrio Pangatian, and two smaller ones hastily organized from warehouses. From these, the Japanese planned to use the P.O.W.'s for various construction projects. But, the angel of death spread his wings mostly over the old Filipino training camp #1 at Pangatian.

Camp #1 had a hospital area consisting of sixty foot long buildings constructed of woven bamboo and nipa grass roofs. Like the wards at Camp O'Donnell, there were no screens over the windows, only thatched shutters which could swing down from a hinged top. The shutters were suitable for blocking the hot sun and heavy rains but did not hold back the flies. The insects swarmed into the wards and crawled upon the faces of the dead and dying. In the first month the wards contained the lifeless forms of 2,500 patients.

The barracks for the other 4,000 American P.O.W.'s were of similar construction. A narrow aisle ran the length, separating two decks of bamboo racks. The floor was of bamboo strips, nailed on a frame a fraction of an inch apart. Since the units were elevated three feet from the ground, the cracks permitted circulation of air.

The stockade at Pangatian sat on flat land on the south side of the highway approximately four miles east of Cabanatuan City. The Japanese had made only a few changes at the camp in preparation for their P.O.W.'s. They enclosed a 600 by 800 yard section with three rows of barbed wire fence, eight feet tall. The fence rows were four feet apart. Inside, they divided sections by single rows of barbed wire fence, six feet tall and contained the P.O.W.'s in the northeast section.

At the front gate facing the highway, the Japanese erected a twelve foot high guard tower and another tower at the northeast corner of the camp. These towers were originally manned by four sentries with rifles and machine guns. They commanded an excellent field of vision over the P.O.W. section, the highway, main gate and a good distance across the open field which stretched north two miles to the Pampanga River.

About half way down the P.O.W. section perimeter on the east was a large open fox hole, slightly elevated above ground level and surrounded with sandbags. From here, four sentries with rifles and a machine gun had perfect vision of the southern half of the P.O.W. area and the eastward terrain which was also flat country.

It was this east area which most concerned the camp commandant. Less than fifty yards outside the fence a small creek cut through a gully running parallel to the fence from south to north. Its bed varied in depth from two feet at the south end of the camp to nearly six feet near the front where it passed under the highway and continued on to the Pampanga River. Fearing that Filipino guerrillas may attempt to approach the camp from this area, the cogon grass was always cut close to the ground and several sentries patrolled on foot, night and day.

At the far southeast corner of the camp, they erected another tower and an elevated fox hole containing a machine gun was at the rear gate.

But most of the camp belonged to the Japanese. They quartered enlisted men and guards in the southeast section and the communication center and transient troop area was in the southwest section. The motor pool was located in the west central area and the northwest section was reserved for officers' quarters, headquarters and barracks for the front gate guards.

Life at Cabanatuan, for those not admitted to the hospital, consisted of five to seven days labor, depending on the mood of the Japanese. Work details were constantly marched or trucked out to cut fire wood, clear bamboo thickets, build air strips and reconstruct buildings damaged or destroyed during the invasion.

By the last of September, 1942, the Japanese officially changed the classification of the Americans from"Captives" to Prisoners of War and began to issue pay in Japanese Occupation Peso currency.

A PFC received 15 centavos a day, N.C.O.'s 25 centavos and officers sometimes as much as ten pesos a day.

With these funds the POW's were free to buy food, fruits and tobacco from the Filipinos who were occasionally allowed to gather along the highway fence or at the main gate. The Filipinos had two prices...one for the Americans, and a highly inflated one for the Japanese. Bananas and other fruits, which the Filipinos had in abundance, were usually given to the POW's only to be confiscated by greedy guards.

Some semblance of a POW command organization began, hampered by the continual shifting of details to and from the other POW Camps in the area and the relocation of numerous groups to Manila or major construction projects throughout Luzon.

The work details suffered such severe beatings that the balance between those in the hospital and those available for work swung back and forth. Actually, none of the POW's were in condition to perform hard labor and when American officers protested the assignment of sick men to details, they were beaten and placed on even tougher labor assignments.

By October, when Japanese Lieutenant Colonel Mori took command of Cabanatuan, the POW's had a farm of over three hundred acres under cultivation. They worked the fields using sticks and hoes made from scraps of metal for seven to ten hours each day. Since there was no irrigation the entire farm had to be watered by hand.

And, when the first small harvest came, the Japanese guards took most of the vegetables. Discovering this injustice, the Filipinos in the area began to leave food at the work sites at night to be smuggled by the POW's back into the camp.

Through it all, however,many of the Americans managed to maintain some sense of humor and even nicknamed their most hated guards by appearance or mannerism,"Half pint, Donald Duck, Big Speedo, Little Speedo...". Jokes about these guards produced a few smiles and an occasional laugh.

In the camp, efforts to organize and improve morale, spear- headed by the clergymen, medics and a few enthusiastic POW's, were successful. First, the clergy finally convinced Lieutenant Colonel Mori that the men should be allowed to worship their God and regular church services were held.

Stoves of clay and metal were built, replacing open fire cooking and the bakers and cooks learned new methods, utilizing the small rations issued by the Japanese.

Meat was mostly the heads and intestines of carabao...350 pounds per week per 2,000 men. Sometimes only fish powder was issued instead of meat and often weeks went by without even fish powder. The POW's devised ingenious traps for rats, lizards and an occasional dog or cat which wandered through the wire fences. The grand total of meat usually averaged five ounces per man every three days.

From the farm the Japanese eventually allowed the Americans to keep the camotes and casava. The POW's stole whatever they could of the okra, peppers, cucumbers, eggplant, onions and radishes.

This was dangerous, for to be caught stealing usually resulted in a fatal beating.

Starting in October, the Japanese made periodic issues of eggs and canned milk, but as the starvation diet continued some turned on their own. A few accepted special favors from the enemy... food for information. Some stole from their buddies and traded for food and tobacco or those hard earned centavos so they could buy necessities from the guards. When caught, these POW's were warned that they may stand trial by court-martial. Cases were prepared and hidden for future reference.

In December, 1942, competition games of golf, baseball and volleyball began and tournaments of chess, monopoly, checkers, and poker were under way with handmade equipment. Prizes were usually one precious egg or hand rolled cigarettes.

But, the POW's grew tired of the activities and when they did, classes in astronomy, radio repair, music, horse raising and cattle breeding caught on. The U.S. Navy POW's who had arrived late at O'Donnell from Corregidor had been allowed to keep most of their musical instruments which they carried on to Cabanatuan. A camp band was established.

These Corregidor POW's managed to smuggle in something far more valuable to morale. Hidden under their clothes and in some of those musical instruments were parts of radio equipment.While others attended classes on how to make dog tags from leather, combs from carabao horn, razors from GI mess kit knives, a special team of technicians began to slowly assemble a radio receiver.

The possession of a radio or even knowledge of the location of a radio would mean instant death. But, these technicians ignored the threat, worked through the nights on their electrical contraption. Unfortunately, they did not have all the necessary parts, especially tubes or wire for a decent antenna. A brilliant plan was devised. They instructed the workers in the power station how to over load the camp electrical circuits and soon every radio owned by the Japanese began to blow tubes.

The guards were then advised that there were a few among the POW's who knew how to repair radios. A steady stream of radios needing repair began to flow to these POW's who reported the name and type of tubes or parts needing replacement. There was nothing wrong with some of the parts and as the replacements arrived from nearby Cabanatuan City or Manila, the POW's retained what they needed.

During this time, small bits of copper wire were stolen and woven into an antenna which was hidden within something the Japanese would never suspicion... a long, heavy rope.

Only one guard inquired about the purpose of the coil of rope. He was informed that some of the POW's had requested permission to commit suicide by hanging themselves. Little by little the radio was assembled into a very compact unit and concealed inside three canteens which had been cut in half. They were hidden in separate areas, to be connected at some future date. But, since so many POW's were transferred in and out of Cabanatuan, it would be almost a year before the engineering marvel would receive its first broadcast.

Lieutenant Merle Musselman arrived at Cabanatuan in June, 1943, and immediately went to work with the other doctors at the camp hospital. The smaller camp #3 where Musselman had been assigned for a year was about to be closed.

Doctor Musselman had heard of the deplorable hospital conditions at Cabanatuan through various members of work details who had been transferred back and forth between the two camps.

But, seeing thousands of bed patients dying slow deaths from lack of medicines and guard brutality shocked the young officer. Visions of those early days at O'Donnell flashed through his mind.

At least at Cabanatuan there were some medicines, (though never enough) and the hospital staff was well organized.

But the black flies, lice, bed bugs and mosquitoes continually spread disease. Handicapped by meager laboratory facilities and lack of cooperation of Japanese officers, the camp doctors and medics worked in twenty-four hour shifts. Soon, deaths resulted among their staff.

The worst slow killer was beriberi. It was probably the most dangerous vitamin deficiency disease encountered at Cabanatuan and was directly responsible for more deaths than any other illness. Chronic in nature, the POW's who suffered from it and did not die were either incapacitated for months or permanently disabled.

Generally speaking, the POW's diet was deficient in all vitamins as a result of their lack of meat and vegetables. The rice issued by the Japanese was of medium mill, most of the Vitamin B containing pericarp removed.

Wet beriberi developed into acute cardiac failure and the dry version of the disease produced painful feet and hands. Some of the unfortunate victims, unable to sleep, spent the night crying , moaning and begging for relief. The pain soon spread up the legs to the knees while the patients suffered additional complications from dysentery, pellagra, worms and malaria chills.

Cool evenings brought slight relief, but during the hot days the pain was completely unbearable. These patients, pathetically moving about the camp grounds, developed a protective gait because of the tenderness of the feet. The weight was placed on the outer side of the foot, each step slow and deliberate. The man looked carefully for a smooth place, then gently set his foot down, flinging his arms upward. So peculiar was the sight of hundreds of men moving in such a manner that it was given a name ... the"Cabanatuan Shuffle".

A few days after his arrival, Doctor Musselman was advised that the last of the precious vitamins and medicines received in Red Cross 1942 Christmas packages were gone. Everyone began to pray that the Japanese would allow 1943 packages to be distributed.

Depressed with the news that the staff was once again out of supplies, Doctor Musselman returned to the laboratory where he found three men busy manufacturing strange looking tablets from handmade molds. The pills were"sulfa tablets", he was informed.

The Japanese guards were constantly trying to buy medical items from the lab, for they also had shortages. As frightened as the guards were of the hospital area, they did often venture into the lab and had been paying handsome prices for the"sulfa". With the money from the sale of the pills, cigarettes were purchased at the camp commissary... cigarettes the Japanese had stolen from Red Cross packages.

The Japanese never discovered that those sulfa pills they lined up to buy from the POW's were actually counterfeited from nothing but starch.

December arrived with its usual pleasant balmy weather in 1943. Two thousand six hundred and fifty-six Americans lay buried in the POW Camp Cabanatuan cemetery.

Now, only 3,844 remained alive.

Chapter 2

"Any nationalist who makes an ally of the Communist is going for a ride on a tiger!"

Luis Taruc, H.U.K. Guerrilla Commander

Nueva Ecija Province

Lieutenant Juan Pajota of the Luzon Guerrilla Force, squatted on his haunches in typical oriental fashion and began to scratch his plan in the dirt as his men joined in a tight circle.

"You must learn this now," the Lieutenant stated."The Japs have a will to fight unlike anyone because they do not wish to surrender. Even if they are wounded, if they can crawl, they will hit back. They may pretend they are dead and strike when you come close. Two of you will aim at each single enemy. We have little ammunition, so aim carefully. The trail the Japs will take is narrow. They will be moving in single file. I will show you positions when we reach our ambush point."

"What about the two ganaps* who are leading the Jap patrol?" one guerrilla asked.

Pajota stared at the ground a moment sickened by the thought that some of his countrymen had sided with the Japanese. He glanced up at the young men around him."They are traitors! They will die also!' His eyes moved from face to face, checking the reaction to his order.

13

"Now," the Lieutenant broke the brief silence. "The ganaps will be leading the patrol. The Japs are clever. They have an alert sense for danger and will force the ganaps to walk ahead. We will allow them all to pass until the last Jap is directly across from me. When you hear my shot at that last Jap... you must shoot quickly!"

The guerrillas split into two groups and moved swiftly, three miles to the ambush point. There they deployed along the trail, concealed by heavy under-brush and bamboo and waited for the enemy. Within an hour the Japanese Patrol approached the site, the two Filipinos leading by some twenty paces, as Pajota had predicted.

When the last Imperial soldier crossed the sights of Pajota's .45 automatic pistol, he squeezed the trigger. The soldier sprang into the air from the impact of the bullet. A barrage of shots followed so rapidly that it was impossible to distinguish individual shots. The seven man patrol crumpled to the ground, all killed instantly.

Now, the guerrillas had five additional rifles. While they divided the ammunition, Pajota sent a man to evacuate nearby Barrio Bacao with instructions for the citizens to mingle with those of the next village of Sagana. If the Japanese intend reprisals on Bacao, they would find nothing but an empty town to burn.

Lieutenant Juan Pajota, a member of U.S.A.F.F.E., had managed to escape Bataan and returned to Nueva Ecija Province where he had been trained by MacArthur's American cadre. His original post was none other than Cabanatuan-Pangatian, now being used by the Japanese as the P.O.W. Camp. At the time of his escape he had only his .45 pistol. His five man squad shared four old bolt action rifles.

His small army began their guerrilla activities against the Japanese in Nueva Ecija as early as May, 1942. In June they discovered a number of other rifles and two water-cooled, .30 caliber machine guns which were much too heavy to carry on hit and run raids. The automatic weapons were disassembled, oiled and hidden until some special mission demanded their devastating capabilities. With each action against the Japanese, the guerrilla arsenal of weapons grew.

Through June, Pajota intensified his intelligence gathering and recruited new members from civilians. He had become known as a determined, cautious leader, thorough in his planning and with simple demands from life. He possessed a serious attitude which allowed no time for dramatics. His "boys", as he affectionately referred to his troops, naturally admired all his traits. The release of men from O'Donnell brought new recruits.

War, the surrender of the Americans, the atrocities committed on civilians by the Japanese, all produced a feeling of uncertainty among the Filipinos. Some questioned if MacArthur would ever return, if America had forgotten them completely. And, understandably, some questioned the wisdom of joining or supporting the guerrillas.

The Imperial Army realized that their pacification program was not progressing well. The Filipinos resented the demand that every citizen bow or kneel when an Imperial soldier passed. They were rejecting the promise of freedom when they learned the beatings, torture and rape inflected on citizens was continuing and Japanese officers were doing nothing to stop it. In fact, Japanese officers were often guilty of the crimes, especially rape and sexual abuse of young Filipino girls.

Shortly after midnight on August 1, 1942, Pajota was awakened by one of his men who advised that an American officer was traveling cross country, heading in the direction of his guerriila headquarters. At 0300 (3 a.m.) United States Army Captain Harry M. McKenzie arrived with Filipino guides to find the guerrillas waiting for them with food.

A conference began in the early morning hours which was to tie Pajota and his men into a growing web of organized guerrilla resistance.

McKenzie, a mining engineer in the Philippines before the war, explained that he had escaped Bataan and, with the help of civilians, was moving north to link up with another American officer... Robert Lapham.

McKenzie was impressed with Pajota's accomplishments and promoted him to the rank of Captain... a"field commission" for which official orders were later drafted. Pajota was instructed to continue his recruitment and break his command into small units. At all times they were to emphasize the importance of supporting the Americans and act to revenge Japanese atrocities.

When McKenzie moved on to find Lapham, Captain Pajota began to commission his most able men as First Lieutenants and placed them in command of units which he called Squadrons. Each Squadron, armed with American Enfield Bolt action rifles, bolos and Japanese weapons had responsibility for a particular vicinity within Nueva Ecija. Captain Pajota maintained command of his army and answered to the American officer, Robert Lapham.

Pajota's area of responsibility consisted of almost thirty square miles which varied in terrain from flat, open fields (mostly cultivated with rice) to dense forest, to the rough high country of the Sierra Madre mountains. P.O.W. Camp Cabanatuan sat almost in the middle of his territory, which he covered on foot or horseback.

Pajota's command was just one guerrilla army which prepared to rain destruction and frustration upon the Japanese. Other guerrilla units, whose commanders were former U.S.A.F.F.E. officers, began activity throughout Luzon and other islands.

Robert Lapham established his mobile headquarters in the northern section of Nueva Ecija. This six foot, twenty four year old blond soldier had successfully avoided capture in Bataan and, with a band of followers, promoted himself from Lieutenant to Major. Captain Mc-Kenzie became his executive Officer.

To their west, Bernard Anderson, an Air Corps Lieutenant, promoted himself to the rank of Colonel and began activities against the enemy. By the end of the war, his army numbered about 8,000 men.

There was a certain charisma about these men which attracted the Filipinos in magnetic fashion. Their status as Officers in U.S.A.F.F.E. played a big part, but , they also possessed the traits of natural leaders. They were handsome, brave, brilliant in their planning, imaginative and determined to fight the Japanese. They had proved themselves worthy of trust.

The Japanese had yet another group to contend with among the troublesome Filipinos. In the middle 1930's, Luis Taruc and a number of socialists broke politically from the American concept of government and began a recruitment campaign among the farmers and small town businessmen in Pampanga, Tarlac and Nueva Ecija Proviences. Their desire was to establish a separate political party by the time Philippine Independence was granted.

To have a Socialist political party would require the backing of a large percent of the population if they expected to have any voice in government. But, Taruc's vision of this new party was a little different from that forming in China. He knew that, for the Philippines, the party must be modified with some Christian- democratic thinking. The country had been motivated by so many generations of Christianity. Being a Catholic, Taruc could not rid himself of his own religious beliefs. The Communists in the Philippines did not agree with Taruc.

17

But, when the Japanese began their conquest of the islands the two groups put aside their differences and joined forces to help repel the enemy. Unfortunately for Luis Taruc and his followers, the future would require them all to be labeled Communist.

With headquarters established at Mount Arayat in the Central Plains, Luis Taruc, at age 28, was appointed Commander-in-Chief of the combined Socialist-Communist group. He formed well-disciplined squads of volunteers from the ranks of peasants into an army which he called the"Hukbo Ng Bayan Laban Sa Hapon" (People's Army to fight the Japanese). As the recruitment for the army continued into the middle of 1942, the organization became known as the"HUKBALAHAP" and, later, the HUKS.

Like Pajota, Commander Taruc divided his army into Squadrons. At least in the beginning, regardless of their political stands, the HUKS and the Luzon Guerrilla Force (U.S.A.F.F.E. guerrilla) had one thing in common . . . the disposal of their mutual enemy, the Japanese.

CHAPTER 3

"I wouldn't take the whole damn Jap Army for one Alamo Scout!"

General Walter Krueger ; Spring, 1944

James Canfield Fisher's concern for humanity and a gifted mind guided him successfully through Harvard Medical School. After his internship, Boston City Hospital assigned Dr. Fisher to their surgical staff where he served for two and a half years until World War II interrupted a promising career.

The only son of novelist Dorothy Canfield Fisher spent his early years in France where his father served for three years as an ambulance driver with the French Army during World War I. After that, James traveled Europe extensively with his parents. In fact, his early schooling was in Europe and when the Fishers finally returned to their native Vermont, young James' friends had a little trouble understanding his heavy French accent.

James was an amiable and curious fellow, full of desire to continue his untiring search for knowledge, doing his part for mankind in the process. He considered World War II only a temporary interruption in life. He never seemed to waste a minute, possessing a marvelous ability to turn every new encounter into something of lasting value. And, armed with an infectious grin, he managed to make everyone he met feel that they were the most important individual on earth.

Like many intelligent men preoccupied with deep thought, Dr. Fisher was terribly absentminded. He had been that way since early childhood, often to the amusement of both teachers and friends. It was not that forgivable fault which produced his overseas assignment during the War. It was the irony of events and that mysterious system of selection executed by some unknown individual in the high commnand of the U.S. military.

By all logical thinking, James Fisher should have been assigned to a medical unit in Europe where his proficiency in those languages would have been most beneficial. At least he should have been assigned to a major medical staff somewhere so his surgical skills could be put to good use. Instead, he ended up in New Guinea as Commanding Officer, Medical Detachment, 98th Field Artillery Battalion, Pack. Captain Fisher did not complain. He shrugged off the peculiarity of the assignment with the thought that he must be needed in an artillery battalion. Why else would fate send him there?

The 98th Field Artillery Battalion, Pack, left Camp Carson in December, 1942, arriving with their 1,000 mules and mountain guns at Brisbon in January, 1943.

Sixth Army Commander General Walter Krueger had planned to use the 98th in the Salamaua campaign but by February, when the Battalion arrived in New Guinea, the Salamaua battles were practically over. Having already crossed the mountains, Allied troops were dealing the Imperial Army a major land defeat. For the time being, the 98th and their equipment were useless in New Guinea.

But, Frank Dow Merrill was busy training a regimental size group of American volunteers in the rough mountainous Burmese jungle and desperately needed the 98th's special equipment to fight the Japanese there. The 98th's mules were quickly reassigned to "Merrill's Marauders". This action left 6th Army at a complete loss for what to do with the troops of the 98th.

A short, husky Captain Fisher went about his duties dwarfed by the former mule skinners in his battalion. With the exception of most of the officers and a handful of men everyone in the 98th was at least six feet tall. Considering the laborious tasks usually confronting a Pack Artillery outfit, the Army had established a minimum height requirement of five foot, ten inches and drafted these tough, healthy individuals from the rural farms or mountainous areas of America.

It would not be easy for men accustomed to a life of hard work to lay around and wait for the Army's new plans. Soon, morale began to slip and Dr. Fisher found his duties far more complex than expected. In the field, personal health is so entwined with spiritual health that the medical officer often supersedes the chaplain. The simple fact was that men sometimes find it easier to talk with one who is more acquainted with the realities of war and life and... waiting.

The low morale situation brought the big men of the 98th to Dr. Fisher and everyone soon developed deep admiration for their medical officer. Yet, when they called him "Captain Fisher", he politely suggested a different title. "Just call me Jimmy", he would say. Not all the men could allow their military courtesy to slip that far. So, Captain James Canfield Fisher became more popularly known as "Captain Jim."

* * * *

In Nueva Ecija Province on Luzon, eighteen year old Jesus Bondoc did not have a rifle, but he was, nonetheless, a guerrilla in Major Robert Lapham's army.

A Squadron Commander had sent Bondoc to the city of Guimba to procure some quinine for the ailing American and when the young guerrilla returned he found the camp in a flurry of excitement. While he was gone some of his countrymen had turned over to Lapham a damaged radio transmitter unit. Not only did the Major manage to repair the equipment, he had even succeeded in establishing contact with MacArthur's headquarters in Australia.

By late August, 1943, Colonel Anderson still operating in a separate area of Luzon, had likewise made contact with Allied headquarters using primitive, practically homemade radio units.

At first, Allied headquarters refused to believe the American guerrillas communication fearing it may be a Japanese trick.   The reluctant Headquarters demanded names of the Americans ' girlfriends, school teachers, and a variety of information to be verified. Often answering in a barrage of typical American profanity (motivated by both frustration and an effort to be believed) the guerrillas finally convinced MacArthur 's staff.

Contact was now established (and maintained) with an Army MacArthur had previously hoped, but could not be sure, existed. It represented the first confirmation that an active, vigorous guerrilla campaign was in full swing on Luzon.

Overshadowing the first communication of important data was the heartbreaking news of the Bataan Death March, the death camps, and the atrocities committed by the Japanese on civilians in reprisal for guerrilla activities. Because of those brutal retaliations, MacArthur was compelled to issue what became known as the "lay low order".

In essence, the guerrillas were instructed to cease their direct attacks on the enemy until arms and munitions could be supplied from Australia. In the meantime, the guerrillas were to sophisticate their units, intensify surveillance, and send as much information on the Japanese as possible.

Two basic factors forced MacArthur to radio the"lay low order". First, the guerrillas with all their small victories considered, might quickly become extinct without adequate weapons. The Allies desperately needed detailed information concerning enemy troop concentrations, troop movements, beach defenses and air base locations before the liberation could be undertaken. Thus, survival of a well organized resistance movement was paramount for intelligence purposes.

Second, MacArthur would need the support of the entire population of the Philippines when the time for invasion arrived. He had the support once and was convinced that it could be maintained with the majority of Filipinos. But, those reprisals for guerrilla activity upon thousands of civilians might jeopardize the feeling of Allegiance to the United States. MacArthur assured the guerrillas however, that they would be unleased on the enemy again...when the time was ripe.

* * * *

Captain Juan Pajota received his orders from Major Lapham. Until otherwise instructed, Pajota and his men were to avoid contact with the Japanese, engaging instead in intensified intelligence gathering.

Using an obsolete map of the province of Nueva Ecija, Pajota began to make his own"Operations Map" to cover each square mile of his area of responsibility. Without the aid of a compass he and several teams recorded every road, trail, river, stream and town on the new map traveling some twenty square miles on foot to do so.

The guerrilla command posts and special landmarks were listed and enemy positions marked on thin paper overlays. Pajota's Operation Map would take almost a year to complete but the end result was surprisingly accurate.

* * * *

A mile north of POW Camp Cabanatuan, the Imperial Army Engineers stayed busy through the rainy season of 1943 reconstructing the bridge over Cabu River at the same site where Filipino USAFFE Engineers had destroyed the old bridge during the retreat in 1941.

Since the reconstruction required much more time than originally anticipated, the Japanese decided to erect a temporary bridge to handle the flow of traffic.

The engineers selected a spot for this wooden bridge some three hundred yards northwest of the highway and detoured vechicles along a dirt track from Barrio Cabu to the river. Once across the river, traffic proceeded on another dirt road at an angle to where it connected, once again, with the highway.

* * * *

When he arrived in Australia from Corregidor, General Douglas MacArthur was appointed Commander-in-Chief of the Southwest pacific Area which gave him control of the entire Allied theater there. Within a few months the aggressive MacArthur was on the offensive.

The Imperial Army had been drilled primarily for the offensive. Defense measures, to the Japanese military, was, at most, only a temporary measure taken until the offensive could begin again. Mac-

Arthur, with his valuable understanding of Asian mentality recognized the importance of turning the table on the arrogant enemy from both a psychological and military point of view.

With all his faults considered, probably the one single factor which distinguished MacArthur as a superb tactician was his decision to counterattack when he did -- and that ability to continue the attack on the enemy when and where they least expected.

In 1942, what America needed in the Pacific was a special plan for victory, an overall consistent aggressive plan to systematically destroy the Japanese capabilities for continuing the war. MacArthur's plan called for a step by step attack up the island chains of the Pacific, bypassing and isolating many enemy held areas but at the same time providing the Allies with land bases for aircraft.

Now, the Allies were no longer on the retreat. MacArthur's forces began a violent offensive along the northern coast of New Guinea. By early 1943, the long battle for Guadalcanal was over, the bloodied island finally written off by the Japanese as a total loss. The future, to the Japanese, was beginning to look gloomy. For the first time since the conception of the Imperial Army, they were now on the defensive.

In June, the Allies landed on Rendova Island and New Georgia in the Solomons and took Nassau Bay in New Guinea. The Japanese, already worried about their over extended supply lines, began to retreat overland in New Guinea, forced from their perimeter at Salamaua. November, 1943, brought the Americans to Tarawa, the key enemy post in the Gilberts. New Britain and Bougainville, largest of the Solomons fell in December. In January, 1944, Japanese positions collapsed in the Marshalls and by then a new word had entered the American vocabulary as a special kind of warfare moved on with astonishing speed and success.. ."amphibious"! But, with all those island victories, there was still an ample supply of Japanese on New Guinea to cause concern for the Allies.

To many in the military it seemed as if Lieutenant General Walter Krueger was born in the United States Army. Emmigrating to the U.S. from West Prussia, Walter Krueger volunteered as an enlisted man in 1898 during the Spanish-American War. While serving in Luzon in 1901 at the peak of the Philippine Insurrection, Krueger was commissioned a 2nd Lieutenant. Later, he was appointed Chief of the newly formed"Tank Corps" in World War I.

Known both for his skill as a tactician and an excellent trainer of troops, the sixty-two year old Krueger was appointed as Commander of the Sixth United States Army early in 1943. By October of that year, his well organized Army had moved to New Guinea and, winning one battle after another, gradually forced the Japanese into that overland retreat.

General Krueger's concern and love for his enlisted men was a well known fact. Having come up through the ranks, unlike most Generals in the Pacific, he could appreciate the hardships the soldiers endured both in training and combat. He looked forward to future invasions, but the loss of a single man weighed heavily on him.

Early in October, 1943, Lieutenant General Krueger studied a special problem confronting his Headquarters. True, his campaign was progressing well. Salamaua and Lae had fallen, but the rest of New Guinea was loaded with Japanese. Sixth Army knew where they were, but exactly how many, their activities, physical condition and morale was not known.

Information was flooding his headquarters in the form of captured documents, prisoners of war interrogation reports, and air reconnaissance. It was all general information...not specific to satisfy Krueger. Air observations were fine, but much could not be seen from the air.

Documents and reports from prisoners or natives were stimulating, but reliability was questionable. To gamble even so much as a company of men on that kind of data did not set easy with General Krueger.

He had also studied the results of a secret experimental group formed by the Navy and decided to discuss the information with his staff.

The"Amphibious Scouts", as the Navy called their team, was formed by Commander William Coultas.

The concept was basically simple, but the missions were some of the most dangerous of the war. A small group of men, all volunteers with special training, would land by night in enemy territory, reconnoiter for several days...weeks if necessary, and bring out first hand information. This temporary unit was composed of men from both the U. S. and Australian Army as well as several Navy adventurers. After considering the success of those early missions by the Amphibious Scouts, General Krueger concluded that the Army needed such an organization on a permanent basis.

To find the right men and keep the program secret at the same time would be quite an undertaking. Commanders must sift carefully through their troops in the Southwest Pacific to find men most suited and, of course, those men must be willing to volunteer. Krueger outlined the basic requirements for the type of men he wanted... courageous, but not foolhardy, rugged, healthy, good swimmers, intelligent and expert marksmen.

When asked what he proposed to call this new unit, he replied, "They'll be called the Alamo Scouts. I've always been inspired with the story of the Alamo and those brave men who died there. Our Alamo Scouts must have the courage and qualifications of Crockett, Bowie and Travis!"

By December 3rd, construction of the training site was well under way near a small native village on Kalo Kalo off the east coast of Fergusson Island. Here, isolated but within one half hour boat ride from 6th Army Headquarters, the Alamo Scouts began their training in secrecy and without interruption. The six week course started with an intensive physical conditioning program, especially strenuous in the sapping heat of the tropics.

Then there were swimming test, rubber boating, marksmanship, emphasizing quick firing from the hip as well as conventional methods, and familiarizing the men with every small weapon in the U.S. and Japanese arsenal. Exercising razor sharp teamwork, the men learned to move like ghosts in the jungle.

Long marches, accuracy drills in grenade tossing, hand to hand combat and courses in blinker signaling, field radio operation and repair, message writing methods (utilizing a variety of codes) and map-compass reading sometimes lasted for a full twenty-four hour period. As a small reward, the Scout trainees were seldom required to stand formal formations and there was rarely a prescribed uniform. Pay was the same as any foot soldier in the Pacific.

Simulated missions with PT boats * dropping them off on deserted islands were repeated over and over, always with enthusiastic support from the Navy.

Conditioning under fire was the final phase. To add realism to the training, live ammunition and full charge explosives were used. The swimming test, for example, included a course requiring a team to swim out in the surf under water for fifty yards, then come up together. Upon a signal the men surface dived while sprays of lead from several Tommy guns whined into the water where they had submerged.

All the trainees who finished the six weeks were good, but some way had to be devised to select the best of the good. This selection dilemma was solved by the democratic process. Each enlisted man candidate was asked to name by secret ballot, three officers, in order of his personal preference, he would be most willing to follow on a mission. He was also asked to name five other men into whose hands he would entrust his life if he worked with them as a team member. Student officers, in turn, were asked which men they would wish to have with them on a mission. To this was added the Staff Officers' recommendations and the total votes were counted. The results was a Scout Team consisting of one officer and six men.

What motivated these men to try out for the Alamo Scouts? Except during combat, life in the Southwest Pacific was often boring. As with any war, there was terrible anxiety, frustration and loneliness haunting the American soldier. Everyone wanted to feel he had contributed something definite and concrete to the winning of the war, to getting it over with as fast as possible. With a small elite unit like the Scouts, one's value could never be doubted. And, typical of young American men, many Scout members were driven by that spirit of adventure.

For the next several months, with the help of the daredevil PT boat crews, the Alamo Scouts investigated enemy positions under the very nose of the Japanese. Dropped off with the rubber rafts at night from the PT boats, Scout teams would paddle through often violent surfs, hide the rafts, carry out their mission and then return to the beach at the appointed hour trusting the Navy would always be there to pluck them from the danger of eventual detection.

Typical of one of their detailed mission reports is the following:"All the enemy observed on the island were in very good health and appeared to be in exceptionally good spirits because of their laughter, talking and playing. Conditions of area along coast from grid coordinates 49.9-62.0 to 52.4-60.8, E and W and from coastal line 150 to 200 yards inland is good firm ground with little underbrush...beaches may be used as road during low tide... the firm ground appears to be capable of supporting truck and tank movement."

Such knowledge gained on hundreds of enemy positions by the daring Scouts was a tremendous value in the planning of many invasions. Within nine months various Scouts had earned a total of nineteen Silver Stars, eighteen Bronze Stars and four Soldiers Medals without losing a single man.

Scout Headquarters once reported to General Krueger that they knew where they could kidnap a high ranking Japanese officer. All plans for a raid on the enemy camp had been carefully drawn and two Scout Teams were standing by, dressed in special camouflage jungle suits.

Krueger studied the report and request with great interest. The capture of the particular enemy officer would have excellent propaganda value but little tactical value. Weighing the odds, he decided the mission was too risky and informed the disappointed Scouts that he could not authorize the raid. When a staff officer pointed out the possible success of the mission might cost only a few men, General Krueger snapped,"I wouldn't take the whole damn Jap Army for one Alamo Scout!"

* * * *

By late January, 1944, the Americans in POW Camp Cabanatuan on Luzon had given up hope for 1943 Red Cross Christmas packages. Word circulated that both mail and those cherished packages had arrived but for unexplained reasons, the Japanese Commandant elected not to release them.

After continual pleading by camp medical officers, the Commandant did finally agree to distribute small supplies of medicine. However, the remainder of valuable goods...vitamins, shoes, blankets, toilet articles and cigarettes would be held for some future date.

But, the Filipinos from Pangatian and other nearby barrios did their best to pass on small Christmas gifts to the POW's with permission from the Commandant. Medical Corpsman Eugene Evers received a broken phonograph complete with hand crank and records. He and his buddies managed to repair the old machine and even made workable needles from bits of wire. The records were cracked but the music was to bring many hours of enjoyment.

The secret radio in the camp, at long last, was in working order. The static filled news broadcast from Australia informed the men of MacAthur's campaign progress and news of the progress in Europe.

But, the majority of prisoners in Cabanatuan were still unaware of the radio's existence and when news of Allied victories was passed from man to man, many were skeptical of the truth.

Numbers of American prisoners at Cabanatuan continued to vary. A head count on a given day could range anywhere from 1,500 to 3,800 depending on how many men were in sufficient health to work the Japanese details. Patients in the camp hospital likewise varied depending upon the numbers suffering recurring disease or injuries from beatings administered by the work detail guards.

Most of the prisoners had now been confined for over nineteen months. Although the death rate was no longer spiraling, conditions in the camp had not improved.

Food... that is, food without meat, was still rationed and medicines remained in short supply.

Chapter 4.

"I'm going to turn you men into Rangers!" Lieutenant Colonel Henry A. Mucci-
April, 1944

A year had gone by since Captain James Fisher and the 98th Field Artillery arrived in New Guinea, and the Army had failed to find some practical use for them. Bored, and with morale dangerously low, the husky fellows occupied their time by making the most of any project.

Dr. Fisher had a passion for carpentry. It was only natural for him to find a spot and erect a "clinic". The site was a small hill on the bank of a fast flowing, shallow stream directly across from Battalion Head- quarters. There, Fisher planned to treat not only the minor ailments and injuries of the 98th, but expand to accommodate the needs of local natives. Members of his detachment offered to help with the construction but Captain Fisher preferred to do the work himself.

Several times a day "Captain Jim" would wade into the clear, cold waters and splash back and forth from Headquarters, usually forget- ting something each trip. His men decided to build him a small bridge.

A day after its completion, men on a detail near the headquarters watched with amusement as Captain Fisher emerged from his clinic, strolled to the stream and began to wade across. As he reached the opposite bank, he was confronted by the detail. They knew he was absent-minded, but this was too much.

"Why didn't you use the bridge?", one soldier asked. Captain Fisher scratched at his close, cropped hair and grinned, "Oh! The bridge... I forgot about the bridge!"

The men of the 98th had wasted away fourteen months through no fault of their own. Without real purpose for existence, only the strong moral fiber of the men and officers held the Unit from becoming a battalion of troublemakers. But, General Walter Krueger had plans for the men of the 98th. The success of the elite Alamo Scouts please him. The small team surveillance of the enemy had yielded magnificient results in the early months of 1944. Now, to complete his well organized 6th Army, General Krueger needed something else.

The invasion of the Philippines would necessitate training another elite unit... a special combat unit for assignments too large for the Scouts. Krueger's colleagues in England planning the invasion of Europe already had such units. They called them Army Rangers.

The most logical group from which to form a Ranger unit in the Pacific was the 98th Battalion of giants.

An army does not convert a bunch of big men into Rangers without considerable effort. The key would lie with intensive training by an excellent cadre and a commander with unusual qualities. A leader must be chosen who could churn the men into an effective fighting force... a leader of special caliber and personality who would gain respect and admiration.

Krueger knew he needed a man with dramatic leadership abilities but insisted that the commander also possess genuine interest and concern for the men. Few of the officers in the 98th were infantry trained. Most had been schooled in artillery. Krueger concluded it would be better to find someone from outside the 6th Army Staff, a stranger who had no obligations or allegance to other officers. The man selected was West Point graduate Lieutenant Colonel Henry Andrew Mucci.

When Colonel Mucci arrived at Fort Moresby to take command of the 98th in April, 1944, he had turned thirty-three. With a high receding hair line, though, he appeared much older. Since his graduation in 1932, Mucci had held a number of less glamorous, less demanding positions. The assignment before New Guinea was Hawaii where he received schooling in jungle warfare and ranger tactics while serving with the Military Police Staff.

The first day of his new command the Battalion was assembled at the parade field while Lieutenant Colonel Mucci stood on the side lines calmly puffing on a pipe. His dark, piercing eyes, accented by heavy brows, studied the men as they formed directly in front of an eight foot platform which stood some four feet high. When the Battalion was called to attention, Colonel Mucci tapped the ashes from the silver rimmed pipe on his boot heel and crammed it, stem first, into his shirt pocket. With a swaggered gate he strutted towards the front of the assembly and in one quick leap, aided by placing his hand on the deck, was standing on the platform.

He stood, a trim small man, with fists clenched and placed on his hips, causing his elbows to jut outward, exposing a.45 automatic hung low in its leather shoulder holster. Mucci raised a hand and scratched at his moustache. Then he shouted.. . "At.. .Ease!"

There was a moment while the man relaxed and waited for what they expected to be a few uninteresting announcements.

"I am Lieutenant Colonel Mucci...your new commanding officer. I'm going to turn you men into.. Rangers! From now on, the 98th will be known as the Sixth United States Army Ranger Battalion!"

35

Mucci paused and studied his men. Then he continued, "For the next few months we will be going through some of the toughest training you can imagine. We are going through it together! You men are big and healthy... you can take it. And... when we're through you'll be the roughest bunch of soldiers in the Sixth Army!"

By the end of the first week a few in the Ranger Battallion requested transfer to other units. A few others were transferred out by Colonel Mucci for various reasons which he held secret between them. Though it was not a requirement, married men were encouraged to give serious thought before they elected to stay in the unit. By the end of the month everyone who remained was a volunteer.

The final Ranger Battalion was to consist of approximately six hundred men. Each of the former artillery "Batteries" became a company containing sixty-three to sixty-five men. A Ranger company consisted of a company headquarters with one officer and three men, two platoons with one officer and thirty-one men. Each platoon was divided with a headquarters, a special "weapons" section of six men, and two "assault" sections of eleven men each.

The assault section had a headquarters of one man, an assault squad of five men and a light machine gun squad of five men. Machine guns actually were Browning Automatic Rifles (BAR). Fire power of a Ranger Company, with their mixture of thirty-two MI semiautomatic rifles, BAR's, MI carbines and Thompson submachine guns (Tommy guns) equaled that of a one hundred and eighty man regular infantry company. The Sixth Rangers had their own Medical Detachment under Captain Fisher, a communications section and a motor pool.

First Lieutenant Robert W. Prince was a likable officer. The men of his "C" Company considered Prince to be a strict disciplinarian fair in his decisions and always expressing concern for their welfare. Officers knew Robert Prince as a quiet, serious man possessing the rare quality of a clam, natural leader. He never wasted time with dramatics or exaggerations. Perhaps this serious attitude left him vulnerable to Colonel Mucci's magic personality. For, Bob Prince, at age 23, was also very impressionable. He received a ROTC commission after graduating from Stanford University and then experienced artillery training at Fort Sill. He was a bright artillery officer, ideally suited for combat. But, fate had held him with the 98th and now fate was about to tie him with the most unusual and exciting officer he had ever met.

Colonel Henry Mucci possessed a natural ability to motivate people. He was a born politician who knew what to say, when and how to say it. He knew the art of leadership and when to turn charming, or dictatorial. To get morale on the upswing while turning the 98th into Rangers would require a good cadre. No one appreciated this fact more than Mucci.

Colonel Mucci looked down his Roman nose at Lieutentant Prince and then broke into a grin as he began their first interview. Since Bob Prince was married, Mucci explained the option to transfer to a different unit, but quickly added, "I need good men like you, Lieutenant. You stay with the Rangers and I promise you'll be two grades higher by the time we are through liberating the Philippines!" Mucci, as usual, was convincing and Bob Prince decided to stay. Not because of the promise of promotions; even Mucci knew it was not the key, but due to the fact that the challenge seemed interesting. And, Prince had become attached to his men of C Company. He would like to see them through the war.

When the Ranger training began with grueling hours of calisthenics, Mucci was there, going through the exercises in the hot sun with the men. Often, he would even be on the platform leading PT. Whatever Mucci told the men to do, he also did. He seemed to be

everywhere... on each twenty mile hike, in the middle of bayonet training, jogging along on the five mile runs before breakfast, crawling
thourgh the mud to participate in attacks on simulated Japanese
pillboxes, firing a variety of weapons and scoring some of the highest
grades.

Some men originally resented their Commander's Napoleonic
personality. They called him "little MacArthur". Yet, unlike generals,
one fact was obvious. Mucci was there to be seen. Often quick
tempered and emotional, Mucci had learned to control the faults.
Those who were critical discovered that behind the Colonel's flam-
boyant front was an individual who was honest and kind to the lowest
ranking soldier. So, the big men of the 6th Rangers, happy to find a
place in the war at last, followed their commander... and learned fast.

Mucci called Charles H. Bosard, "the kid", but not because of his
age. At twenty-six, Bosard was, in fact, a few years older than most
of the others. The nickname Mucci bestowed on the lst Sergeant of
F Company was in reference to Bosard's size. Yet, the wiry five foot,
six inch Bosard could move about with speed as he maintained
relentless pressure on his men in the field. Typical of so many tough
lst Sergeants, Bosard's size had nothing to do with his ability to train
and lead. Somehow, at the end of practically every training day, Sergeant Bosard managed to find a few quiet moments and maintained
a field diary.

"May 8, 1944 - Having a big general inspection today - Have been
firing all our weapons, going over Misery Hill, through Torture Flats,
landing nets, obstacle course - ran about ten miles. We are all darn
good swimmers now - 250 yards with a 50 pound pack. June 4 -
Working very hard -going through grenade course and bayonet
course. Getting ready for amphibious training."

* * * *

During mid August, 1944, Luzon guerilla Major Robert Lapham received confirmation on his radio that MacArthur and the U.S. Navy were ready to supply the guerrillas in the Philippines with those promised weapons and munitions. The only possible way this could be accomplished was by submarine.

Major Lapham requested Captain Pajota to select a suitable site for the rendezvous.

Colonel Bernard Anderson also was promised delivery of supplies and selected the mouth of the Masanga River on the East Coast of Luzon. To reach this scheduled point, Colonel Anderson and his men successfully avoided Japanese patrols as they crossed fifty miles of open country on foot. Once in the safety of the Eastern mountain range, they were able to move down to the coast, make contact with the U.S. Nautilus, and return with the valuable equipment without incident.

Pajota suggested a cove known as Debut Bay, about midway along the east coast of Luzon. It is a narrow cove with waters deep enough to easily accommodate the Nautilus. Surrounding the cove, heavy forest, providing excellent concealment, stretched up into the high Sierra Madre Mountains.

Major Lapham and Captain McKenzie arrived at Debut Bay and along with Pajota, established a temporary headquarters... and waited. When the Nautilus arrived, she was able to maneuver to within twenty-five yards of shore and docked at a raft Pajota's men had constructed of bamboo.

The joy of the two American meeting with fellow countrymen for the first time in almost two and a half years was, understandably, overwhelming. The excitement continued as the Filipinos began to unload a fantastic assortment of weapons and supplies.

There were Thompson submachine guns,.45 caliber "grease guns", MI carbines and Browning Automatic Rifles (BAR's) plus what seemed to be an unending quantity of ammunition. The small, light-weight carbines with their fifteen and thirty round magazines were perfectly suited for guerrilla warfare and the little Filipinos.

Numerous cartons of a very special item were unloaded... American cigarettes. The U.S. Psychological Warfare teams had not missed a trick. On each pack was the picture of General MacArthur, and clearly printed beneath his profile were his words, "I SHALL RETURN!" The Cigarettes would be handed out all over Nueva Ecija.

Major Lapham, Colonel Anderson and some of the other American guerrillas could have evacuated the Philippines on the Nautilus and left the fighting to the Filipinos. No one would have condemned them. Each American was plagued with at least one tropical illness. That was enough reason to leave. Each had been in the combat zone since December 1941 - almost three years under the most trying con-ditions.

MacArthur's Headquarters had already commended them highly for their outstanding sacrifices. The ranks they bestowed upon them-selves, qualified by their duty and performance, had been recognized by the U.S. Army. It was a small reward, but they asked for no more... only the privilege to continue to serve their country. Whatever motivated these men of unusual caliber, their decision to stay and fight rather than evacuate certainly impressed the Filipinos.

But, now that the guerrillas knew subs could deliver supplies they proposed an interesting question. If the Nautilus could get in and out of Debut Bay, and the Guerrilla commanders would not leave, then why must the sub return empty? Could it evacuate the American P.O.W.'s at Cabanatuan?

The idea was not completely new. Colonel Anderson had drawn attack maps and all the plans for a raid on the P.O.W. camp. Major Lapham, whose command area actually included the P.O.W. camp, likewise had maps and plans. He and Captain Pajota discussed the idea many times during August and September of 1944. If the attack on P.O.W. Camp Cabanatuan was executed at once, over 3,000 Americans could be set free.

Pajota's squadrons and Lapham's other units in Nueva Ecija could easily overpower the Japanese garrison at the P.O.W. camp. The evacuation of 3,000 sick men across the mountains to the sea while under pursuit by the Japanese, of course, presented the greatest worry. Most of the P.O.W.'s were not capable of walking that distance. They would have to be carried.

In the Guimba area, Major Lapham had another brilliant guerrilla captain... Eduardo Joson. An average size Filipino with a pleasant personality, Joson was an excellent organizer and a fearless leader. With the help of Joson and Pajota, Major Lapham knew enough civilians could be mustered to carry the P.O.W. 's. Assuming the guerrillas could deliver all the 3,000 P.O.W.'s to the sea, another major problem would face the Navy.

It would be impossible to risk the twenty or thirty subs required to evacuate all the men at once. Never could enough sea planes be expected to land and take off in enemy waters without detection. However, it was believed that one or two subs might be able to shuttle the P.O.W.'s far out to sea to a waiting transport ship. The American guerrillas knew the time for an Allied invasion of the Philippines must be close at hand. Would the Japanese execute the prisoners at Cabanatuan? Based on past performances of the Imperial Army in Bataan and O'Donnell, there was good reason to study the future of the Cabanatuan inmates with great concern.

Colonel Anderson pleaded by radio with MacArthur's Headquarters. In order to save the P.O.W.'s, a raid must come immediately. Anderson was ordered to "hold off". Major Lapham also presented his plan by radio, and he too was instructed to "hold off".

The risk, in the eyes of Headquarters, was too great. No one doubted the guerrilla's ability to overpower the Japanese garrison. Nor, did Headquarters feel that Anderson or Lapham would be unsuccessful in delivering at least a large percentage of the P.O.W.'s to the ocean. But, the U.S. Navy could not yet guarantee a successful evacuation by sea.

* * * *

At P.O.W. Camp Cabanatuan, cigarettes were at a premium. The Japanese, in a generous mood, turned over to the prisoners shredded leaves of tobacco which had been processed by the Imperial Army while manufacturing insect repellent. From this the Americans rolled an ample supply of cigarettes. For those who had never been able to rid themselves of the habit during twenty-eight months of confinement, the garbage was better than nothing.

The death toll leveled. Now, only a few a month withered into death from beriberi, malnutrition, dysentery and malaria. These numbers had to be added to those who were failing fast from the beatings. Maintaining the list was complicated by the continual rotation of men for work details. Some names were simply missing from rosters of returning work groups. It was seldom possible to ascertain if these men were dead or sent to other details elsewhere in the islands.

By September, 1944, P.O.W. Camp Cabanatuan had become a mixing bowl of Allied prisoners. A few American civilians who were interned in other prisons in Manila suddenly found themselves in Cabanatuan. There were a few British, Norwegians and Dutch, most of whom had been plucked from the sea by Japanese naval vessels.

Several Navy P.O.W.'s had constructed a large gong, bent into the shape of a triangle from scrap iron. Taking turns at standing "watch", they struck out the time of day. The resulting sound had a strange similarity to navy "bells".

Also in September,1944, the fourteen month old "lay low order" imposed on the guerrillas in the Philippines was lifted. The new instructions received by radio came as welcome news to the men who were forced to play hide and seek with the Imperial Army for so long... "Destroy all enemy lines of communication, harass, delay and destroy enemy troops and supply movements..." Now, the guerrillas were on the offensive again. There was good reason for the change in strategy. General MacArthur had been advised by Washington. His plan to invade *Leyte, was approved and was to begin October 20., 1944.

* * * *

Second Lieutenant San Pedro's men enthusiastically carried out the orders of Captain Juan Pajota. The temporary wooden bridge spanning the Cabu River, about a mile from P.O.W. Camp Cabanatuan, was no longer in use now that the Japanese had reopened the main bridge. The Guerrillas proceeded to destroy the temporary bridge anyway. When they had completed their task they moved to their next objective.. the main bridge.

The Imperial Army was proud of the new Cabu Bridge which stretched some eighty feet across the river at the main highway. They had devoted almost two years working on its reconstruction.

Like large brown termites, the Filipinos chopped into the wooden girders until they had cut a little more than half way through each beam. Then, they withdrew into the brush. Around 1 p.m. an Imperial Army truck loaded with supplies, left Cabanatuan City headed for Bongabon. By 1:15, the truck passed theP.O.W. camp and continued north, passing onto the Cabu Bridge. As the guerrillas expected, the weight of the truck was sufficient. The bridge, with the vehicle, crashed into the river. The next day, the Japanese engineers were once again at the river removing the damage and hauling fresh lumber for their second reconstruction of Cabu Bridge.

Chapter 5

"People of the Philippines... I have returned!" General Douglas MacArthur

October 20, 1944

On October 3rd, Lieutenant Colonel Henry Mucci called his officers into the "war room" for a briefing. At 0800, October 9th, the Battalion formed in front of their headquarters before moving to their point of embarkation. At 5 p.m., their convoy pulled out for sea and proceeded for Hollandia.

A few days out to sea, Captain Bob Prince (Mucci had kept his promotion promise) and the other company commanders reluctantly invited Colonel Mucci into their quarters for a game of Bridge. They considered Mucci to be a lousy Bridge player and even maintained a record of his losses.

"Why don't we play Hearts?" Mucci asked as he sat down. Prince shuffled the cards and no one answered.

"I'm tired of Bridge," Mucci persisted. "Let's play Hearts!"

"This will give you a chance to cut what you owe." Prince smiled as he began to deal. "Besides, your game of Hearts is nothing to brag about either."

Colonel Mucci, disgusted with the game selection, sat through one hand after another. Finally, after two hours of losing he stood and tossed his cards on the table. "To hell with Bridge! I'm not going to play with you guys anymore!"

The Colonel stormed from the room. The steel door slammed behind him and laughter broke out among the staff.

On October 15th, the winds, reaching gale proportions, lashed at the Allied convoy, but on the 17th, as naval guns hammered away at three small islands selected for the Rangers attack, the sea suddenly became calm.

Under an overcast sky the first assault waves of Rangers approached what appeared to be perfect beaches. A hundred yards off shore their landing craft grounded on coral reefs forcing the men to wade the rest of the way. By noon, all of C Company were on Dinagat and had established their Battalion Command Post, thus far completely unopposed. Three platoons then moved out to find the Japanese and gain control of the upper end of the island. Company D landed on Guiuan and Company B, reinforced with a platoon from the motor pool, landed on Homonhon, also unopposed. Within an hour they were combing the jungle for the enemy.

During the next three days, the Rangers killed over seven hundred Imperial Army soldiers, destroyed several radio installations and set up valuable navigation lights to guide the arriving convoy heading for Leyte.

To take Leyte and its valuable airfields General MacArthur planned to commit 200,000 men of General Krueger's 6th Army along with 2,500 combat aircraft from the Far East Air Force and 1,500 aircraft from the 7th and 3rd Naval Fleet.

General Tomoyuki Yamashita arrived at his new headquarters in Manila in early October to assume command of the Imperial Army's 14th Area Operations. By October 20th, the Japanese had fewer than one hundred and fifty conventional combat planes throughout the Philippines. Of Yamashita's 500,000 man Army, about 200,000 were scattered in the Southern Philippines. Only 20,000 were on Leyte on October 2Oth to greet the giant Allied Army invasion force.

By mid afternoon of the 2Oth, the Allies had established a large beachhead on Leyte's eastern shore. Just before 2 p.m., General MacArthur was joined by staff officers and newspaper men in a landing barge.

Touching sand some fifty yards off shore, the barge's door splashed down and the party, led by MacArthur, waded ashore. The Field Marshal stepped before the microphone of a portable radio. His rough voice cracking with emotion, he began his speech... "This is the Voice of Freedom, General MacArthur speaking. People of the Philippines; I have returned! By the grace of the Almighty God, our forces stand again on Philippine soil..."

By the end of October, the Allies had secured the Leyte valley. By December lOth, the Japanese had lost 50,000 men, including reinforcements Yamashita committed. The remaining Japanese were sick, short of food and ammunition and no longer functioned as organized units. Yet, for the next twenty days they would hold until finally hunted down by Filipino guerrillas or American patrols. Almost none survived. Now... Luzon could be liberated.

* * * *

At P.O.W. Camp Cabanatuan, the canteens containing the homemade secret radio were placed together and the rope with its antenna was connected. The P.O.W.'s who kept the secret of the radio could not believe their ears as the rebroadcast of MacArthur's speech from Leyte came through.

It was too dangerous to keep the radio going for any length of time. The operators worked in shifts. Each shift transported the radio to a new location. Still, most P.O.W.'s did not know of the radio's existence.

But, American planes had been spotted flying over at high altitudes and all the prisoners began to hold to the hope that liberation was close at hand.

During the last week of October, 1944, over 1,800 American prisoners of war, mostly from Camp Cabanatuan, were packed into the lower level of a 5,000 ton freighter in Manila Harbor. A few hours out into the China Sea, the vessel was spotted by a U.S. submarine who had no way of knowing of the freighter's human cargo. Direct hits were scored by two torpedoes. Within minutes, the ship... and its prisoners, disappeared beneath the waters. Only five American P.O.W.'s survived and were picked up by Chinese fishermen. Meanwhile, the Japanese Imperial Headquarters ordered the evacuation of all Allied P.O.W.'s in the Philippines to continue as fast as practical.

Captain Pajota reported the departure of that first group of American P.O.W.'s from Cabanatuan to Major Lapham. Once again, Pajota and Lapham reviewed their plans for a raid on the P.O.W. camp. If they could attack now, while the Japanese's attention was on Leyte and the defense of Luzon, it was possible to rescue the 2,000 P.O.W.'s remaining. A number of radio messages shot back and forth between Major Lapham and Colonel Anderson. They both agreed. A raid on the camp must come now. It may be the last chance.

Another radio plea for permission to carry out the attack went to MacArthur. Again, Allied Headquarters radioed the guerrillas to "hold off". Headquarters still felt that it was impossible to furnish naval support for evacuation of prisoners. The invasion of Luzon was two months away. The guerrillas were assured that the rescue of all Allied P.O.W.'s would receive top priority once that invasion began.

Pressure was on the Japanese Engineers to finish repairs on the bridge over the Cabu River. Their Headquarters insisted that the highway from Cabanatuan to Bongabon be open for heavy military traffic. On November l5th, the Engineers tested their new bridge by permitting two tanks to follow one another across its wooden structure. All were satisfied that specifications had been met. The bridge would support armor. The road to Bongabon was once again open.

The new Cabu Bridge, constructed of heavy timber, was approximately seventy-five feet long and twenty-one feet wide, spanning the muddy river about ten feet above the water. The engineers had included a chest-high wooden handrail along both side edges. Now, the Japanese hoped that the bridge would not fall victim to the guerrillas again or be destroyed by American planes which were appearing over central Luzon with alarming frequency.

Three days after the new Cabu Bridge was completed, a sleek U.S. P51 fighter buzzed P.O.W. Camp Cabanatuan at a low altitude. As the fighter climbed straight into the western sky, the prison area became wild with excitement. Men poured out of their nipa barracks and began waving hats, bits of cloth... anything to attract the attention of the American pilot. The pilot banked to return for a closer look.

As the plane approached, a Japanese tank rolled out from a shed in the center of the compound with its machine gun firing at the sky. The pilot's eyes fixed on the tank and his finger moved to his machine gun control button. The dirt around the tank erupted in small explosions as.50 caliber bullets raked the area.

Like a mad hornet, the P51 roared over, climbed almost out of sight, then dove at the camp at an 80 degree angle. Again, the compound was chopped with bullets.

A small puff of blue smoke sprang from the tank. The fighter pulled out of his dive, leveled off and turned once more. The pilot saw something unexpected. While the Japanese rushed to extinguish the fire in the tank, the P51 returned, only much lower and at a reduced speed. As she flew over, one wing tilted earthward. The craft leveled and the other wing dipped. Then the plane screamed upward and disappeared in the clouds.

The pilot's recognition of white men in the compound came only a moment too late. One P.O.W. lay on the ground, a piece of his shoulder ripped away by a stray .50 caliber bullet. He was rushed to the camp hospital and after an hour's surgery, his buddies were informed that he would survive. While the surgery was in process, other P.O.W.'s assembled pieces of cloth and spelled out on the ground three letters large enough to be seen from the air ... "P.O.W".

Later that afternoon, the Camp Commandant issued two orders. The first was for the prisoners. There would be no more waving at American airplanes . . . punishment is death. The second order was directed at his garrison troops. There was to be no more firing at American planes. Since the Allies now knew there were Americans in the camp, future attacks were unlikely.

For the next thirty days, several American planes passed over P.O.W. Camp Cabanatuan. Unmolested, they took time to wave their wings at the men below. Now, all of the 2,000 P.O.W.'s had hope for survival... providing the Japanese did not have other plans.

On the morning of December 15th, the Americans landed on Mindoro. The invasion of Luzon was to begin on January 9, 1945. The Japanese no longer possessed an effective air force or navy in the Philippine area to stop the Americans.

Chapter 6

"Go to Manila... Go around the Nips, bounce off the Nips but, go to Manila!"General Douglas MacArthur - 1945

In Manila, on December 12, 1944, a group of more than 1,600 American P.O.W.'s were loaded into a converted ocean liner for evacuation to Japan. Again, many of the prisoners were from Camp Cabanatuan. Before the vessel could pull into the Bay it was sighted by U.S. planes returning from a mission. The fighters broke from formation and dove in for the attack.

With the noise of the battle erupting above and exploding bombs in the bay around them, panic spread in the dungeons of the liner. For many who had survived the Death March and the concentration camps of O'Donnell and Cabanatuan this new hell was too much.

Low on fuel and ammunition, the U.S. planes were forced to call off the assault. But before they did, more than one hundred of their countrymen suffocated or were trampled to death as men scrambled over one another in an effort to claw through the ship's steel walls. During the night the liner maneuvered through Manila Bay and out into the China Sea. By dawn, she was far up along the west coast of the Bataan Peninsula, scarcely more than a mile from Subic Bay. But, with the dawn, the U.S. planes returned, now determined to finish the enemy ship.

Trapped in the dark holds, the P.O.W.'s climbed upon one another to reach the upper deck. To drive them back, Japanese guards opened the hatches and began to fire rifles into the screaming crowd. Suddenly the ship ran aground in the sand less than a quarter mile off shore. The Japanese then decided to allow the P.O.W.'s to climb out. In the sky, horrified U.S. pilots recognized Americans and called off the attack.

The surviving 1,300 prisoners who swam ashore were quickly rounded up and held in various areas around the ruins of Subic Naval Yards until a new plan for evacuation could be instituted.

By the end of 1944, only a little over 500 Allied P.O.W.'s were left at Camp Cabanatuan. The majority of these were much too sick to send anywhere.

A change had developed in the behavior of the guards at Cabanatuan. Their arrogant and belligerent attitude towards the P.O.W.'s was not replaced with kindness. But, the prisoners detected a nervous and worried appearance in their faces. The activity of the sentries became haphazard, and they seemed to ignore the presence of their captives. Work details and beatings, for the most part, ceased. Red Cross Christmas packages marked "1943" were distributed to some of the men as the first P.O.W.'s departed in late 1944. A few of the 500 who remained in the camp found themselves in the possession of American-made shoes from those packages. The majority stored the shoes for some future use, electing to move about the camp barefooted or with handmade sandals as they had done for so long.

* * * *

Captain Juan Pajota was not an officer wrapped in complexities, nor had he an obsession for greater power or glory. He considered himself simply a field commander in the Army of the United States leading men in an unconventional war.

Captain Pajota limited his power because he believed he was only one link in the chain of U.S. military authority. His sworn duty to uphold the Constitution of the United States did not include establishing himself as a war lord.

Undoubtedly he understood his enemy. He had fought them in close quarters continually for three years. Yet there was a new enemy emerging which he did not completely understand. This enemy was his"Kababayan," some of his fellow countrymen, who also fought the Japanese. Now this group was turning on the U.S.A.F.F.E. Guerrillas. This enemy was the Hukbalahap...the HUKS.

It was not that the HUKS had always desired to war with the guerrillas who were controlled and supported by the United States. Nor was it the HUKS' goal to war with the Americans. To the contrary, Commander Luis Taruc and his followers still held to their basic committment of driving the Japanese from the Philippines.

But, it had become increasingly evident to Taruc that his hard earned victories in various battles with the Japanese may be completely ignored by the Americans once liberation was accomplished. The dream he had for a separate political party now lay in jeopardy unless MacArthur recognized them as a popular movement among the people.

The friction between the strong Communist members of the Huks and the somewhat middle of the road followers of Taruc reached a kindling point. The strength of the Huks, the Communists believed, must be impressed upon the Americans, else their party stood no chance for political survival. To be recognized, they must win battles with the Japanese and for this they needed modern weapons even if it required the destruction of other guerrilla units. Consequently, guerrillas functioning under Colonel Anderson and Major Lapham in both Pampanga and Nueva Ecija Provinces discovered the danger of two enemies... the Japanese and the Huks.

It was almost January lst before the Japanese could spare the time or ships to evacuate the 1,300 American P.O.W.'s who survived the December l2th U.S. aircraft attack on the prison ship at Subic Bay.   These P.O.W.'s along with a few hundred taken from various work details about Luzon, were divided into two groups. 1,000 were packed in the hold of a large freighter and the balance crammed into smaller ships.

In Manila the Japanese held over 3,500 Allied civilians at Santo Tomas University and approximately 1,300 civilians at the old Bilibid Prison. Another 2,200 civilians were interned at Los Banos Prison on the south shore of Laguna de Bay about forty miles from Manila. Most of these civilians were Americans... men, women, and children who were trapped in the Philippines during the Japanese invasion. They were a mixture of businessmen, educators, engineers, journalists, and dependents of the U.S.A.F.F.E. force. With the exception of Camp Cabanatuan, there were only a handful of American military P.O.W.'s still scattered about Luzon.

The Civilian prisoners were, by comparison to the Cabanatuan P.O.W.'s in reasonably good physical condition though the majority suffered from malnutrition and lack of adequate medical attention. The Japanese calculated that the civilian prisoners would present no real embarrassment either for the Imperial Army or Tokyo should Luzon fall to the American forces. Japan had every right, they felt, to hold civilian prisoners. After all, American born Japanese were still being held in"detention camps" in the United States.

So the last load of American prisoners leaving by ship virtually eliminated the remaining military personnel, except for those at Cabanatuan. As before, little preparation had been given to the care of a the P.O.W.'s crammed inside the ships. Over ten a day would die from lack of water during the trip to Japan.

Again, U.S. planes, unaware of the ship's contents, assaulted the vessels, scoring a direct hit on one with bombs. Two hundred and sixty-five Americans were killed in the brief attack.

* * * *

Most of the Imperial l4th Area Army Commander Tomoyuki Yamashita's sixty years had been devoted to the military service for his Emperor. The world once called Yamashita the"Tiger of Malaya" after his brilliant but brutal victories in that jungled part of Asia. His troops had smashed Singapore, dealing the British one of their worst defeats in history.

Yamashita understood Western mentality and strategy. He knew the secrets of breaking American fighting spirit by permitting his army to commit atrocities. His army thrived on winning... on the offensive, and each warrior deserved to draw blood in any way he desired.

Although Yamashita had over 250,000 soldiers under his command on Luzon, Imperial Headquarters had not given him control of the large group of Naval troops stationed around Manila. Nor did Yamashita have the superior army he once commanded on the mainland of Asia. More than half his Luzon force was poorly led and short of supplies and munitions.

Yamashita calculated correctly that MacArthur would attack at Lingayen Gulf where General Homma's invading armies had landed three years earlier. Other than a small delaying force, Yamashita did not plan to meet the Allies at Lingayen.

The best, he figured, was to delay the American's conquest of Luzon and inflict as many casualties as possible. Thus, mainland Japan would have more time to prepare for an inevitable invasion.

Yamashita planned to leave the Central Plains area defended by only small delaying forces while the bulk of his quarter million men moved to three mountain strong holds. The majority of these men began a withdrawal from previously assigned positions to the rugged wilderness of northern Luzon. To defend the hilly area east of Manila, the second largest force prepared fortifications in cliffs, caves and tunnels. The mountainous terrain just west of the Central Plains which overlooked Clark Field is where the third, but smallest force withdrew. If the Americans moved down the Central Plains for Manila, as Yamashita expected, their flank could easily be threatened.

As for the Allied strategy, to attack Luzon, Vice Admiral Thomas Kinkaid's Seventh Fleet, consisting of more than 850 vessels, was in charge of providing protection and delivering General Krueger's 200,000 man Sixth Army. While this major assault was under way, Admiral Halsey's Third Fleet carriers would launch their aircraft to strike at Formosa and Northern Luzon. General George Kenney's Far East Air Force would bomb and strafe Luzon from its new bases on Mindoro and Leyte. Kenney was to move his airplanes up to Luzon as soon as engineers completed construction of bases.

The battle for Luzon was to become the largest in the Pacific. Against the largest Japanese force ever assembled on one island, more American fighting men were to be committed than in North Africa or Italy.

On January 4th, four large landing craft (LCI's) containing the Sixth Ranger Battalion joined the forty mile long convoy heading for Luzon. At 0700, January 9, 1945, the Allied forces entered the calm waters of Lingayen Bay. The Navy began their barrage of the beaches while aircraft pounded suspected positions further inland.

At 0930, the first wave of American liberating forces hit the Luzon beaches almost completely unopposed. By nightfall over 68,000 soldiers, including MacArthur, were on shore.

The Sixth Rangers were disappointed when they learned that they must wait until January lOth before going ashore. At noon that day, the first landing craft carrying A Company beached in a surf which had churned up ten foot waves over night.

DWAKS* were called in to deliver the Rangers and by 1600 (4 p.m.) all companies were ashore. The battalion moved 1,000 yards inland and found Colonel Mucci with the advance"quartering party" standing in an area he had selected for bivouac site.

Everyone was ordered to dig in and get some rest. The next morning the battalion moved further inland, establishing a new perimeter near the town of Dagupan. Then, the Rangers moved two miles south of Dagupan to the vicinity of Calasio and began to erect a"semi-permanent" camp. It would be three more days before the battalion received their first combat mission.

No sooner had General Walter Krueger settled in his new headquarters than he found himself in the presence of some very distinguished guests.

On hand to welcome the Sixth Army Commanding General was guerrilla leader Colonel Bernard Anderson, still wearing his 1941 Air Force cap and Major Robert Lapham, wearing his old campaign hat. New orders were issued for the guerrillas,"...Effective at once you and all elements of your organization are placed under command of the Commanding General, Sixth United States Army." The war was not yet over for the Americans who had survived the hardships of a thirty-one month guerrilla campaign.

By January lOth, the slow and careful advance of the American forces into Luzon was making good progress against light enemy resistance.

On the right (southern) flank, moving towards Tarlac, Clark Field and San Fernando was Major General Oscar W. Griswold's XIV Corps.

Major General Innis P. Swift's I Corps began to push north into the mountains towards Baguio and east towards San Jose. It was in these mountains that the Americans would run head on into the largest concentration of more than 158,000 Japanese soldiers.

As the I Corps entered the hills, the Japanese opened up with a heavy bombardment from a series of caves, pillboxes and tanks. Short of fuel, the Japanese had buried their armor on the mountain sides leaving only their turrets exposed. The I Corps advance slowed and MacArthur became impatient.

General Krueger explained that he was worried about his flanks, fearing that a fast drive for Manila may leave his lines of supply vulnerable.

"Go to Manila," MacArthur ordered."Go around the Nips, bounce off the Nips, but go to Manila!"

Of all the Allied troops fighting their way inland from Lingayen Gulf, none had a greater variety of combat experience than the men of the Signal Corps' Photographic Service.

The average strength of a combat photography unit was one officer and five enlisted men. The enlisted ranks were comprised of two still and two motion picture photographers, plus a utility man. Each unit was self sustaining, packing thirty days of field rations, plus their cameras and film. For protection, each man carried a.45 caliber automatic pistol and, under certain conditions, was issued a carbine or MI rifle. But, their cameras were their most prized possessions, seeming often more valuable than life itself.

Now separate photo units began to push along with the Army, employing their special technique of becoming almost part of the countryside to obtain accurate, candid photos. It became the responsibility of"Unit F" of the 832nd Signal Service Battalion to go with the Sixth Rangers and record every action on film, no matter how dangerous the mission.

At dusk, January I5th, the Ilocanos' in Pangasinan began a discussion about the strange new American war plane. It was time for the"Nangisit law wa-law wa" to appear as she had each evening for the last three days. The machine was a dreadful looking thing which thundered into the evening sky to kill the Japanese. She did not return until almost dawn.

None of the Filipinos had ever seen such a weird looking airplane before. It became a game to stand outside and count them as they flew over. Some of the children tried to stay awake until the killers returned. But it was impossible to count them once the darkness gained control of the land. Then the killers could not be seen...only heard. The Filipinos named the airplane as it appeared to them,"Nangisit law wa - law wa"... " black spider." The Americans called her the"Black Widow"! The" Dark Lady," the "South Pacific Sandman." Whatever they called her, the P61 Night Interceptor Pursuit Airplane had proven to be one of the most valuable aircraft in the Pacific war.

Painted glossy black, the P6I's twin 2,000 horsepower radial engines were mounted in the wing in low slung nacelles which tapered back into twin tail booms. A long, podshaped fuselage projected front and back of its inner wing sections and was accented by a long blunt nose and a greenhouse type, two level canopy. Though capable of reaching speeds of 375 miles per hour, she could circle at extreme- ly slow speeds without a stall. Altitude ranges were just as impres- sive. She was comfortable at 30,000 feet or at tree scraping, one hundred foot levels.

One of the secrets of the craft was a new"spoiler" type aileron. It permitted her to function at very low speeds (stalling speed was 75 miles per hour) and out turn practically all other aircraft. Another was her armament. The P61 had four.50 caliber machine guns contained in a top dorsal turret and four 20 mm cannons in a front belly bulge below her fuselage. The pilot could command all eight guns forward, producing more fire power than any other fighter.

Her crew was a pilot in the front seat, a gunner in the seat direct- ly behind him and a special observer in the top, third seat. The ob- server and the duty he performed was what made the P61 especially interesting and deadly. He was the Radar Observer (RO), reading and interpreting the instruments receiving signals from a radar device mounted in the long blunt nonmetallic nose of the fuselage.

Radar was something new in World War II. It was the secret which allowed the P61 to see in the dark and find her enemy.

Perhaps those spider-like lines and the black finish contributed mainly to the P61's arachnoidian name. But like the deadly spider, the fighter also had a lethal bite with her four.20 mm cannons. Any enemy plane caught in her radar web stood little chance for escape.

Army engineers worked fast, starting January 9th, and by the l3th, completed an airstrip built of pierced steel planking (PSP) on the sand just one hundred yards inland from the waters of Lingayen Gulf. This was to be the new home of the 547th Night Fighter Squadron.

The 547th was composed of some sixteen P6l's. The unit was granted tremendous latitude and freedom which enabled them to perform services of air cover throughout the China Sea area. This activity occurred at night or during extremely unfavorable flying conditions when day fighters were grounded.

The Allied invasion of Luzon was about to produce a new hunting field and additional admiration for the 547th. With their air power virtually nonexistent, the Japanese Imperial Army took to the roads mostly at night. It was then, so the Japanese thought, that their convoys and troops would be safe from American aerial attack. But the Black Widows were about to change all of that.

The personnel of the 547th were just as unique as the equipment they flew. Highly motivated and creative in both officer and enlisted ranks, over 90% were hand picked and screened carefully before acceptance. By January, 30% of the pilots were on their second or third combat tour. Some had even flown with the RAF and RCAF in Europe. The 547th were the"old men" in the Air Force. Their average age was twenty seven.

Innovations had become a trademark of the squadron. Its members developed many amazing ideas in the way of tactics, and demonstrated for the first time the use of radar as a means of conducting safe instrument landings. Years later, their system would be perfected into what is now known as"Ground Control Approach" (GCA).

Chapter 7

"You had better get down on your knees and pray! Dammit... don't fake it! I mean...PRAY! And, I want you to swear an oath before God... Swear you'll die fighting rather than let any harm come to those POW's!"

Lieutenant Colonel Henry A. Mucci, Jan. 1945

On January l6th rumors prevailed around 6th Army Headquarters that the Rangers were going to be assigned their first mission on Luzon.

Suddenly, as it happens during combat operations, it was no longer a rumor. A reconnaissance patrol consisting of three officers, nine enlisted men, one Filipino guide, and one radar technician, all under the command of Captain Arthur Simons of B Company, boarded two PT boats and headed out into Lingayen Gulf for a little dot on the map known as Santiago Island.

Santiago, 6th Army G2 (Intelligence) believed, was ideally situated for a radar station which could detect enemy planes should the Japanese attempt to approach Lingayen Gulf from Formosa. The Rangers were cautioned that they may find over 4,000 Imperial soldiers on Santiago.

At 2200 hours (10 p.m.), the Ranger patrol disembarked from the PT's and began to row their rubber boats towards what they had been told was Santiago. Unfortunately, someone had made a mistake. They were dropped near Saipar Island some two and a half miles from their destination. When the error was finally discovered, the patrol had to row their tiny boats for two more hours.

Once on Santiago, the Rangers split into two smaller units and soon learned from the excited residents that there were no Japanese on the island. All the enemy had pulled out for the mainland the day before. Captain Simons located a suitable spot for the radar station and the Rangers returned to make their report to Colonel Mucci.

Wanting to insure the security of the island, 6th Army Headquarters then requested Mucci to furnish two companies who were to draw rations and prepare for a twenty day stay on Santiago. Captain Simons was senior by date of rank and having already accomplished the reconnaissance mission was rightfully entitled to the assignment. On January 19th, B and E Companies departed Ranger headquarters for an uneventful trip aboard a LSM.

When they landed with a bulldozer, a truck, and a jeep, the natives greeted them with a joyous welcome. No one had expected to see so many Americans and such interesting equipment on their small island. After the wild reception, the Rangers got down to serious business and by January 21st the radar station was operational.

As luck would have it, the Santiago mission was to eliminate B and E Companies from participating in one of the most dramatic and rewarding assignments ever placed upon a Ranger Battalion in World War II.

Around 1500 hours (3 p.m.) on the 16th, a complement of Imperial Army soldiers, accompanied by several engineers, passed by POW Camp Cabanatuan and stopped to check Cabu Bridge to be sure that the Filipinos had not been up to their sabotage tricks again.

The Japanese were now making good use of the major artery connecting Cabanatuan City and Bongabon for their troop movement north. Cabu Bridge must remain open and support both armor and trucks until after February 2nd, at which time, Imperial Headquarters figured the withdrawal to the mountains would be complete.

On the l6th, the soldiers were also looking for a good bivouac area. They found it along the northeast side of the Cabu where large trees and bamboo thickets provided ample camouflage for troops and vehicles.

The POW compound, a mile to the south, was considered much too conspicuous for a large contingent of transient troops.

* * * *

Shortly after the Rangers settled in their new base, a few Filipinos from a nearby Barrio entered the camp with gifts of fresh papaya, bananas, and coconuts. They asked if there was a doctor among the Americans, explaining that a woman in their village was about to give birth. In the confusion of the Allied invasion, the local midwife had disappeared.

Captain James Fisher jumped at the opportunity and accompanied by Staff Sergeant John Nelson of the medical detachment, followed the Filipinos to the Barrio.

In a nipa hut on the night of January 2Oth, by the flickering light from a coconut oil lamp,"Captain Jim" helped the young Filipina give birth to her first child. With gratitude, the new mother bestowed the best honor possible to the American by requesting him to be the godfather for her child.

A few days later, Jimmy Fisher stood in a church built of bamboo cradling the infant in his arms. While other offices assisted, a Filipino priest performed the baptismal service. Afterward, a smiling Captain Fisher announced to the priest,"This is the new generation of Filipinos...those who must build a free Philippines."

The Rangers seized upon the chance to tease the godfather." Did their doctor"overcharge the patient"?

Captain Jim took it all in good stride, remarking that, due to his usual absent-mindedness, he had forgotten to issue the bill.

* * * *

At Pangatian a strange series of events began to unfold in POW Camp Cabanatuan beginning Jaunary 6th three days before the Allied invasion of Luzon.

In the early morning hours of the 6th, the POW's were awakened by a tremendous amount of activity on the Japanese side of the compound. By noon, the guards had packed up and pulled out of the camp leaving their quarters deserted except for a few soldiers who were sick and unable to travel. Other than those Japanese, the POW's were left practically unguarded for the next several days. Naturally, discussions began as to the possibility of making an escape.

The Allied prisoners remaining at Cabanatuan now totaled between 518 and 520; a combination of U. S. Army, Marine, Navy, and civilian personnel, plus a few British and Norwegian civilians, British Army and Navy, and Dutch Army men.

Their physical condition had continued to deteriorate, some were without limbs and more than fifty percent could not even walk. Actually, less than fifty men were strong enough to walk out of the camp. Their only chance for escape would be to evade the Japanese soldiers long enough to make it safely to nearby Filipino villages.

If a breakout was attempted, they calculated that probably half would be shot by the guards before the fences were cleared. Only about ten should expect to survive once other Imperial soldiers were called in to hunt them down. A final argument against the wisdom of a break was the revenge expected upon those left behind. None wished to gamble 500 lives against the slight possibility that ten may successfully escape.

On January 7th and 8th, a few more Japanese soldiers drifted into the camp but on the 9th, when the shelling began at Lingayen, those troops also took off, leaving about twenty armed guards at the compound. Generally, these Japanese remained to themselves. Except for the sentries at the towers and front gate, all stayed under cover inside their barracks.

On January l2th, the prisoners came up with a bold plan. They had noticed that the remaining livestock had been transferred inside the compound from the large buildings on the opposite side of the south fence. The Japanese placed the animals in a corral just across the center road on their side of the camp.

If escape was impossible, the POW's decided that at least they could face whatever the future held on a full stomach. A team of fifteen, the strongest of them all, volunteered to make a daring attempt to crawl through the fence, cross the center road and raid the corral. Success, they felt, would be based mostly on the apathetic attitude of those new guards.

The POW"slaughter team" waited until dark, slipped through the single fence row and dashed towards their selected target...a Brahma steer. In seconds, like a pack of hungry dogs, the team was upon the steer, slicing away with crude knives made from scrap metal and bamboo. The beast was butchered on the spot and every bit of the carcass carried to the POW area where cooks had already begun the fires. That night, the prisoners enjoyed a meal of meat. For most of the men, it was the first meat they had tasted since the Americans' retreat into Bataan in December, 1941... 1,120 days ago.

Several Japanese guards had watched the slaughter with a peculiar fascination. The POW's knew that if they had tried such an act a month before, while the regular guards were present, everyone would have been shot.

As a result of their action, by January 23rd, the POW medical staff reported that the majority of men were now gaining weight and strength.

But more Imperial soldiers began to arrive bringing the contingent of guards to over one hundred and the nipa barracks on the enemy side of camp were continually filled with troops moving in one day and out the next. Even though the condition of the POW's was beginning to improve it now was impossible for anyone to consider escape.

During those many months in captivity, at least fifty percent of the POW's had attempted to carry on some semblance of military custom and tradition. A certain percent simply said"to hell" with military tradition, figuring such behavior ridiculous when basic survival was difficult enough.

Some officers actually managed to maintain records of"good deeds," valor, and misconduct. When that large number of POW' s left Cabanatuan in late 1944, the records were turned over to the remaining men for safekeeping.

A few"Courts Martial" were held and recorded on scraps of paper for processing should they ever be liberated. The trials ranged from realistic proceedings against officers and men accused of stealing food from fellow prisoners or accepting favors from the Japanese, to the absurd. One starving man was tried (by the offended) for stealing and eating his officer's pet cat which had (unfortunately for the cat) slipped into the compound through the barbed wire.

Other men continued to keep records of deaths. The doctors maintained logs of diseases, the effects of malnutrition, and the treatment conducted, mostly without drugs and under the most adverse medical conditions. A total of one Colonel, twelve Lieutenant Colonels and several Majors composed the high ranking staff at the camp.

As the days drifted by they began a serious campaign to gather and file all the records. The records were hidden in various places about the camp while everyone waited for the Japanese--or the Allies to decide their fate.

* * * *

At 1900 hours (7 p.m.), January 25th, Battalion Commander Tomeo Oyabu called his Imperial Army unit to a halt at the crossroads, just east of Cabanatuan city.

Oyabu had orders to stop at this small suburb known as Sangitan and receive final instructions for his march. Now he would learn if his unit must proceed north to San Jose or northeast past the POW Camp to Bongabon.

Divisional Commander Naotake knew that there were entirely too many security leaks at the Imperial Army Provincial Headquarters in Cabanatuan City to issue orders until the units were on the move. With the Americans advancing steadily from the west and increasing guerrilla activity throughout Nueva Ecija, the Japanese intended to exercise every possible precaution to keep their troop movements secret from the nosy Filipinos.

Cabanatuan city was the hub of Imperial troop movements. Division Commander Naotake was frustrated trying to handle it all plus preparing the city for a delaying defense against the Americans.

General Yamashita left Naotake five battalion size units plus the division headquarters to serve as a rear guard in Nueva Ecija while the main body of the Army positioned itself in northern Luzon. Naotake must also cope with the many logistical problems of other units, not under his command, filtering through Cabanatuan as they proceeded north.

To delay the American forces, Naotake had orders to hold all main highways, running south to north through Nueva Ecija for another week until the last of Yamashita's troops safely evacuated the Manila area. In essence, the Naotake command was expendable.

Without air reconnaissance the Japanese could not determine accurately just where the major strike of the Americans would come. Cabanatuan City must be held since it sat dead center to the wave of advancing American units. Gapan, fifteen miles to the south could be sacrificed. Soon all Imperial forces scheduled for the northern withdraw should be safely through Cabanatuan. There would be no need to hold Gapan.

San Jose, twenty-five miles north of Cabanatuan City and Bongabon, twenty miles east must be held. Therefore, Naotake decided that the primary defense should be placed equally at Cabanatuan City and San Jose. Bongabon (furthest from the Americans) would be of secondary concern.

Battalion Commander Oyabu's unit consisting of a little over eight hundred men, had rested all day in Cabanatuan City while Naotake decided where to send them. The word finally came for Oyabu to move to the Sangitan at dark. Either the twenty-five miles to San Jose or twenty miles to Bongabon would be an easy one night's march for the battalion.

Since its beginning, the Imperial Army lacked the motorized equipment enjoyed by Western militaries. To overcome this problem the Japanese foot soldier had received extensive training to build his resistance and endurance. As early as boot camp the soldiers were trained with a twenty-five mile march, often beginning before daybreak and ending with each man being required to run laps around a parade field. The marching exercise continued, even increased, through advance training assignments and carried over to post assignments.

With uniforms which seldom fit (and usually in deplorable condition) the little soldiers' marching stamina had amazed Western observers for years before the war. Carrying his heavy ten pound rifle, ammunition, bayonet, canteen, first aid packet and his own food rations, a fully trained Japanese soldier could easily cover thirty-five miles a day on a cupful of rice, usually, flavored with dry seaweed or fish powder.

Commander Oyabu picked up the phone at the crossroads' guard station and gave his code name to the officer on the other end of the line.

"Dokuho 359... Dokuho 359, reporting!"

The voice from Naotake Headquarters issued the orders,"Dokuho 359, proceed to San Jose! Follow route through Pinaganaan, Talavera, Baloc... highway clear. . . small enemy units approaching Guimba. Report to Battalion Commander Inoue at San Jose for coordinated defense. Kimpeidan Headquarters now here. Kinpeidan proceed to Pangatian Prison camp. Kinpeiden will then proceed to Bongabon. Dokuho 359 and Inoue battalion must hold San Jose..."

Commander Oyabu now had his orders. He had no way of knowing that the San Jose assignment would be cut short.

* * * *

Around daybreak on January 26th, advance reconnaissance units of the U. S. 6th Division, I Corps, occupied the town of Guimba in Nueva Ecija. Within hours, outposts were established another nine miles east along the Licab River.

To the south of Guimba, La Paz fell to the Americans giving them a solid line, over eighteen miles wide, with the town of Licab in the center. The Allies had moved their wide front some seventy-eight miles east of 6th Army Headquarters and were now ready to launch a major drive towards San Jose and Cabanatuan City.

The push of this big wedge, to this time, had met with little enemy resistance. But, 6th Army Intelligence knew that large enemy forces were waiting for them at both San Jose and Cabanatuan City. They also knew that remnants of enemy units were making good progress, moving at night and resting during the day, as they withdrew north.

General Krueger continued to worry about his over extended line. With units engaged with the Japanese in the mountains both north and south of the Central Plains the front line could be cut off should the enemy make a desperate thrust at his middle. MacArthur's orders, nonetheless, were unchanged. The drive to Manila and the Philippine Sea must continue with all possible speed.

General Krueger calculated that his eastern front could take San Jose by January 29th and Cabanatuan City by February lst. From these two points, his men could then sweep in on Rizal City and Bongabon, cross the Sierra Madre mountains and be at the Philippine Sea by February 3rd, thus severing both Luzon and the Japanese withdraw. The eastern front must accomplish all of this while General Griswold's XIV Corps continued his dash for Manila.

Guerrilla Major Robert Lapham's knowledge of the terrain and Filipino activities was invaluable to Sixth Army Intelligence Section (G2) through early January. Now, with Guimba in Allied hands, the Americans were truly in Lapham's backyard where he had operated since 1942.

At 1500 hours (3 p.m.) on January 26th, Colonel Horton White, 6th Army G2 and his assistant, Major Frank Rowale were ready to meet with Bob Lapham and discuss, once again, a subject which had been near all their hearts for a long, long time...the Japanese POW camp at Pangatian, Cabanatuan.

When Sixth Army units entered Nueva Ecija Province Filipino runners reported to Lapham routinely. The situation near POW Camp Cabanatuan had become increasingly alarming. G2 was well advised of Japanese troop movements in and around Cabanatuan City. They knew that the POW Camp was being used for transient troops and that at least three hundred Allied POW's were still in the camp.

Intelligence Chief, Colonel Horton White, a big man with a calm disposition and a pleasant youthful face, joined Majors Rowale and Lapham at the map spread over a field table in the G2 tent.

"It's too big a job for the Scouts to handle," Colonel White agreed,"but, they can sure help." He turned to Bob Lapham and explained."Two of our Alamo Scout teams have already had experience raiding a Jap POW camp...admittedly, it was a much smaller one and the Navy delivered them to within a mile of the objective. The teams were commanded by Lieutenants Rounsaville and Nellist. Lieutenant Dove planned and coordinated the entire mission. We'd better get them in on this, Frank."

"They are on their way over here now, sir," Major Rowale replied.

Excellent." Colonel White nodded his head."How many guerrillas can we depend on, Bob?"

Major Bob Lapham pointed to a spot on the map several inches southeast of Guimba."Captain Edwardo Joson has over a hundred armed men here... near Lobong..."

" But, that's still more than twenty miles from the stockade," Rowale noted.

"Yes," Lapham continued."But...Joson is a good organizer and knows that country like the back of his hand. He can lead your men to... here." Lapham pointed to an area he circled with his finger.Balangkare and Platero. Captain Juan Pajota has more than three hundred armed men you can rely on."

"Well, Colonel...What do you think?" Rowale grinned.

"I think we had better get the 'Old Man's ' opinion!" Colonel White replied.

Within a few minutes, Alamo Scout Lieutenants Tom Rounsaville, Bill Nellist and John Dove arrived to be briefed on G-2's plan.

His buddies did not call him the"All American Boy" because he was from Hollywood or because his weight lifter physique or physical power aided him in achieving some of the highest ratings in the Alamo Scouts. Nor was the title bestowed upon Lieutenant John M. Dove when he won the Bronze Star after his first mission or the Soldiers' Medal for saving the lives of two other Scouts. John Dove did not drink or smoke and even refused coffee. He was tough, intelligent, hard working, and clean living. It was no wonder that the devotion of his men reached hero worship proportions, for he was the ideal

73

of every American boy. But the war in the muggy jungle heat of the South Pacific and the secrecy shrouding Scout operations never allowed the record of their deeds to reach the outside world.

During October, 1944, Lieutenant Dove had mapped out the entire rescue plan for thirty-two civilian Javanese being held by the Japanese at Moari in New Guinea. Two Alamo Scout teams were delivered under cover of darkness by Navy PT boats. The raid on the prison camp was a complete success. The entire Japanese garrison was liquidated and the liberated Allied prisoners (including some women and children) were safely aboard the PT boats in thirty minutes. The Scouts did not lose a single man.

One of the two teams Lieutenant Dove selected for that raid was commanded by a twenty two year old veteran parachutist from the IIth Airborne Division, First Lieutenant Thomas Rounsaville. This team consisted of five other men. PFC Frank Fox and Sergeant Harold Hard, both expert shots with the MI rifle were big, rugged individuals. PFC Francis Laquier possessed the ability to slip through the night with the quietness of a shadow. To Laquier, hunting came as instinct.. .an instinct for survival in the wilderness which he and all his American Indian brothers seem to possess. Tech Sergeant Alfred Alfonso, an American-Filipino from Hawaii was nicknamed"Opu" (fat), but his stocky build did not slow him down. He could move with cat-like precision through the underbrush.

Perhaps the last member of Rounsaville's team was one of the most interesting personalities. PFC Rufo Vaquilar had not really volunteered for the Alamo Scouts. He immigrated to California from the Philippines at age fifteen and at the"old age" of thirty-eight did not even expect to end up in the war. But the military had other ideas. He, like many American-Filipinos, soon found himself drafted and sent to New Guinea. Once he arrived, the Army informed him that he was to try out for the Scouts.

It was believed logically that these Filipinos could be of tremendous value when the Allied Army returned to the Philippines. Vaquilar preferred to carry the light weight MIAI folding stock carbine and a.45 automatic pistol. He had qualified as an " expert" with the big handgun. Always relating amusing stories concerning his past adventures (even one about a"run-in" with the law), Vaquilar was, indeed, a colorful character. No one knew if there was any truth to those stories. It didn't make any difference. He was doing his job as a member of a special group of men who had selected him to fight with them.

The second team was commanded by one of the best shots with the MI rifle in the Scouts, First Lieutenant William Nellist. Also from the llth Airborne, twenty-six year old Nellist carried his six foot, two hundred pound frame with the speed of a football halfback. His team likewise consisted of two eager and most capable Filipino-Americans...PFC Sabas Asis and Staff Sergeant Thomas Siason.

During the Moari raid, Nellist's team was also composed of Corporal Andy Smith, Tech Sergeant Wilber Wismer, PFC Gilbert Cox, and Private Galen Kittleson. Other than the Filipinos, twenty year old Kittleson was one of the smallest men in the Alamo Scouts. Yet his favorite weapon was the Thompson sub- machine gun. He was a true artist with the heavy weapon. He could squeeze off single rounds, fire short bursts or rake an area with thirty or more slugs with the deadly accuracy of a rifle.

At long last Major Robert Lapham's dream for an attack on the POW Camp was becoming a reality. Everyone was in agreement. The Sixth Rangers would be perfect to conduct such an attack.... with reconnaissance assistance from the Filipino guerrillas and the Alamo Scouts. The idea was presented to 6th Army Commanding General Walter Krueger, who listened with attentive enthusiasm.

"When do you wish to execute this?" General Krueger directed his questions to Colonel White.

"We don't have much time,Sir," White answered."The closer our lines move on Cabanatuan City the shorter the minutes of life run for those prisoners. I would say we make our final plan tomorrow with Colonel Mucci...by noon...and suggest that the Rangers strike at dark on the 29th. After the 29th our chances of finding POW's alive are slim."

General Krueger did not hesitate to respond."Get Colonel Mucci. It looks risky. But, it's a wonderful enterprise. I don't want a lot of casualties with this...and, I don't want those POW's dead, either!"

* * * *

At his headquarters in a small Barrio near the POW camp, Captain Juan Pajota unfolded the note from Major Robert Lapham which a runner had delivered. A simple strip of graphing paper eight inches wide, the note's appearance was no different than the others received by Pajota from his American commander during the thirty-three month's campaign against the Japanese. Like most of the directives, this one was handwritten with a pencil.

"Captain Pajota, Send immediately the 50 land mines in your possession.They are badly needed for a specific mission assigned us. Suggest you bring them personally for additional instructions and orders.

<u>RUSH</u>

Major Lapham"

76

The word"Rush" was underlined three times, but this was not what impressed Pajota.

If Major Lapham desired land mines (which had remained concealed since their delivery by U. S. submarines a few months earlier) then there was something of unusual interest about the "mission. " If explosives were needed for a simple sabotage job, Lapham would not have requested mines. There was only one logical conclusion. Plans for a major assault (or defense) were under consideration.

Captain Pajota instructed Sergeant Pacifico Tuallo," Go to Lapham! Tell him we will be on the way with the mines as soon as we can uncover them and load up. I will leave this place before 1200... noon, tomorrow. If you cannot find Lapham at Guimba, then go to Captain Joson at Lobong. Joson will accompany you to Lapham!"

* * * *

It was almost 2100 hours (9 P.M.) on the 26th when General Walter Krueger decided to get some sleep. As the weary General approached his tent the tall soldier standing guard at a position of"parade rest" snapped to attention, saluting with an MI rifle.

General Krueger stopped and looked up into the face of the young man."Stand at ease!" Krueger said, his voice reflecting fatigue. The guard relaxed.

"What's your name, Ranger ?" Krueger asked the startled soldier who was unaccustomed to being addressed by three star Generals.

"Proudfit, sir! PFC William Proudfit, 2nd Platoon...F Company!"

"How tall are you, Proudfit?"

"Six foot, two and a half inches, sir!" PFC Proudfit barked, staring straight into space.

"Without your boots?"

Proudfit's eyes glanced down quickly at the 6th United States Army Commander and noticed that the General was smiling.

"Yes, sir!"

"Boy!" Krueger exclaimed."I'm only five foot, six. I wish I was as tall as you. Where are you from, son?"

"Des Moines, Iowa, sir!"

"Iowa...good place, Iowa. Getting enough to eat, Ranger?"

"Yes, sir!" Proudfit replied.

"You look like it!"

Proudfit's clean shaven face finally broke into a grin.

General Krueger reached into his shirt pocket and produced a cigar."Care for a smoke?"

"No, sir! Thank you, sir"

" I mean when you're off duty." Guard change is in a few minutes, isn 't it?"

"Yes, sir," Proudfit acknowledge."But...I don' t smoke, sir!"

"Hum... I see. Well then, get some rest. And, son..."

"Yes, sir."

"You men keep up the good job. But don't take any unnecessary chances!"

Proudfits' eyes returned to the General,"Yes, sir!...You, too, sir!"

At 1130 hours (11:30 A.M.) on January 27th, Lieutenant Colonel Henry A. Mucci left his Battalion headquarters near Calasio and made the two mile ride to 6th Army headquarters at Dagupan by jeep.

Naturally, the moment the men learned that their Colonel was on the way to G2, rumors began to spread through the Ranger camp with exciting speed. A new mission, everyone knew, was in the making and the game was to guess what it may be and which company would get the assignment.

By 1150 hours all introductions had been made in the G2 Intelligence Command tent, and the officers were ready to begin their business. Those present for the hour long meeting were 6th Army Intelligence Chief (G2) Colonel Horton White, his assistant, Major Frank Rowale, Guerrilla Commander Major Robert Lapham and Alamo Scout Lieutenants John Dove, Thomas Rounsaville, and William Nellist, and, Lieutenant Colonel Mucci.

Colonel White began."Colonel Mucci, your Rangers are needed for an important mission. We want you to hit a large Jap POW Camp and free our boys. This is a tough one... Your men are the best qualified to pull the job off! I'm going to turn most of this meeting over to Major Rowale."

Mucci received the news calmly, and lit his pipe.

It had already been decided that lst Lieutenant John Dove would serve as liaison between the two Scout teams selected for the mission (Rounsaville and Nellist's teams). In this capacity, Lieutenant Dove was to attach himself to the Rangers and move with them.

As the meeting progressed, every known detail concerning the current Japanese troop movements, the enemy situation at POW Camp Cabanatuan and Cabanatuan City was discussed at great length.

The Rangers, Colonel Mucci was told, must make a cross-country march, attack the camp at night, liberate the Allied prisoners and return safely with them to American lines. Just how he planned to accomplish this was left entirely up to him.

The selection of the two Scout teams was based on their prior experience in raiding a Japanese prison compound. Since Lieutenant Dove did most of the planning for that mission it made sense to attach him to the Rangers. Mucci could exchange ideas with Dove while on the march.

But the successful Alamo Scout raid had been conducted under entirely different conditions. Their raid, being of smaller scale, required fewer men. The mission was carried out in jungle territory and the Scouts had the advantage of being delivered and picked up by PT boats.

This new mission was far more complex. The Scouts and Rangers must walk almost thirty miles through practically open country in the Central Plains...and all of that country, once they left Guimba, was still in the hands of the Japanese. Enemy garrison troops at POW Camp Cabanatuan were estimated to be over two hundred in number. Japanese troops of battalion-size were camping from time to time at Cabu Bridge which was only a mile from the POW compound.

At Cabanatuan City, four miles south of the compound, enemy forces estimated to be of division strength were gathering and could be expected to move along the road which ran in front of the compound. Japanese tanks were known to be at all these locations. They were moving after dark along the roads leading north and east from Cabanatuan City.

To make the situation even more hazardous, Mucci was informed that the entire mission must remain"top secret". The Air Force would not be told of the mission unless the Rangers requested air cover.

Upon hearing this, Colonel Mucci removed the pipe from his mouth and stared at the dark-complextioned Major Rowale."Then, we will maintain radio silence."

"Yes, Colonel," Rowale replied, his brown eyes showing no emotion. "Unless it is an extreme emergency or you are forced to make a change in plans. The entire misson is so delicate we can't even risk transporting your men by any kind of vehicle. One tip to the Japs...and, I'm afraid you'll find nothing but dead American prisoners when you arrive at the camp."

"And, the tanks. You think there are tanks in the camp?" Mucci expressed the concern felt by everyone present. Foot soldiers fighting off tanks, especially while trying to carry sick men, presented a very dangerous situation.

"Well...we have good reason to believe there are tanks in the camp," Rowale answered."Major Lapham's guerrillas report that at least two tanks were hidden in or around metal buildings. " Major Rowale paused and handed Colonel Mucci a six by twelve inch aerial photograph of the POW camp area."You see this spot...here, at the center of the compound to the right of the camp road?"

"Is this the best photo you have?" Mucci exclaimed as he squinted his eyes to study a two by two inch section on the photo which was the camp.

"I'm afraid so. I have copies for you fellows," Major Rowale nodded to the Scout Lieutenants."now...our boys think they see a tank in the shadow of this building. The tank sheds... or motor pool section, if you wish...are the only metal buildings in the stockade. They are corrugated iron. All the other buildings are bamboo, nipa and wood...except for the chapel over here near the drainage pond. It's concrete. Apparently there's nothing there worth worrying about. Even if there are no tanks in the camp, you must be ready for armor moving up from Cabanatuan City!"

"A few bazookas should do the trick on the tanks in the stockade," Mucci said assuredly."But, what about this road between Cabanatuan City and Bongabon?" He pointed to a line on the large topography map given him a few minutes earlier."You say the road is heavily traveled. We have to secure that road and cross it to hit the camp. If it's traveled continually by armor even bazookas won't make the job easy!"

Rowale looked up at Colonel White. Mucci had just touched on a point which concerned G2 the most. Regardless of the best plans, the entire mission depended on surprise, exact timing and... luck. Luck that enemy traffic on the main highway passing the POW camp would be light enough to permit an attack. And, luck that no one would tip off the Japanese that an attack was pending.

"Colonel Mucci," Major Rowale interrupted the brief silence,"I guess we can't predict how heavy the traffic will be on that road . Major Lapham feels that his guerrillas in the area may have some dope on the subject when you arrive in the camp area.The guerrillas infiltrated the staff of the Philippine Constabulary operating out of

82

Cabanatuan City long ago. They know a great deal about the troop movement. But...of course, if your raid is already under way and the Filipinos learn of a Jap unit moving up... it may be too late for them to warn you."

"I'll plan accordingly," Mucci stated.

Rowale continued. "To ease your mind a little...you'll have air cover for your return trip once you request it and the Black Widow Night Fighters will be out on the prowl between now and the time the mission is over. They don't know about all this, yet, but they are covering every major road and giving the Japs hell each night. We'll tell them to stay clear of the camp...unless you radio that you need them."

"How about the weather?" Mucci asked.

"Looks good!" Colonel White answered. "Should be dry and warm with scattered medium to high clouds on the 29th and 3Oth. And. .. you'll have a full moon."

Mucci grinned."And, what about our advance units out of Guimba?"

Colonel White shifted his large frame on the field stool."We will coordinate this with the 6th Division...the lst and 2Oth Regiments. You fellows can identify yourselves by two green flares. We hope, Colonel, that your walk back won't be so long as the one going over. Our lines should move up a few miles during your absence."

"I'll need more than one company," Mucci said."With Bravo and Echo companies on Santiago, I'll take Charley company and probably a platoon from Fox company..."

"Well...you'll have some good help Colonel," Major Lapham injected as he tilted his old campaign hat back from his forehead."When you step off from Guimba some of my guerrillas will take you to Joson...Captain Edwardo Joson's headquarters down near Lobong. He has over a hundred armed men who can serve as your flank guards and guide you to Captain Juan Pajota near Platero. Joson's men know every trail between Guimba and Pajota's area and... Pajota knows every inch of his territory.

He was even based at that compound before the Japs invaded. He'll bring you up-to-date on the Jap situation when you arrive. These Filipinos have fought a long hard war, Colonel. It's been mostly hit and run... attack and hide. It's cost them their homes and many have lost members of their family. So, they are looking for a chance to even the score... they are excellent fighters. The villagers will want to feed your men in every barrio you enter. You can trust everyone of them except... the Huks."

Mucci frowned."What about the Huks?"

Major Lapham rubbed his pointed chin."Well, originally we got along with the Huks. At least we tolerated one another. They were killing Japs just like we were. But, for the last year my men and the Huks have been tangling... "

"It's all political, you know," Major Rowale interrupted."The Filipinos have been fighting amongst themselves over whose going to run the country after the war."

"Leave the Huks to my men, if you can," Lapham suggested."Joson and Pajota know how to handle them. They'll know where the Huks are. If anything, the Huks will probably want to get in on the act. They know that the officers under me are commissioned in the United States Army... that my guerrillas are sworn members of our Army. The Huks resent that fact."

When Mucci had all the information he felt he needed he stood up. "OK...you say this is to be done on the 29th. That doesn't give us much time."

"Tomorrow at dawn," Rowale replied. "You'll truck to Guimba and then move out when you are ready. The Scouts will leave tonight and establish contact with this fellow, Pajota. They'll reconnoiter the area and be ready to report to you when you arrive in the morning of the 29th."

Mucci looked at the Alamo Scouts. "Will that give you fellows enough time to get all the dope we'll need? You'll need to travel all night and part of the day, just to get there!"

Lieutenant Nellist replied. "We'll do our job, sir!"

"Then," Mucci stated, "we'll strike after dark on the 29th! Just be sure we have that air cover coming back!"

* * * *

Shortly after noon on the 27th, Sergeant Pacifico Tuallo arrived at Sixth Army Headquarters with his message for Major Lapham.

When he reported that Captain Pajota would be on the way with the requested land mines, Tuallo was informed to get some rest and prepare for a new assignment.

At dusk, the Sergeant must return to Platero and tell Pajota to "keep the mines and prepare all squadrons to be ready to assist the Americans. They will attack the POW camp at Pangatian!"

A runner had already departed for Platero with the same message. But, Sergeant Tuallo would have the honor of leading the Alamo Scouts cross-country to find Pajota.

* * * *

Not long after he finished lunch on January 27th, Tech Sergeant Norton Most sat at his radio and stared dreamily out at the waves which rolled onto the dark sandy beaches of Santiago Island.

Life for Sergeant Most and the members of B and E Company had been relatively dull for the last few days, but they could not afford to drop their guard for one minute. The Rangers remained at the "alert" for a possible Japanese commando attack on the radar station. The radio teams worked in shifts, ready to relay an emergency warning should enemy planes approach over the China Sea.

Suddenly, Norton Most's radio came alive. He began to rapidly record the coded message from Battalion head- quarters. The message was for Sergeant Most. It was an order to return immediately to Ranger Headquarters and join a "special mission." Sergeant Most knew that there must be something especially important about that mission, else another radio man could fill the position.

Sergeant Most spent the next several hours journeying to Calasio and, once at Battalion headquarters, learned the details of the "special mission".

The Battalion's comnication officer, Lieutenant Smith, informed Norton Most of the plans for the raid. The two men reviewed the technical requirements surrounding the assignment. The new, lightweight SCR 694 radios would be put to test under difficult conditions. But, the SCR 694 was designed for such purposes.

Lieutenant Smith was pleased that his entire Communications Section had volunteered for the mission. From them all, he selected Sergeant Most, Tech 5 William A. Lawver and Tech 4 George R. Disrud to actually go on the raid. Tech 4 Disrud, like Norton Most, was a qualified radio"operator". If Most was killed, Disrud could take over.

The rest of the men in the Communications Section were scheduled to operate relay stations.

The radio men were told to try and get a few hours sleep before the mission.

* * * *

Japanese Battalion Commander Tomeo Oyabu strained to hear his new orders coming in on the static filled radio phone. It was 1700 (5 P.M.) January 27th.

"Yes..! This is Dokuho 359. We have established defense positions at San Jose."

"Dokuho 359... Dokuho 359. There is a change in plans! You are to return at once to Naotake Headquarters! Guimba is in enemy hands! Commander Inoue will remain at San Jose. You, Dokuho 359, proceed to Bongabon, then south to Cabanatuan City.

Commander Oyabu glanced at his map. According to these new orders, he could not return by the same march route his unit traveled from Cabanatuan City to San Jose less than thirty hours before. Now, he must move twenty-two miles southeast to Bongabon, then another twenty-five miles south to Naotake Headquarters at Cabanatuan.

It was too late to pull his men from their positions and move to Bongabon before daylight, he explained to Naotake. Oyabu requested permission to wait until dark the next day. If they traveled all night they could make the south side of Bongabon by dawn the 29th. Then, they could continue the night of the 30th and reach Cabanatuan City the morning of the 3lst. This way his Battalion would not be caught on the highway during daylight hours by American planes.

Commander Oyabu continued to present his idea by phone... "Dokuho 359 request permission to bivouac at Prison Camp Pangatian night of January 30. There I await instructions for movement to desired defense positions at Cabanatuan City."

Naotake Headquarters realized that the Oyabu Battalion could easily make the four miles march from the POW Camp to Cabantuan City in perhaps an hour, but, that idea presented another problem. There were already too many troops scheduled for rest at the POW camp.

"No! Dokuho 359. You must reach vicinity of Cabu River before morning of January 30. Kinpeidan Headquarters unit resting at Camp Pangatian. Kinpeidan will depart Pangatian Camp at 1000 hrs., January 30 for Bongabon. Road must be open for Kinpeidan movement. Suggest you bivouac vicinity of Cabu River. At 1100 hrs. road will clear... depart Cabu River at 1100 hrs. for Cabanatuan City..."

Battalion Commander Oyabu, like all good Japanese officers, did not question the final orders. If Dokuho 359 Battalion must pull out and march over forty miles to the Cabu River, they would do it. His men could rest all day along the banks of the Cabu and be in condition to continue the remaining four miles to aid in the defense of Cabanatuan City.

Oyabu's battalion simply had to wait for that headquarter's unit to pass over Cabu Bridge on their journey northeast from the POW camp. He could then cross and head south to Cabanatuan.

American forces were still at least three or four days away from Cabanatuan City, the POW camp and Cabu Bridge. At least, that was what Dokuho 359 believed.

* * * *

When Lieutenant Colonel Henry Mucci returned to his Ranger base it was mid afternoon of the 27th. He immediately informed Captain Robert Prince of the details of the mission, instructing him to prepare his C Company and advise F Company Commander, 1st Lieutenant John F. Murphy to get his 2nd Platoon ready.

"My wonderful Captain Prince", as Mucci was later to describe his C Company commander, would be second in command (under Mucci) and responsible for most of the plans and organizing the mission.

Colonel Mucci planned to hold an"officers call" and stated that he would address the troops scheduled for the raid later in the day. Then he retired to his tent to get his own affairs in order.

Within a few minutes, Mucci was visited by F Company's First Sergeant.

"Hi, kid!" What's on your mind?" The Colonel greeted the wiry little Sergeant Charles Bosard.

"You know what's on my mind! I want to go on this mission!"

"No, kid...not this one!"

Colonel..."

"No!" Mucci snapped."And, dammit, that's final! Your 2nd Platoon sergeants will be enough NCO's."

"I'm the kind of man you need to pull this thing off, and you know it!" Bosard continued.

"No...you're too valuable. I don't want you shot up!" Mucci looked at Bosard and the Sergeant noticed the Colonel's eyes were misty."I don't want anyone shot up." Mucci added in a quieter tone."If we don't come back, where would F Company get another good First Sergeant like you, kid?"

"God damit, Colonel! I trained these men. They're my boys as much as yours. If you're their father, I'm their mother. I deserve to go with them!"

Mucci grinned one of his big broad grins."You want to be my bodyguard? If you go, you'll have to stay close to me. I want to keep an eye on you the whole time... you'll be in there with your knife cutting some Jap and getting yourself shot up."

"I don 't give a damn what you assign me... just let me...!"

"OK... OK!" Mucci began to laugh."You can go! Now, get the hell out of here,. Remind Prince I'm going to address the men in a few minutes!"

"Yes, SIR!" Bosard replied.

Before midnight another twenty-five officers, NCO's and   men approached Colonel Mucci hoping to persuade him to take them along on the raid. Each received the same story from the Ranger Commander, who had become increasingly emotional by the over-whelming numbers of volunteers. They were all good men, he told them, but he could not take everyone. There would be other missions. Their time would come.

Nonetheless,"A" Company First Sergeant Ned Hedrick, Staff Sergeant Richard Moore of F Company and Sergeant Harry Killough of E Company managed, somehow, to change his mind.

The Battalion Executive Officer, Major Garrett, tried to con- vince Mucci to stay behind, insisting it would be wiser to send him, instead. That discussion did not last long. Lieutenant Colonel Mucci had made his final selections and he was going to lead his troops. Nothing...and no one would change that decision.

The Rangers of Company C, Company F (2nd Platoon), medics, radio operators...everyone scheduled for the raid assembled in front of the Battalion headquarters to hear what Colonel Mucci had to say.

When their commander appeared from the tent wearing his soft, round "yard bird" hat, they noticed he was also wearing his .45 pistol on the hip, rather than in the shoulder holster.

Colonel Mucci studied the excited faces of his men and began his speech in an unusually calm tone."As you know by now... we have been given a tough but rewarding assignment. We 're going to hit a Jap POW stockade and free a few hundred of our boys the Nips have held for almost three years..."

A few whistles and muffled" wows!" came from the men.

"All those prisoners," Mucci continued,"are sick and dying. They are what's left of our troops who held out on Bataan and Corregidor... and if we don't free them now, you can bet they'll be killed by the Japs before our front reaches their area.

"We'll be behind enemy lines the entire trip, but, we'll have Filipino guerrillas to guide us and help with our mission.

"You fellows are the Eight Ball company...you are really behind that eight ball now! This isn't going to be easy. Nothing has been easy so far but this is a most dangerous assignment.

"If you feel lucky...you're welcome to come along. If not.. . I promise no one... repeat, NO ONE, will ever say one word to you about your decision to stay back. Naturally, I think married men should stay home for this one, but it's up to you to decide.

"Before you make that decision, you had better pay attention. This mission is top secret ! Other than the guerrillas and a few Alamo Scouts, we'll be alone and on our own. Our Air Force doesn't know about this mission yet. We'll need to avoid our boys as much as the Japs. They may mistake us for Japs. But...we'll have air cover on the return trip."

Now Mucci began to speak louder, the words rolling fast with dramatic impact. "We'll have to attack at night so the darkness can cover our withdrawal. We are going to jump that stockade right between two big Jap forces which will be only a few miles away. There are over one hundred and fifty Japs in the camp itself!

"Use your knives when you get inside if you need to! We want no Americans in that camp killed...especially by our own bullets!

"You're going to bring out every God damned man even if you have to carry them out on your back!

"Those prisoners will probably be confused and scared. Some may not wish to leave. Remember what they have endured over those long months with the Japs. You will be gentle with those

92

prisoners, but if they refuse to leave, kick'em out if you must ... but, get them out ALIVE!

"You'll be carrying extra rations besides your three day packets ... extra chocolate. I don't want to see any of you guys eating that stuff. It's for the POW's you release...OK! ?

"Before daybreak we'll be trucked about seventy-five miles north-west of here to a town called Guimba. Near there, we'll meet the first guerrilla group who will serve as our escort.. . and, from there we walk through Jap country, all the way... no sleep... then we attack and walk back!

"Jungle greens will be the uniform, and soft caps. No helmets this time. They make too much noise. Those who wish to carry an extra.45 can do so. You might need'em for close in fighting.

"Now! One last thing. I don't want any damned atheists... any non-religious men to go on this mission. We are going to gather around the Chaplain in a few minutes. You are all going to church if you plan to go on this raid!

"You had better get down on your knees and pray. Dammit, don't fake it. I mean...PRAY! And, I want you to swear an oath before God... swear you'll die fighting rather than let any harm come to those POW's!"

Colonel Mucci exercised an abrupt"about face" and disappeared inside his command tent leaving his men practically spellbound. Everyone went"to church" and swore that oath and no one requested his name be scratched from the mission.

After Colonel Mucci's speech, Ist Lieutenant John W. Luddeke assembled his five-man team... Unit F of the 832nd Signal Service Battalion. The men were disappointed to learn that only three of them could go on the mission.

"OK, men. That's the dope as I know it," Lieutenant Luddeke said."This is for volunteers only."

All five men raised their hands.

"Well, I thought so."

The Lieutenant removed the liner from his helmet and dropped five small folded pieces of notebook paper into the steel pot. "Weiner, you shouldn't go anyway. But, to keep this fair, you can draw in the lottery if you wish."

PFC Morris Weiner cursed his bad luck under his breath. He had fallen off a truck a few days before and broken his finger.

"Ready to draw? Look for the marked paper and then show it to me l" Luddeke instructed.

"Darn, I lose" PFC George Woodruff exclaimed as he held up a blank paper."I'll see you lucky bums later."

The"winners" were Tech 4th Class Frank J. Goetzheimer, Corporal Robert C. Lautman and PFC Wilber B. Goen.

Twenty year old Corporal Lautman at five foot seven inches and one hundred and forty pounds was not the smallest man in Unit F. In fact, he was a good two inches taller than his tough little comrade, Tech 4 Frank Goetzheimer.

What Frank Goetzheimer lacked in physical stature, he made up with energy, photographic skill and determination. He was already "jump qualified" having successfully completed the rugged paratrooper school. With a boyish face, twenty-two year old Geotzheimer, the"little fellow with the big name", unfortunately had the biggest load of equipment to carry. His ten pound.35 mm Eyemo Bell and Howell movie camera, plus ten rolls of movie film at five pounds each and the weight of his web equipment with a .45 automatic pistol equaled half his body weight.

"What are you taking this time, Bob?" Goetzheimer asked Corporal Lautman as the men prepared for the mission.

"The Rolli," came the reply as Robert Lautman buckled his pistol belt from which hung a.38 caliber police special revolver. He had traded his heavy. 45 service automatic long before to a Navy friend for the revolver.

The little 2.25 inch twin lens"still" camera Lautman planned to take was usually preferred over the standard, but heavier 4 x 5 Speed Graphic for tough assignments where great distances must be covered on foot. PFC Wilber Goen, nonetheless, planned to carry the Speed Graphic.

* * * *

Late in the afternoon of January 27th, the first section of Japanese Kinpeidan unit consisting of approximately fifty men had boarded two troop transport trucks, pulled out of Cabanatuan City and proceeded to the crossroads at Sangitan suburbs. There they turned northeast and headed directly to their destination . . . POW Camp Cabanatuan at Pangatian.

Along the road they passed the bulk of their unit, some one hundred and twenty-five men, who were marching to the camp.

By 2100 hours (9 P.M.) the entire Kinpeidan headquarters unit had bedded down in their transient quarters area inside the compound with orders from Naotake command to remain in the camp until after dark, January 30th.

For these Imperial soldiers the next few days would be easy duty. The detachment of about seventy-five guards at the stockade continued as sentries, unassisted by the transient troops.

The presence of this headquarters group at POW Camp Cabanatuan was the very reason why Battalion Commander Tomeo Oyabu and his Dokuho 359 unit was ordered to bivovac at the Cabu River. Naotake Command did not wish Dokuho 359 and the Kinpeidan unit to merge either at the camp or along the road. But, fate was about to merge the two Japanese units in a common destiny.

* * * *

At dark on January 27th burr haired Alamo Scout Lieutenants Tom Rounsaville and Bill Nellist shook hands with their friend, 1st Lieutenant John Dove.

"Take care of Mucci and the Rangers, Johnny," Lieutenant Nellist said with a teasing grin.

"You fellows stay out of trouble. I'll see you in a couple of days," Dove replied.

Tom Rounsaville turned to look at the two Scout teams who were chatting and adjusting rifle slings. "We haven't lost a man yet... since the beginning. The Scouts haven't lost a man, " he said.

"And, we're not going to lose anyone on this mission either," Nellist added with cool confidence.

Rounsaville tossed the MI to his back, forcing his arm through the loop in its sling. "How many Japs did G2 say are in that camp?"

"About two hundred... give or take a few," Dove answered. "Maybe another thousand at Cabu River... and at least a division at Cabanatuan City."

"Well," Rounsaville replied,"with thirteen Scouts and a hundred Rangers... it should be a fair fight!"

By 1900 hours (7 P.M.) the two Scout teams, guided by Sergeant Pacifico Tuallo and several other Filipino guerrillas, left Guimba for their twenty-four mile cross-country march to Platero.

For this mission, First Lieutenant Tom Rounsaville's team consisted of Sergeant Harold Hard, PFC Franklin Fox,Filipino-American Rufo Vaquilar, Hawaiian-Filipino PFC Alfred "Opu" Alfonso and American Indian PFC Francis Laquier.

First Lieutenant Bill Nellist's team was composed of his two Filipino American members, PFC Tom Siason and PFC Sabas Asis. PFC's Gilbert Cox, Wilbur Wismer, Andrew Smith and Galen Kittleson, the Tommygun expert, completed the group.

Perhaps by modern standards the equipment carried on the mission by the photography unit, radio men, Rangers and Scouts seem primitive. Yet, it was the best available at the time and far superior in quality and function to anything the Japanese on Luzon possessed.

All the Scouts, dressed in their faded green battle fatigues with baggy pants and soft caps were literally a walking arsenal. Each carried a.45 automatic pistol and extra magazines of ammunition , a wide blade trench knife, a few hand grenades and four bandoliers of ammunition for their rifles. The Filipino members carried their preferred lightweight MIAI, folding stock, carbines and PFC Kittleson, lugged his Thompson submachine gun.

The deadly nature of their work and several months of dangerous missions behind enemy lines had produced thirteen young men who began this assignment with the seriousness of it all etched in their faces. As individuals, each was quite capable of carrying out the assignment alone should anything happen to the other team members.

The Scout operations before Luzon had been mostly in the jungles and usually during the hours of darkness. Now, they must depend on the Filipino guerrillas to guide them through open, enemy held country during daylight and darkness without being detected. They must cover almost thirty miles on foot, set up plans with Captain Juan Pajota, reconnoiter the camp area and be ready with detailed information and suggestions when Colonel Mucci arrived with his Rangers the morning of the 29th. The Scouts would have only about thirty-five hours to accomplish their part of the mission.

By 2000 hours (8 P.M.) on the 27th, the two Scout teams were deep within Japanese territory.

Captain Pajota waited for the Scouts at Balangkare, a few miles north of Platero, well advised by the bamboo * telegraph which moved ahead of the Americans. When he met them at dawn on the 28th, Pajota was not disappointed.

The new generation of Americans... these giants which had come to liberate his country, were everything Pajota had hoped for. The Alamo Scouts (which he had never heard of before January 26th) were tough, intelligent individuals. Most of all, they were dead serious about their assignment and interested in his opinions. He would never forget their names or personalities.

* * * *

When Lieutenant Colonel Mucci entered his Battalion Surgeon's tent he found Doctor James Fisher busy checking a large assortment of medical equipment. It was almost midnight.

Captain Fisher hardly noticed his visitor, hesitating only a moment to scratch at his close chopped black hair, then continued to stuff surgical instruments into canvas bags which simply could hold no more.

"What are you doing, Jimmy?" Colonel Mucci finally inquired.

"Got to finish getting these aid satchels ready. I understand the guerrillas have a doctor. Maybe he can use some of our excess equipment."

Mucci watched as Captain Fisher searched through a large wooden trunk.

"Now...where in hell did I put those forceps?"

"Is that it on the table?" Mucci asked.

"Yeah! Just where I left them."

Fisher spread a web belt on the table and began to fumble with the hooks of a trench knife sheath as he attempted to attach the weapon.

"Where do you think you are going with that, Jimmy?"

"Why... with my men, of course."

"Oh no! No, Jimmy. Not you." Mucci hook his head,"I heard you had some fool notion about going. This will be too tough a mission...and, surgeons...especially good ones are hard to come by in the Philippines!"

Fisher's face flushed."Colonel, you are taking over a hundred men a long way..."

"Yes, and how many of your medics?" Mucci inquired.

"Four"

"Who are they?"

"Sergeant Johnny Nelson, Corporal Martin Estesen, Corporal Bernie Haynes... and, Corporal Bob Ramsey." Fisher continued, determined to make his point,"and, they are good...really experts. But, suppose some of our boys get hit bad. My medics can't be expected to perform surgery out there under a banana tree or in some nipa hut... but I can! If any of our boys are hit real bad, their chances of making it back to our lines alive are next impossible... you know that. What are you going to do, Colonel leave a trail of dying men all the way back? Our medics can take care minor wounds...maybe even more. But, you won't have time for anyone but a qualified surgeon to do serious work."

Lieutenant Colonel Mucci stood silent for a moment, his unlit pipe protruding from the corner of his mouth. He reached up slowly, grasped the bowl and pointed the stem at Captain Fisher. "You said yourself that the Filipinos have a doctor."

" Yes," Fisher replied."But, you can't expect him to follow you about the country."

"All right, Jimmy. I know there is no way of talking you out of it. But, I'm telling you now...you are not getting anywhere near the camp when we attack!"

Captain Bob Prince waited until he has alone in his tent, the night of the 27th, to remove his boots and carefully unroll the heavy army socks. Now he could doctor his blistered feet without anyone noticing the dangerous condition. Those blisters must remain his secret, else Mucci or Captain Fisher may confine him. Nothing, certainly not blistered feet was going to hold Bob Prince back from the mission. He planned to carry some GI foot powder in the deep pockets of those baggy green combat fatigues. Somehow, he would make the march over to the POW camp and worry about walking back later.

Before him, on a blanket, lay the necessary tools of war of a Ranger company commander... a. 45 automatic pistol in its shoulder holster, web belt with canteen, first aid packet, pouches with extra .45 caliber shells in their magazines, and the trench knife. Next to that assortment of equipment was his MI rifle, two bandoliers of clip ammunition (with two packs of cigaretts crammed in one bandolier pocket), several flares, a "Very" flare pistol and a compass.

By his side lay the aerial photo of the camp area and the topological map of Nueva Ecija Province.

Actually, the map which Colonel Mucci and Captain Prince were to rely on was constructed from three separate maps, carefully assembled by 6th Army's G2 section. It consisted of Quadrangles "Zaragoza 3357111, Cabanatuan 335711 and Papaya 3457111".

With contour intervals indicated at twenty feet and a scale 1:50,000 (one inch equaled 50,000 actual inches on the ground), it represented the best that the military had in 1944.

It appeared to be extremely accurate. Towns, roads, trails, rice ponds, swamps, rivers, streams, bridges, barrios...everything seemed perfect.

Captain Prince had noticed that the map indicated the area directly across from POW Camp Cabanatuan to be heavily wooded. But, the aerial photograph taken a few days before showed that same area to be open grass land, dotted with rice ponds.

This would mean that the Rangers must expect little or no concealment while they crossed that last mile to the camp. It might also indicate the beautiful map may have other critical errors.

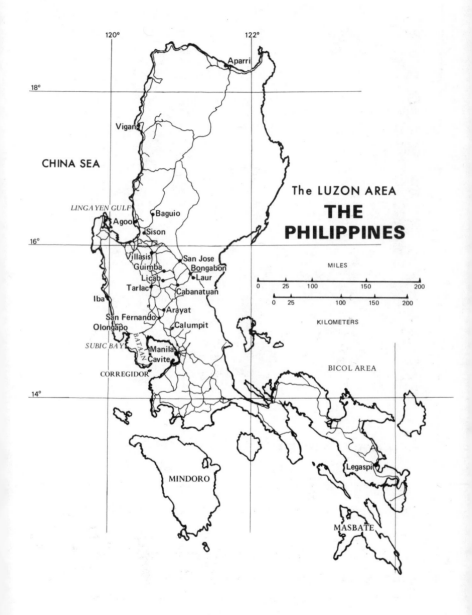

CHINA SEA

The LUZON AREA
THE
PHILIPPINES

Aparri

Vigan

LINGA YEN GULF

Baguio
Agoo
Sison
Villasis
Guimba
Licab
Tarlac
Iba
San Fernando
Olongapo
SUBIC BAY
BATAAN
Manila
Cavite
CORREGIDOR

San Jose
Bongabon
Laur
Cabanatuan
Arayat
Calumpit

MILES

0	25	100	150	200

0	25	100	150	200

KILOMETERS

BICOL AREA

MINDORO

Legaspi

MASBATE

U.S. educated, Imperial Army Colonel S. Aoyagi stands next to the POW Camp O'Donnell cemetery monument his "Public Relations" group erected in late September, 1942. . . dedicated "to the memory of gallant Filipino soldiers who died here". . as a pacification effort directed at surviving Filipinos the Japanese released. The cemetery held the remains of over 38,000 Filipinos and 2,000 Americans who died at O'Donnell from beatings, starvation, disease and executions. Colonel Aoyagis program became a failure. (Photo courtesy of Josefa Hilado Torre, R.N.)

Cabanatuan prison hut constructed of bamboo and nipa.

(U.S. Army photo)

"They built the nucleus of a guerrilla command which gained them a well deserved place in the history of unconventional war." Colonel Bernard Anderson, American Guerrilla, with pants rolled up, prepared to meet a U.S. supply submarine, 1944. (Courtesy - Col. Anderson.)

"There was a certain charisma about these mem which attracted
the Filipinos in magnetic fashion." Major Robert Lapham,
American Guerrilla, January, 1945.

"Having come up through the ranks, he could appreciate the hardships the soldiers endured both in training and combat." Lieutenant General Walter Krueger, Commanding General, United States Sixth Army. 1945 (U.S. Army Photo)

MAJOR JUAN PAJOTA
FEBRUARY, 1946

"He had become known as a determined, daring, yet cautious leader." Juan Pajota as a Major. February, 1946.

"Lieutentant Colonel Henry A. Mucci possessed a natural ability to motivate people. " 1944

"They were motley looking bunch of fierce fighters dedicated to serving the United States and ridding their country of the Japanese for good." Some of Captain Juan Pajota's "boys". Sergeant Benigno Barca on the left. January, 1945   (U.S. Army Photo)

"They were the kind of soldiers everyone liked . . . " Tech 5 Francis "Father" Schilli (left), Corporal Roy Sweezy (center), unidentified Ranger (right). Taken a few weeks before the raid.

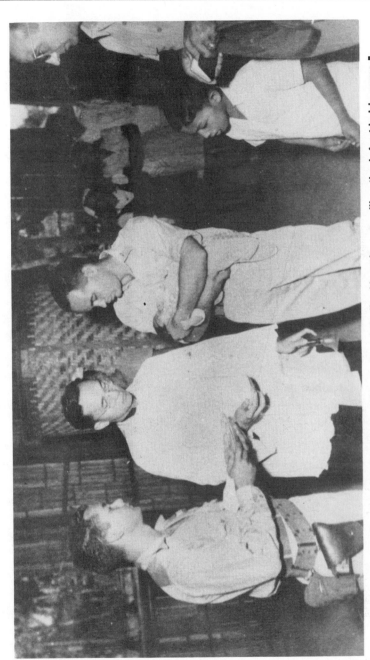

"A few days later, Jimmy Fisher stood in a church built of bamboo cradling the infant in his arms."
Captain Fisher with infant. Luzon, Jan. 1945.

The last photo taken of Captain James Fisher, M.D. (foreground, with hand on belt as he chats with Captain Bob Prince (center, cap and M1 rifle) in Platero. About three hours before the Raid. January 30, 1945

One of Captain Pajota's squadrons crosses the Pampanga River enroute to their positions at Cabu Bridge. About 6 P.M. January 30, 1945. Note the wide variety of equipment and weapons and the "medic" carrying a bamboo pole (just entering the water at the left bank). (U.S. Army Photo)

Less than two hours before the Raid. Rangers crossed the Pampanga River at the sand bar. January 30, 1945

"Nagisit law wa - law wa", also known as the "Hard to Get". P61 Black Widow of the 547th Night Fighter Squadron. January, 1945

Pilot of the "Hard to Get" Lieutenant Kenneth Schrieber (second from the right) and Radar Observer Lieutenant Bonnie Rucks (second from left) 1945. Also in the photo are Colonel R. L. Johnson (right) and Staff Sergeant John Crowe (left).

Enlargement of the original air photo of POW Camp Cabanatuan used to plan the raid. Lietuenant Nellist's marks are still visible. #1 is the tank shed area, #4 is the communication area and the guard towers, front (highway) and rear are circled. The creek bed through which F company passed to reach the rear of the camp is in the lower left of the photo. The white line through the center (left-right) is the result of age when Captain Prince folded the original.

An additional enlargement of the POW Camp gives a clearer view of the tank shed area (#l) and communication area #4) which was also a Japanese troop section. Zigzag defense trenches are directly above "#4".

Alamo Scout team leaders Ist Lieutenant William Nellist (left) and Ist Lieutenant Tom Rounsaville. After their return from the Raid, February, 1945

Captain Robert Prince, C Company Commander 6th Rangers (left) with Colonel Horton White, 6th Army G2. (U.S. Army Photo.)

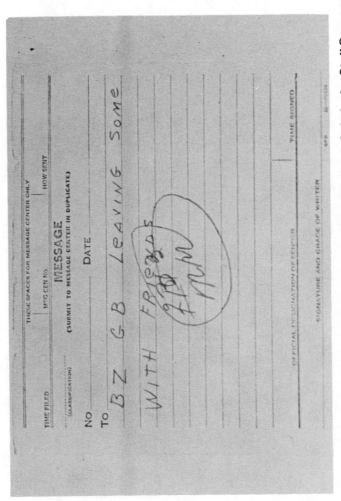

THESE SPACES FOR MESSAGE CENTER ONLY

TIME FILED | MSG CEN NO. | HOW SENT

----------(CLASSIFICATION)----------

MESSAGE
(SUBMIT TO MESSAGE CENTER IN DUPLICATE)

No _____ DATE _____

TO __ BZ GB Leaving Some
WITH FRIENDS

SIGNATURE AND GRADE OF WRITER

OFFICIAL DESIGNATION OF SENDER | TIME SIGNED

Photograph of original radio message sent to T/4 James Irvine at Guimba by Staff Sergeant Norton Most from Platero. It reads, "Mission accomplished - Starting back - Leaving some with friends." Note the time was corrected from the civilian "11:03" P.M. to read in military "2303" hours. January 30, 1945.

One of the first photos taken by Combat Photo Unit F of liberated Allied POW's, Northwest of Balangkare, just after dawn, January 31, 1945 (U.S. Army photo.)

Liberated POW's and one of the carabao carts as the column rests near Sibul. Morning of January 31, 1945. (U.S. Army Photo.)

Only a few hours of freedom. Part of the Allied column take a break. (U.S. Army Photo.)

Members of the 6th Rangers discuss the Raid while a former POW looks on. January 3l, l945. (U.S. Army photo.)

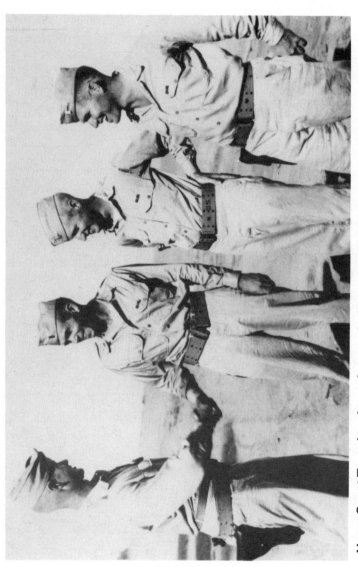

Alamo Scout Team Leaders a few weeks before the Raid on POW Camp Cabanatuan. Left to Right: Lt. William Nellist, Lt. Thomas Rounsaville, Lt. Robert Sumner and Lt. John Dove. (U.S. Army Photo.)

"With a small elite unit like the Scouts, one's value could never be doubted."

6th Army Alamo Scouts who were on the raid. Standing, left to right: PFC Gilbert Cox, PFC Wilbur Wismer, Sgt. Harold Hard, PFC Andrew Smith, PFC Francis Laquier. Kneeling, left to right: PFC Galen Kittleson, PFC Rufo Vaquilar, 1st Lt. William Nellist, 1st Lt. Thomas Rounsaville and P FC Franklin Fox. (On the Raid but not in this photo: 1st Lt. John Dove, PFC Tom Siason, PFC Sabas Asis, PFC Alfred Alfonso.) February 1, 1945 (U.S. Army Photo.)

President F.D. Roosevelt meets with a group of Rangers and Alamo Scouts selected after the raid on Cabanatuan to visit the States to assist in a Bond Drive and news media interviews. This photo, taken in the Oval Office, in early March, 1945, a few weeks before the President's Death. From left to right: First Sgt. Robert Anderson, Staff Sgt. Clifton Harris, Staff Sgt. Theodore Richardson, PFC Leland Provencher, Sgt. Harold Hard (Scouts), PFC Leroy Myerhoff, PFC Carlton Dietzel, PFC Charles Swain, Staff Sgt. William Butler, First Lt. Melville Schmidt, Capt. Robert Prince, Sgt. Gilbert Cox (Scouts). (U.S. Army Photo.)

"Doctor Captain James C. Fisher Memorial Park" Photo of the area on the outskirts of Barrio Balangkare where Captain James Fisher and Corporal Roy Sweezy were originally buried. Today the area is rice land. (February, 1945 - Courtesy Juan Pajota)

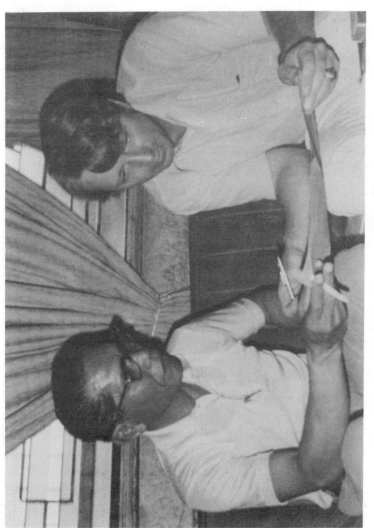

Major Juan Pajota with Author. . . . Manila, 1976 (Author's Photo)

Official or Unofficial, these patches are often associated with two elite combat units. . Left, U.S. Army 6th Ranger Battalion (Sixth Army) and Right. . .Alamo Scouts (Sixth Army.)

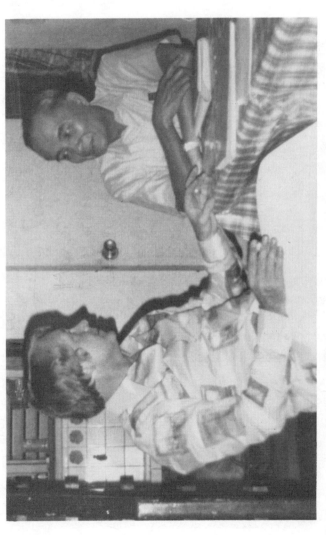

During a rare interview at a secret location near Manila, Commander Luis Taruc (right), founder and leader of the HUKBALAHAP, answers Author's questions concerning World War II HUK Guerrilla activity. Originally a "Socialist" group, the HUKS evolved into the Communist New People's Army (NPA) after Commander Taruc surrendered to the Philippine government. (Author's photo.)

Captain James Fisher Memorial in the center of Barrio Balangkari was designed so those who helped the Americans had a place to dry their rice. 1976. (Author's Photo.)

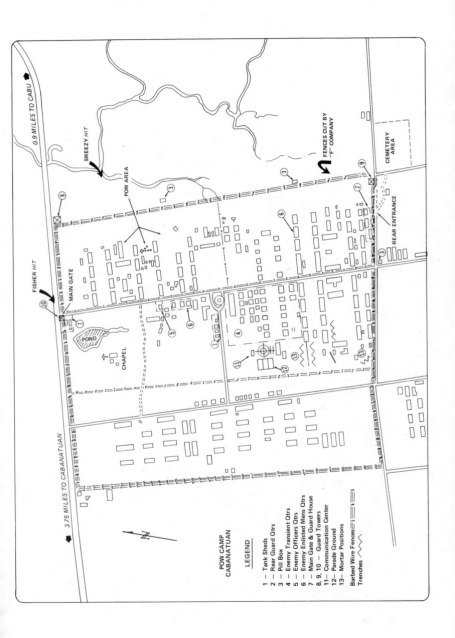

POW CAMP
CABANATUAN

LEGEND

1 — Tank Sheds
2 — Rear Guard Qtrs
3 — Pill Box
4 — Enemy Transient Qtrs
5 — Enemy Officers Qtrs
6 — Enemy Enlisted Mens Qtrs
7 — Main Gate & Guard House
8, 9, 10 — Guard Towers
11— Communication Center
12— Parade Ground
13— Mortar Positions

Barbed Wire Fences
Trenches

0.9 MILES TO CABU

SWEEZY HIT

POW AREA

FENCES CUT BY
"F" COMPANY

CEMETERY
AREA

REAR ENTRANCE

FISHER HIT

MAIN GATE

POND

CHAPEL

3.75 MILES TO CABANATUAN

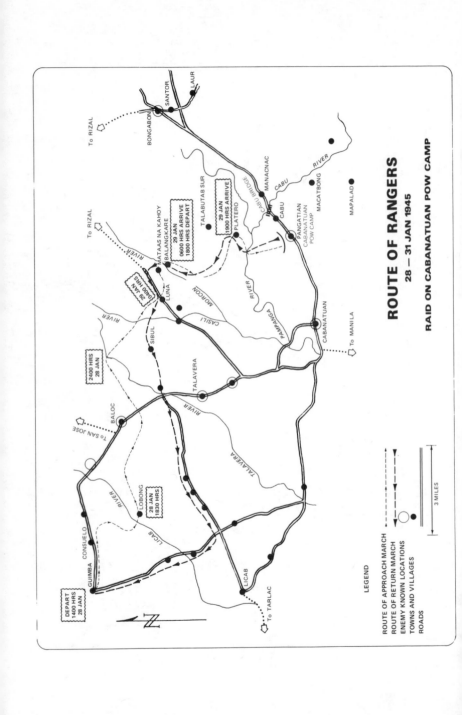

ROUTE OF RANGERS

28 — 31 JAN 1945

RAID ON CABANATUAN POW CAMP

LEGEND

ROUTE OF APPROACH MARCH
ROUTE OF RETURN MARCH
ENEMY KNOWN LOCATIONS
TOWNS AND VILLAGES
ROADS

3 MILES

DEPART
1400 HRS
28 JAN

GUIMBA

CONSUELO

LOBONG

28 JAN
1830 HRS

LICAB

To TARLAC

BALOC

To San Jose

2400 HRS
28 JAN

TALAVERA

LICAB RIVER

TALAVERA RIVER

29 JAN
0400 HRS

SIBUL

LUNA

CASILI

MORCON RIVER

PAMPANGA RIVER

CABANATUAN

To MANILA

MATAAS NA KAHOY
BALANGKARE

29 JAN
0600 HRS ARRIVE
1800 HRS DEPART

To RIZAL

RIVER

TALABUTAB SUR

PLATERO

29 JAN
1900 HRS ARRIVE

CABU BRIDGE

MANACNAC

CABU RIVER

CABU

PANGATIAN
CABANATUAN
POW CAMP

MACATBONG

MAPALAD

BONGABON

SANTOR

LAUR

To RIZAL

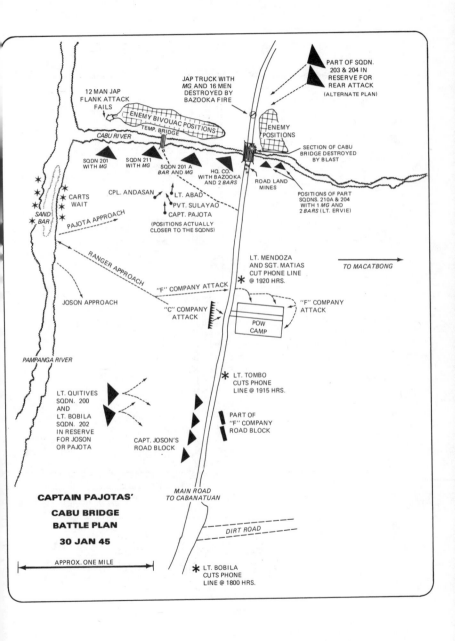

12 MAN JAP FLANK ATTACK FAILS

JAP TRUCK WITH *MG* AND 16 MEN DESTROYED BY BAZOOKA FIRE

PART OF SQDN. 203 & 204 IN RESERVE FOR REAR ATTACK (ALTERNATE PLAN)

ENEMY BIVOUAC POSITIONS

TEMP. BRIDGE

CABU RIVER

ENEMY POSITIONS

SQDN 201 WITH *MG*

SQDN 211 WITH *MG*

SQDN 201 A *BAR* AND *MG*

HQ. CO. WITH BAZOOKA AND 2 *BARS*

SECTION OF CABU BRIDGE DESTROYED BY BLAST

CPL. ANDASAN

LT. ABAD

PVT. SULAYAO

CAPT. PAJOTA

(POSITIONS ACTUALLY CLOSER TO THE SQDNS)

CARTS WAIT

SAND BAR

PAJOTA APPROACH

ROAD LAND MINES

POSITIONS OF PART SQDNS. 210A & 204 WITH 1 *MG* AND 2 *BARS* (LT. ERVIE)

RANGER APPROACH

LT. MENDOZA AND SGT. MATIAS CUT PHONE LINE @ 1920 HRS.

TO MACATBONG

JOSON APPROACH

"F" COMPANY ATTACK

"C" COMPANY ATTACK

"F" COMPANY ATTACK

POW CAMP

PAMPANGA RIVER

LT. TOMBO CUTS PHONE LINE @ 1915 HRS.

LT. QUITIVES SQDN. 200 AND LT. BOBILA SQDN. 202 IN RESERVE FOR JOSON OR PAJOTA

PART OF "F" COMPANY ROAD BLOCK

CAPT. JOSON'S ROAD BLOCK

CAPTAIN PAJOTAS'

CABU BRIDGE

BATTLE PLAN

30 JAN 45

MAIN ROAD TO CABANATUAN

DIRT ROAD

APPROX. ONE MILE

LT. BOBILA CUTS PHONE LINE @ 1800 HRS.

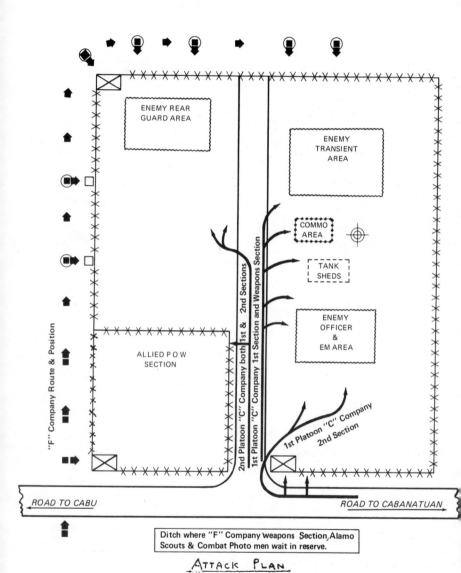

ENEMY REAR
GUARD AREA

ENEMY
TRANSIENT
AREA

COMMO
AREA

TANK
SHEDS

ENEMY
OFFICER
&
EM AREA

ALLIED P O W
SECTION

"F" Company Route & Position

2nd Platoon "C" Company both 1st & 2nd Sections

1st Platoon "C" Company 1st Section and Weapons Section

1st Platoon "C" Company
2nd Section

ROAD TO CABU

ROAD TO CABANATUAN

Ditch where "F" Company weapons Section, Alamo
Scouts & Combat Photo men wait in reserve.

ATTACK PLAN

CHAPTER 8

"God bless Ameereka. . ."

Barrio Platero Reception Committee

January 29,1945

Shortly before daybreak, at 0500 hours, on January 28th, 1945, a small convoy of "6 x 6" trucks, two jeeps and a command staff car containing one hundred and twenty-one menbers of the United States 6th Army Rangers left Calasio. Within a few minutes they were at the 6th Army Headquarters area near Dagupan.

During the short stop at Dagupan, four members of Combat Photo Unit F, 832nd Signal Service Battalion climbed aboard while a number of Rangers loaded several bazookas, rockets, anti-tank rifle grenades and additional ammunition.

In less than twenty minutes the convoy was on the move again, proceeding to Guimba, seventy-five miles away. For the next hour and a half, as the vehicles bounced and jerked along the narrow, bomb cratered highway, some Rangers actually managed to get a few minutes sleep. Practically none had slept the night before.

At 0715, the convoy arrived at Guimba. Major Robert Lapham was on hand to greet them. While the Rangers adjusted equipment and checked their weapons, Lapham introduced Colonel Mucci to the Filipino guerrillas who would guide them to Captain Edwardo Joson ' s headquarters at Loborg.

The men were allowed three hours rest, then a hot lunch, and another hours rest before Lapham bid them farewell and"good luck". Bob Lapham wanted to accompany Mucci but G2 considered his knowledge of the country, which forward units of Sixth Army were preparing to cross, much too valuable to gamble his life now. After all, Lapham had already served his country far beyond that could be expected of any man. Mucci would be in good hands , Lapham knew, with Joson and Pajota .

The Rangers drew a two days supply of "K" combat rations (food) and added the cans to the weight they must lug on the long march.

As Mucci had instructed, uniforms were the usual faded green combat fatigues and soft cap . No rank or insignia was worn. By now each man was familiar with the faces of his buddies, their rank, squad and nicknames. Automatic weapons were prescribed according to particular assignment, however, rifle-men had a personal choice of the MI or MI Carbine. The Weapon Section men carried BAR's instead of light machine guns. Most Non- Commissioned Officers carried a Tommygun and at least one .45 pistol. Captain Prince and Lieutenant Murphy carried both an MI and a .45 but Captain Jimmy Fisher and Lieutenant Colonel Mucci wore only a .45. The other Lieutenants, including Comnunications Officer Clifford K. Smith and Combat Photo Unit F Commander John W. Lueddeke carried MI's and .45's and all medics, either a Carbine or MI plus a .45. A number of the men wore two or more .45 pistols. Every man had two bandoliers of ammunition, the large trench knife and at least two hand or rifle grenades.

* * * *

A dull olive colored four door command staff car bumped to a halt beneath the shade of a large tree about a mile southeast of Guimba

. In the back seat of the canvas topped vehicle sat radio operator Tech 4th Class James M. Irvine and before him, mounted to the rear of the front seat was a SCR 284 field radio which would serve as the base communication link between Sixth Army and Mucci's Rangers during the mission. . James Irvine must remain awake and alert for two days to be ready should Mucci be forced to break radio silence prematurely with a message for help or a change in plans.

The communications section was in complete agreement. If Sergeant Norton Most flashed a message back to Guimba,"hand" key, rather than voice, transmission would be used. Realizing they must operate on the outer limits of their radio's capabilities, the communication men did not wish to take a chance with voice transmission. The human voice could become completely distorted or saturated with static during a crucial message. A modified version of Morse code, dots and dashes, clicks or pauses would be used. Various code letters had been specially designated for the mission. The combination letter"BZ", for example, represented the word message,"mission accomplished". With the exception of the new code, everything else was to be routine.

What worried Tech 4 James Irvine, though, was the fact that he had less than four hours sleep the night before. It would not be easy to stay awake during the hot days and balmy evenings ahead. But, Irvine had thought of an idea. Instead of wearing a soft fatigue cap, he brought along his steel helmet. If sleep conquered him, his head would fall forward, the helmet striking the metal case of the radio . The alarm system should work. But, Irvine had no way of knowing that the number of hours he must remain alert would exceed the period of time for which everyone planned.

At 1400 hours (2 P.M.) Colonel Mucci and his men left Irvine at the radio car and began the first leg of their march to Lobong.

After leaving Guimba, the Rangers now on foot, proceeded two miles east along a dirt road, then swung south of the town of Consuelo, then through two or three miles of grassland until they reached the banks of the Licab River.

The Filipino guides knew just where to cross the river. Though the water was less than knee deep, sloshing along through a thick bamboo forest and more grassland with wet boots made for very uncomfortable walking.

After another quarter mile the guides called a halt. The front of the Ranger single file line suddenly was in the presence of some one hundred armed Filipinos.

The natives were clad in a variety of uniforms ranging from old USAFFE khaki to the simple clothes of rice farmers. TheRangers had reached Barrio Lobong. . .the headquarters of guerrilla Captain Edwardo Joson.

As planned, Captain Joson and eighty of his armed soldiers joined the Rangers. The combined force, now totaling two hundred, departed Lobong at 1830 hours (6:30 P.M.). Joson advised that he must leave twenty armed men to protect his village headquarters from possible Huk attack.

With the exception of a few who would guide Mucci toBalangkare, the guerrillas were dispatched far out on both flanks. Neither Huks nor Japanese would be able to attack the force without advance warning.

When the group entered a heavy forest east of Lobong, they were over six miles into enemy territory.

* * * *

Nine miles south of Guimba, near the town of Licab, Corporal Vance O. Kiser of F Company and a detail of four other Rangers erected a radio relay station camp. Complete with antenna wire strung in treelimbs, three pup tents, an SCR 694 radio and hand crank generator. The equipment and activity of the American team was too much for the curious and hospitable Filipinos.

A few minutes after the camp was operational, at about 1800 hours (6 P .M.), excited natives from a nearby barrio began to arrive with fresh eggs, fruits and a chicken. In return, the Rangers traded their "K" rations. Everyone was delighted with the exchange -- the Americans glad to give up the tasteless canned goods for "real" food, and the Filipinos happy to receive such fancy gifts. Not only did the villagers love the processed food, they planned to put the empty cans to good use.

The existence of this Licab radio station was important. If reception difficulties occurred between Guimba and Colonel Mucci the Licab station was now ready to serve as a relay transmitter for either group.

* * * *

It was dark. The rangers had journeyed five and a half miles from Lobong. They were out of the thick forest. Now, they entered flat land and chest tall grass. They halted for a ten minute break in a bamboo thicket about one half mile south of the town of Baloc.

Before them, stretching at least, two hundred yards, was more open grass country through which cut the National Highway connecting Cabanatuan City and Talavera to the south and San Jose in the north. This was the first of two major roads the Rangers must cross. G2 had warned Mucci that both arteries may be heavily traveled by

Imperial Army troops at night. G2 was correct. The sounds from heavy vehicles moving north on the road could easily be heard by the Rangers as they crouched in small groups, concealed by the bamboo.

"What do you think, kid?" Colonel Mucci asked as he crawled up next to lst Sergeant Charles Bosard.

" Where in hell have you been sir?   You said I'm suppose to be your bodyguard and I haven't seen you since we left Guimba!"

Sergeant Bosard knew very well where Mucci had been during the march. . . everywhere. The Battalion commander was like a "mother hen" moving up and down the column of his men all after- noon, covering almost twice the distance of everyone else while ex- ercising constant control and issuing words of encouragement.

"We're going to have to leapfrog that road, one at a time if we are all going to get across safely tonight. Look at that!" Bosard pointed to a Japanese tank sitting ominously in the moonlight at the side of the road about a hundred yards to the north."Looks like they are guarding something . . . or waiting for someone," the Sergeant added.

"Yeah, I know," Mucci replied. Prince indicates that there is a ravine and a small bridge near the tank. The Nips may be guarding the bridge.. . or else, just taking a break. Prince thinks we should go through the ravine and dash. . . one at a time through the field on the other side for that bunch of trees over there. I agree.It's our only chance to make it without being spotted on the road. If we try to cross anywhere else we can be easily seen by either that tank. . .or any other Jap coming up the road."

"Sounds OK by me!" Bosard replied.

"Good! Spread the word back! We'll start crawling through this grass for the ravine. See you in the woods!"

Corporal James B. Herrick of C Company clutched his MI rifle as he crawled through the high grass towards the ravine on the west side of the National Highway. Several Rangers had already slipped through the shallow gully which ran under the bridge where the Japanese tank stood guard.

As Corporal Herrick moved closer to the bridge he could not only see the tank but clearly hear the voices of its unsuspecting crew.

Now, he was directly under the bridge, his heart pounding so loud he feared the enemy would hear it . His hand moved to the left pocket of the fatigue jacket and pressed against his chest. In that pocket he carried something he read each day. . . a small New Testament Bible his mother had given him.

Slowly. . . cautiously, Herrick crawled into the grass on the other side of the road and continued to creep along for another fifty yards. Then, crouching low, he sprang forward to run for the trees a mile away on the moonlit horizon.

It required over an hour for all the Rangers and Captain Joson's men to cross the National Highway, but they managed to do it without alerting the enemy tank crew.

After regrouping, Colonel Mucci assured himself that everyone was accounted for, they started northeast through the woods towards the Talavera River, carefully avoiding villages and their noisy dogs.

* * * *

Imperial Army Divisional Commander Naotake realized his situation in Cabanatuan City was rapidly becoming critical. A review of the field intelligence reports indicated that the advancing American forces would be in a position to strike at his city by February 2nd . . .maybe even twenty-four hours earlier. One of his five Battalions, Inoue, was under attack by forward U.S. units at San Jose and Commander Oyabu's Dokuho 359 Battalion was on the move somewhere between Bongabon and the Cabu River.

Naotake figured that if he could get all his Battalions to the city in time, his total force of over 6,000 combat troops could hold the Americans beyond that February 2nd date.

The task of holding the western suburbs of Cabanatuan he assigned to two Battalions. . . Nimomija and Muta. The Matsumoto Battalion was to hold the outskirts on the north. But to effectively accomplish this mission Matsumoto must have reinforcements. Naotake expected the major blow to come from the Allies at the north.

Around 9 P.M., January 28th, Naotake headquarters radioed Commander Inoue to withdraw from San Jose, as Oyabu had done earlier, and retreat via the fastest route to Cabanatuan City. The only possible route would take Inoue through Baloc and Talavera. If those men made it, they could link up with Matsumoto at the northern perimeter.

But, Naotake was realistic. They knew it was doubtful if Inoue could arrive unscratched. Somewhere along the National Highway, as his men passed other units heading north, the Americans would surely catch him.

Therefore, the only real hope for reinforcements lay with a complete and successful movement of Oyabu's Dokuho 359 Battalion which, by now, was well on the way at a safer distance east of the National Highway.

If Cabanatuan City was to be held, Oyabu must reach the Cabu River and be ready to move into position with Matsumoto before midnight, January 30th.

* * * *

A few minutes before midnight on January 28th, the Rangers reached the banks of the Talavera River, traveled parallel to its waters up stream a mile and then began their crossing. They had marched over three miles from the National Highway . . . fifteen miles since leaving Guimba.

With the exception of a ten minute break each hour, and the wait at the National Highway, there had been no other rest. But, the Rangers spirits were extremely high. So it is with most elite units assigned a mission. The usual"bitching" and complaining often experienced in other foot soldier units simply did not exist in the Rangers or Alamo Scouts. These men were basically volunteers, trained to perfection. They thrived on such assignments. One man later described the march to this point by stating,"Everyone was excited . . . as if we were going on a Sunday picnic!"

The men all knew C Company's Staff Sergeant Lester Malone loved to tease and the big Oklahoma farm boy was often the brunt of jokes, himself. As soon as the Talavera was crossed, one of the Rangers noticed that Sergeant Malone had been unusually quiet for the last mile.

"Hey, Twister!" The Ranger called to the Sereant."What's the matter with you? The old cowboy getting tired? How do you feel?"

"I feel great!" Malone replied."I feel like nothing in the world can hurt old Twister!"

"Well. . .something worried us ," another Ranger said."We weren't sure cowboys could walk this far."

"I tell you what," Malone responded in his heavy western drawl. "You give me your address . . . don't you all forget, now! And, I'll go see the wives of anyone who gets shot up!"

After the Talavera, the Rangers followed Joson's men through another heavy forest for three miles, then spread their single file line as they entered more open grassland.

As they began slipping through the tall grass the front troops suddenly heard a loud"thud" like noise and fell forward, releasing the safeties on their weapons. Seeing the front men drop, everyone immediately"dove for cover."

For a few moments there was no sound other than the warm evening breeze rustling the tall cogan grass. Then there came another loud"thud" . . . and a third . Rifles, BAR's and Tommyguns Swung from one point to another, ready to fire, But nothing could be seen in the moonlit field.

Several more minutes passed before a voice broke the silence, ". . .it's birds! Big dead birds falling!"

Something had killed the birds in flight. They never discovered what caused the act of Nature that produced some very anxious moments.

The men were on their feet again and after a mile reached the Rizal Highway, the second, and last major road they must cross. Again, enemy traffic was heavy as a steady stream of vehicles moved out from the town of General Luna heading north. And, as before, Japanese tanks were waiting at various points off the highway, spaced several hundred yards apart.

The Rangers waited for a break in the traffic flow. Then using their leapfrog technique, they crossed the road one at a time and dashed another mile through grass to the cover of trees.

Gasping for breath, lst Sergeant Charles Bosard sank to his knees and rolled over next to the trunk of a large tree for a few seconds rest. To his surprise, he discovered he was next toColonel Mucci.

"Boy! That was a close one," Mucci panted.

"Sure . . .was ."

Colonel Mucci began to think aloud."You know. . .those guard towers at the stockade . . ."

" Yes. . .?"

"I've been thinking . . . we may have to do a knifing job on the Japs in the towers before our boys can crawl in close. You'll have to do it, Kid. It'll take someone small . . . good . . . nerves of steel. That's you, kid. . .you'll have to do it!"

Sergeant Bosard stared at the Colonel without answering.

Mucci sat silent. Then, shaking his head, said,"No. No, forget it, Kid. That would be down right suicide. We'll have to think of some other way."

The Rangers now traveled east a mile and a half, forded the Mor-can River, continued east for a mile, turned south along a dirt road another mile, then southeast into more open, flat country. It was al-most dawn, January 29th. They had but three miles left to travel to the rendezvous with the Alamo Scouts . . . Balangkare. Twenty-four hours had elapsed since they left their Battalion headquarters. They had walked twenty-two miles, POW Camp Cabanatuan was another five miles from Balangkare.

The Rangers were tired, but this was not what worried Colonel Mucci. He planned for his men to rest until dusk in either Balangkare or Platero. The matter which concerned him most was the report the Alamo Scouts would give on the Japanese troop movement near their target. Had the Scouts obtained all the knowledge necessary? Or, for that matter, did they even reach their objective? Were they still alive?

* * * *

Since the late hours of January 27th and throughout the 28th, the Bamboo Telegraph moved the"alert mobilization" orders of Captain Juan Pajota and his Squadron Commanders to every town and bar-rio in eastern Neuva Ecija ."Mobilize at once . . . Squadron Com-manders move to meet at Platero . . prepare for combined action. . .we will help Americans with major assault. . . Seventy-five men needed at Balangkare by daybreak. . ."

From the Sierra Madre mountains, from Bakero and Bagong Sikat in the north came First Lieutenant Juanito Quitives and his Squadron 200 with one hundred men and First Lieutenant Regino Bobila's Squadron 202 consisting of over one hundred men.

From the area of Macatbong and Cabu, Lieutenants F. Bernardo and Ricardo Mendota brought their one hundred man Squadron 201 and four hundred and thirty men of Squadron 201 followed First Lieutenant Jose Hipolito to their designated assembly point.

One hundred and fifteen men of Lieutenant Villaruman's Squadron 203 and another one hundred and thirty men of Squadron 204 assembled near Manacnac, only two miles northeast of the POW Camp.

Squadron 211's thirty-six men with Lieutenant Toribio Paulino moved from the south towards Platero and Balangkare. And, around Platero the twenty men of Headquarters company began preparations for some very special guest. In all, more than 1,000 Filipino guerrillas, sworn members of the United States Army, mobilized to the orders of their commander.

Some of these men moved cross country in large squads, traveling first south, then north, then southwest, producing deceptive confusion for anyone trying to learn of their true destination. Others traveled alone. From the isolated farms, small towns, barrios and secret command post camps they came, most walking, a few riding carabaos or horses .

Only about five percent, mostly officers and NCO's who had served with USAFFE in 1941 through 1942, wore khaki uniforms. About one third were armed with rifles (both U.S. and captured Japanese weapons), U.S. Carbines and .45 caliber automatic pistols. The rest carried only their bolos. A few still had their round, U.S. World War I type helmet or army soft fatigue caps . The majority were their native buri hat*. They were a motley looking bunch of fierce fighters dedicated to serving the United States and ridding their country of the Japanese forever.

The maneuvers of Pajota's squadrons would have impressed any student of military tactics. If each man or squad were replaced with a tank symbol on a tactical map, the calculated movements might strangely resemble a gigantic army of armored vehicles preparing to advance on a particular objective. Pajota's plans were basic in concept yet ingenuously designed for his type of warfare on the terrain most familiar to him. The only difference between this activity and previous missions was the fact that, for the first time, his entire command - every squadron - must function as one complete unit. This all-out effort was intentionally designed to place the guerrilla leader in a position where success would most likely be guaranteed. With a slight stretch of the imagination, Pajota was now functioning as a Corps Commander, positioning his squadrons as if they were small divisions and battalions, though they lacked, of course, the usual Corps advantage of numerical strength, armor, mechanized equipment and artillery. Without the benefit of radio equipment, his units were exercising effective communication, nonetheless, through use of the Bamboo telegraph runners.

Pajota had guessed how the Americans intended on using his men in a general way. He would be ready for a number of contingencies.

Strangely, it seemed as if everyone in central and eastern Nueva Ecija had a good idea of what was coming except the Japanese . Asian cleverness was on equal terms as wits of the Japanese and Filipinos locked head on. Information bounced about via the Bamboo Telegraph, men and weapons moved from one place to another and back again , members of the Constabulary in Cabanatuan City suddenly disappeared, revealing finally by their absence allegiance to the United States or membership with the guerrillas. Entire families began to evacuate barrios, assembling in one town or village, only to split up and evacuate again.

At first it must have appeared to Naotake Headquarters in Cabanatuan City that complete disorder had finally befallen the Filipinos. The Japanese always suspicioned that the conquered Race was on the edge of chaos anyway.

But, the Imperial Headquarters was too preoccupied with the defense of the city and the logistical problems of the transient troops to worry much about what the Filipinos were up to now. After three years of occupation, the Imperial Intelligence Section, as efficient at forcing information from the natives as they were, still did not completely understand them.

By January 29th, the Japanese command, frustrated with the approaching Allied lines, guessed that if anything of particular importance was developing among the residences of Nueva Ecija, the"Makapili" would inform as they always had. Unfortunately for the Japanese, there were not many Makapili left to inform. By now, most realized their mistake in helping the Japanese and had a change of heart. Others had been assassinated by townmates or guerrillas. Those few Makapili remaining were much too frightened of the Japanese, the Americans and the guerrillas to reveal anything.

The guerrillas realized, however, that if just one Makapili decided to talk to the Naotake Command the entire mission would end in a terrible disaster.

* * * *

At exactly 0600 (6 A.M.), January 29th, Lieutenant Colonel Henry Mucci and his Rangers arrived at the outskirts of small barrio Balangkare. There, in a grove of trees bordering a rice field on the northwest edge of the village, they found Alamo Scout Lieutenants Tom Rounsaville and Bill Nellist waiting for them. Everyone was

117

relieved to learn each group had experienced little difficulty during the last thirty hours and completed the journey undetected by the Japanese. The Scouts reported that their two teams had arrived at Captain Pajota's headquarters without incident and had been working since the previous afternoon with Pajota's Intelligence Officer, First Lieutenant Carlos Tombo, gathering as much information as humanly possible. Some of the Scouts were still out on reconnaisance patrol, covering the many trails which zigzagged from Balangkare to Platero, from Platero to the main road in front of the POW Camp. They had traveled the Pampanga river banks north and south, the rice fields across from the camp and even circled the camp itself, but, at a safe distance. What they revealed to Mucci was very disheartening.

There simply had not been sufficient time to gather all the data required to plan a raid on the stockade. The terrain at the camp area was much too flat and open for anyone to get close enough to procure accurate information on the strength of the enemy force and their activity. But, even more distressing was the news that for the last twenty-four hours the main road in front of the camp had been heavily traveled by Japanese forces heading north. At least two or three hundred Japanese were bivouacked along the northeast bank of the Cabu River a mile north of the camp. Pajota's men reported that a division of Japanese were at Cabanatuan City, less than four miles to the south.

The Scouts, of course, had not been to the big city. There was enough to worry with in the immediate area. Mucci was obviously upset and disappointed. Unless the situation changed for the better he knew he may be forced to postpone the raid. He now demanded more detailed information on the garrison and the enemy troops stationed there. Even if the road was heavily traveled at night he may order the raid to go on as scheduled regardless of the risk. But, before that decision could be made, they needed a complete description of the camp. While Colonel Mucci, his officers and Scouts discussed their hazardous and frustrating situation, a group of Filipinos approached the grove of trees by a trail leading out from the barrio . One man was riding horseback on a horse about the size of an American pony. The rider was dressed in a faded khaki uniform and fatigue cap with no rank or insignia A .45 automatic pistol hung from a web belt and over his left shoulder was slung a U.S. MI Carbine. When the group reached a point about twenty-five yards from the Americans, the rider dismounted, and, flanked by two other men, walked directly up to the Ranger Commander.

"Lieutenant Colonel Mucci?" the little Filipino inquired.

"Yes . . I 'm Mucci."

The Filipino snapped to attention amd saluted."Sir! I am Captain Juan Pajota. Welcome to Balangkare!"

After a brief exchange of introductions, Pajota was invited to sit down and join the meeting. Mucci immediately informed,"We plan to attack that POW Camp tonight. . .at dusk"

Pajota stared into Mucci's face, trying to determine if the Colonel was serious. After a moment, he could control himself no longer."Sir! Are you committing suicide?!"

Mucci's narrow eyes flashed at the comment which bordered on disrespect. He glared at the Filipino." Of course not!"

"Well, Sir," Pajota tried to explain his bluntness."You must know the enemy situation from your Alamo Scouts . My own scouts have been reporting to me every hour . Another Jap unit is approaching Cabu Bridge from the North. . .Battalion size. If they stay at Cabu River there will be over 1,000 Japs at that place." Pajota's serious face warped with a frown."This is a very tough assignment you have been given. There are hundreds of Japs in the camp . . .and tanks.

And, maybe five hundred POW s . Only a few POWs can walk. They must be carried if you are going to take them out. But. . .I have a plan for the prisoners . My men are organizing a team of Carabao carts for you to use to move the POWs. . ."

Mucci, still irritated by the"suicide" comment, listened, nonetheless , without interrupting .

"Allow me to show you, Sir. . .this map." Pajota produced from his shirt, the Operations Map he had so carefully constructed during the long resistance campaign. He began to unfold it and added,"I have wanted to attack this camp for a long time . I was ordered not to do it even though Major Lapham and I had plans for a successful raid."

Colonel Mucci glanced at the Filipino's map and with his natural diplomatic ability, recognized the opportunity to melt the icy atmosphere which held since the beginning of the meeting."Where did you graduate, Captain. . .West Point? That's a very good map !"

As usual, the Colonel's insight into human nature paid off. Pajota grinned with pride."No, Sir. I was trained by General MacArthur's USAFFE."

At that time Colonel Mucci showed Pajota a sketch of the camp drawn from the aerial photograph and his large topography map. Of course, Pajota knew most of the camp features by heart, having once been stationed there. But, he had never seen such a beautiful map as the one the Colonel now unfolded. He noticed, at once, that some of the town's names on the Ranger's map were misspelled, but it did not seem polite or necessary to call anyone's attention to the errors

Colonel Mucci then began to outline his general plan for the attack, explaining that all his Rangers and Scouts would be required to handle the assault on the camp. Captain Joson's eighty men were to set up a roadblock south of the camp.

Several Rangers from F Company with bazookas would assist at that position.

"How many armed men do you have here?" Colonel Mucci directed his question to Pajota.

The guerrilla leader replied with the truth. At least the figure he gave represented the number in the immediate area . . . "ninety men with weapons and one hundred sixty unarmed men." Since Mucci had not inquired about the total number serving under Pajota, the complete strength was not revealed. Pajota had suspicioned that his squadrons would be assigned to a holding action along the road somewhere, but he was not sure just where. There was no sense committing more men than Mucci needed.

Pajota also did not reveal that he had four old water cooled .30 caliber machine guns, hoping the Rangers would turn over more such weapons for his use. To his surprise, the Rangers had no machine guns.

Now, Pajota learned of his assignment. His armed soldiers must hold the Japanese camped across the Cabu River from crossing the highway bridge and reinforcing the Imperial troops at the stockade. The unarmed Filipinos would assist the Rangers by moving the POW's from the Pampanga River area. They would also serve as runners, litter bearers and carabao cart drivers. Pajota assured Mucci that he could muster at least four hundred unarmed men to help in and around Platero. But, he still did not reveal that he had decided to assign Squadrons 200 and 202 to be in reserve near Joson's roadblock and Squadrons 203 and 204 to positions near Manacnac behind the Japanese at Cabu Bridge . Most all of the men in these"ghost" squadrons were armed.

Colonel Mucci was full of questions for Pajota.

"What's the distance from here to Platero?" he asked.

"Five kilometers. . .about two and one-half miles." Pajota replied.

"And . . . from Platero to the Pampanga River?"

"One kilometer. . .about one half mile, Sir."

"And . . . from the Pampanga to the front gate of the camp?"

"More than four kilometers . . .two miles, Sir, depending on what route you elect to take."

"The front gate to your position at Cabu Bridge. . .how far?"

"About a mile, Sir."

"Good!" Mucci nodded. It all checked with the distances indicated on his large map.

"Captain Joson!"

"Sir:"

"You will form your roadblock at this spot near the road. . . 800 yards southwest from the camp. You are to stop all enemy traffic from 1930 hours, . . .understand!" Mucci pointed to his map .

"Yes, Sir." Captain Joson replied.

On and on the meeting went, Mucci shooting questions between puffs on his pipe, stopping now and then to think, then snapping orders while everyone listened. The staff was told that he would announce his final decision later, after the Scouts reported back and everyone assembled in Platero. There would still be time to either proceed with raid or postpone it.

In the meantime, both Pajota and Joson's men must undergo an orientation on the use of the bazooka. Most of the Rangers could try and rest in the shade for the day.

* * * *

While Mucci and his staff met with the guerrilla leaders at Balangkare a new unit of Japanese troops settled down in the bamboo groves on the east side of the Cabu River only three miles away.

It was 0730 (7:30 A.M.) and Pajota's scouts accurately predicted the arrival of Battalion Comnander Tomeo Oyabu and his Dokuho 359.

Oyabu was pleasantly surprised when he discovered that a force of over three hundred soldiers were already camped in the woods along both sides of the highway on that east bank of the river. He was especially delighted to learn that these men were from a variety of units, including remnants of a tank company, complete with four tanks and a truck with a mounted machine gun at its cab top.

These fragment units were commanded by four junior officers who had no orders other than to retreat north the next night and attempt to link up with General Yamashita's main defense group. But, the young tank officer expressed concern to Oyabu. All his vehicles were low on fuel and he doubted if they could make it any further than Bongabon. He had not yet decided where to make his stand against the Americans.

123

Oyabu solved his dilemma. He immediately assumed command of everyone in the area and issued his own orders. They all would rest for another day and then move to the defense of Cabanatuan City at 9 P.M., January 30th . . . not Bongabon .

Oyabu's Battalion, Dokuho 359 now consisted of a little more than 1,175 men.

* * * *

One mile south of the bivouacked Oyabu Battalion, the one hundred and seventy-five man Kinpeidan Headquarters unit continued their rest at POW Camp Cabanatuan.

Other than curiosity, they had little interest in the Allied POW's contained inside the barbed wire fence across the road. Nor did they have much to do with ninety-five guards at the camp. To the men of Kinpeidan Headquarters, those Japanese, Korean and Formosans assigned to guard the prisoners were beneath the dignity of the regular Imperial Army.

Kinpeidan's men were mainly interested in resting and leaving the area just as soon as their orders indicated they should. Everyone could hear the big American guns thundering in the distance. The thought of having to wait until the next night was not an easy one to sleep on.

* * * *

At Balangkare, the day wore on for the Rangers who were finding it difficult to nap due to the tremendous excitement and hospitality of the Filipinos.

C Company PFC Mariono Garde, of Mexican descent, was, despite the generous gifts of fresh fruits, a little disappointed. He had tried his Spanish, on several Filipinos only to learn that no one spoke the language.

"What the hell is this?" Garde complained to his buddy as he shifted his heavy BAR from one shoulder to another."Spain ruled this country for hundreds of years and not one soul around here speaks Spanish!"

"Maybe no one bothered to teach them," came the reply. "Why don't you start a Spanish class, Garde, you got nothing to do all day anyway!"

A few hundred yards away, Staff Sergeant August Stern and other members of C Company's Special Weapons Section began to train the guerrillas in the use of the bazooka.

With his fatigue jacket unbuttoned, the Filipinos noticed that Stern was wearing a Saint Christopher medal with his dog tags and that, along with the American's hairy chest, brought considerable interest. The Filipinos figured every American was a Catholic, just like themselves, but they did not know U.S. soldiers wore religious medals.

The Filipinos were even more impressed with the peculiar looking pipe the Americans called a bazooka and found it difficult to believe that its little rocket actually could yield as much destructive power as Stern said it would. They laughed when the Sergeant cautioned that"fire comes out both ends" of the tube. They must take care to aim and point the weapon in the correct direction but also stand clear of the"back blast" when the rocket fires.

What gave Sergeant August Stern his laugh for the day was when he discovered Captain Bob Prince admiring an egg and trying to decide how it should be prepared. It was the first real egg the C Company Commander had seen in a long time . Stern would never forget the look on the young captain's face when he was told to "poke a hole in the point and suck everything out!"

Tech 4th Class Frank Goetzheimer was disgusted, and his buddies of Combat Photo, Unit F, were equally frustrated.

"What's the matter , Frank?" PFC Bob Lautman asked his friend. "You look like you just discovered your Bell and Howell got busted."

"It might as well be broken," Goetzheimer replied."Those fellows never stopped long enough on the way over here for me to get even a single foot of film. Now they say they are positive the raid will be after dark. Hell! We can't get any shots in the dark with our equipment ."

"Yeah! I know. I don't think Goen got many shots on the march. I know I didn't . We're beginning to get some good ones now.You're right. If Mucci pulls this thing off after dark, we'll just be spectators.

At age twenty-four, C Company Commander Captain Robert Prince was, indeed, a remarkable young man.

There had never been a mission during his short military career like the one now facing his men. Even had he been a soldier by profession, he would not have had the benefit of knowing how to conduct a raid on an enemy POW camp right in the middle of hostile forces. No such action had ever been attempted in the history of the United States Army.

Nor did Captain Prince even have the advantage of seeing one of those many"war movies" flooding the entertainment market in the States. Regardless of how corny those productions, millions of people back home were learning how movie star commandos planned make-believe attacks .

Colonel Mucci had placed the responsibility of the Rangers breaking into the camp completely upon Captain Prince. The plan must be his own, original and perfect. One mistake, one miscalculation, one man failing to carry out an assigned job and everything could fail. And, if it failed, Bob Prince knew there was no second chance . . . all the POWs would be dead.

He realized that even in failure, they could inflict heavy Japanese casualties. But this was not positive thinking. Prince understood his orders perfectly. No American, especially a POW, was to die. To insure this, every Japanese in the camp must be killed quickly.

Colonel Mucci, with his decision to turn the bulk of the planning over to his"wonderful Captain Prince", had selected the right man. Prince, above all, was not reckless. He was an intelligent cool nerved, positive thinking individual who went about his work with the calm disposition of a college professor preparing a lecture. If there would be a problem during the raid it would not come from poor planning. A problem could only arise from an improbable accident.

Perhaps it was this serious aspect of Bob Prince's personality which attracted and impressed Juan Pajota. The two men were very similar in the manner in which they confronted life's problems .

Copies of the POW camp's design had been distributed to all officers . They and their NCO's must study every detail of the camp and be ready to make changes as information became available from either Pajota's men or the Alamo Scouts.

Now, Captain Prince, sleeves rolled to the upper arm, his fatigue cap pushed far back on his head, was ready to coordinate plans with Captain Pajota.

It was agreed that the guerrillas would provide the perimeter security around both Balangkare and Platero and continue this protection until after the raid. They discussed the matter of evacuating civilians not involved in the support effort and the problems concerning carabao carts and food preparation for approximately 650 men.

Prince also passed on a message to Pajota from Colonel Mucci. All dogs in the area of Platero and barrios on the attack route were to be tied and muzzled and chickens penned up to avoid any alarm being sounded by nervous animals as strangers (the Americans) passed by.

Pajota stated that he had already ordered his Executive Officer, Captain Luis De La Cruz, to inform the villagers to keep their dogs inside.

An evacuation plan, of Pajota's design, was also ready for execution. Civilians residing along the attack route, primarily at Calawagan and Comunal (population, less than 100) were to move southwest of Platero. Later, the people of Cabu, near the bridge, were to pull out one family at a time, southeast for Macatbong. And, those few in Pangatian, next to the POW camp, were to move southeast to the Sierra Madre Mountains.

At 1600 hours (4 P.M.) Sergeant Norton Most was given orders to break radio silence and send Guimba base the message. . ."Request air cover along planned withdrawal route, commencing 1900 hours ." Sergeant Most tapped out the message and, as planned, received no acknowledgement . The message was expected by Tech 4th Class James Irvine at his radio in the Command Staff car near Guimba and the Sixth Army members who waited there with him . The message simply meant everything was proceeding on schedule.

A few minutes later the Rangers divided into two groups. Flanked by Captain Joson's men on one side and Captain Pajota's men on the other, the force left Balangkare for the two and one half mile walk to Platero.

About half way, the march came to a halt. The Alamo Scouts were assembled off the trail under several large trees and were ready to report on the results of their days reconnaisance.

Despite their rest, the Rangers looked exhausted. Green uniforms were caked with dust and sweat. Perspiration soaked their soft caps and trickled down from close cut hair. A two day growth of beard was clearly visible.

Colonel Mucci, his fatigue shirt sleeves rolled up almost to the arm pits and beads of perspiration covering his high forehead directly under the narrow brim of his cap, sat down to listen to the Scouts.

The Scouts were even a sadder sight to behold. Their loose fatigues, completely soaked with sweat, had turned almost a brownish black from dust and mud. Again, their report was disheartening. They confirmed what Pajota's men had reported. . . . 200 Japanese soldiers were in the POW camp, at least 800 to 1,000 Japanese were camped near Cabu bridge. Even worse, an enemy unit estimated to be of division strength was beginning its way northeast towards Bongabon along the main highway. No one knew for sure just how many Japanese troops remained in Cabanatuan City.

It was the large unit on the move which caused Colonel Mucci to make the decision. The raid must be postponed.

Sergeant Norton Most and the commo men set up their SCR 694 radio. As the generatar operator began to turn the hand crank, the

129

message was tapped out. . ."New developments . . . twenty-four hour delay!"

Actually, most everyone along that trail to Platero breathed a sigh of relief. The risk of executing the raid while a Japanese Division passed, was much too great to guarantee success and a full night's rest would certainly be welcome .

* * * *

Tech 4 James Irvine lifted his steel helmet momentarily to scratch his curly black hair. Not counting the sleepless night prior to the Rangers departure, he had now been awake for thirty- five hours at his radio post in the staff car near Guimba without relief.

Suddenly, his radio came alive and began to click a message, startling him with the shock of an alarm clock on a rainy morning . Quickly, he scribbled out the coded words on a standard yellow message sheet.". . . New developments . . .twenty-four hour delay."

This time Irvine tapped a reply" . . .message acknowledged". He then relayed the information to 6th Army headquarters at nearby Guimba .

Within a few minutes, Mucci's message was reported to   General Walter Krueger.   The 6th Army Commander, his face expressing deep concern, muttered to his aide,"I wonder if I've sent those men on too rough a mission this time!"

There was something always frightening about typical combat radio messages. By necessity they could not elaborate. And years of experience receiving such brief, blunt words will never relieve the anxiety of a commander. General Krueger would not sleep that night. It was as if there were no other battles on Luzon. . .no other units on a mission but Colonel Mucci and the Rangers. Through the night the General paced the floor of his tent and studied maps of Nueva Ecija. His only instructions were . . . he must be notified immediately if another radio message arrived from Colonel Mucci.

* * * *

It was 5:30 P.M. when sixteen year old Victoria Targa came running to the house of her girl friend in Barrio Platero .

On the flat black dirt in front of the home, an elderly lady bent forward with her hand broom made from rice straw, fanatically sweeping the yard clean. Typical of each homemaker in the barrios the yards were always cleared of leaves and trash (usually imaginary) several times a day.

"Have you heard?" Victoria shouted to her friend, pausing only a moment to catch her breath."The Americans are coming! They are coming already. . . from Balangkare!"

"How do you know?" her girl friend grabbed for Victoria's hand with usual Filipino affection.

"Captain Pajota's soldiers . . . I heard them talking."

"How many Americans?" the old lady interrupted while continuing her vigorous sweeping.

"I do not know. A hundred, maybe . Of course . . . at least one hundred. Captain Joson and his men are with them."

"Only one hundred! Jesus, Mary, Joseph!" the old lady swore. "They will need more than one hundred to kill all the Japanese!"

The woman's words fell on unattentive ears The long awaited news moved through the village at lightning speed . Now the two teenagers were surrounded by other young girls who giggled and shouted with uncontrollable excitement.

"The Americans are so tall. They are like giants! They take one step for every two of Captain Pajota's!" Victoria reported what she had heard.

More giggling followed.

"Their noses are long and pointed. . ."

"What! Not flat?"

More giggling.

"And their eyes are light . . . so is the hair! They have hair on their arms . . . all the way to the hands . . . and, hair on the chest"

"Tell us, Victoria! How do they feel? Have you ever touched American?

"Oh, no! Of course not!" Victoria covered her mouth with an open hand to politely cover her laugh.

"Then," another girl announced as she twisted fast to twirl her skirt,"I will touch one and tell you how they feel!" She tossed her long raven hair with a quick snap of the head and strutted gracefully away from her townmates.

"Come! We must hurry, now! Mr. De La Cruz is preparing the reception, already. He is waiting for us!"

* * * *

It was almost dark when the front ranks of the Rangers entered Platero. They halted suddenly, causing those behind them to bunch up and fan out some twenty-five yards on both flanks.

"What the hell's going on up there, Pat? What's everybody slowing down for?" Twenty-five year old PFC Bill Proudfit asked Sergeant Patrick Marquis who was directly in front of the tall Iowan.

"I'm not sure. Take a look at that! Looks like some kind of reception."

"Wow!" another Ranger exclaimed."Look at all them girls! Reckon they're for us?!"

What had caused the Rangers to stop in their tracks was a reception composed of twenty girls ranging in age from fifteen to twenty-three. The Filipinos were neatly lined in two straight rows blocking the main dirt road which led into Platero. Each girl held a bouquet of bright colored flowers and around their necks hung leis of sweet smelling white sampaguita blossoms. They were all dressed in white, some wearing short sleeved, long skirted "Traje de Bodas", others wore a modified "Maria Clara" with long skirts and long sleeves sloping down in bell shaped form to the elbows. A few even wore the exotic "Balintawak" with its wide flat sleeves reaching from the elbow and extended high above each shoulder. The natives costumes represented the very best formal dress owned in the family.

Some girls had their long black hair fixed eloquently atop the head in true Spanish style. Yet, for others, it simply hung straight to the shoulders or down to the center of the back. Pre-war school principal, Luis De La Cruz, now Executive Officer and Captain in Pajota's army, had specially selected the girls for their beauty and talent from a number of nearby barrios.

It was twilight and the beautiful picture of white dresses, brown skin and shiny black hair became etched in the minds of all the Rangers. What happened next was something none of the Americans would ever forget.

As the four Combat Photo men, thirteen Alamo Scouts and one hundred and twenty-one rugged foot-sore Rangers moved closer to the"reception committee", the girls, with heavy accents, began to sing. . .

"God bless Ameerka

Land dat I love

Stan beside her. . .and guide

her Thru de night with a light from aboved.

From de mountain . . . to de preere

To de oocean, white with de foam

God bless Am. . .meer. .re. . .ka

My home, sweedt . . .home

God bless Ameereka

My home . . . sweedt . . . home!"

"Can you beat that," Sergeant Marquis murmured,"after all these people been through . . . they think of us!"

PFC Proudfit cleared his throat and glanced around, noticing that several of the big men's eyes were wet."My God! . . . it's beautiful."

In a few seconds the girls began to sing again,

"Land of de morn -ing, child of the sun returnimg

With fer-vor burn-ing, thee do our souls a-dore.

Land dear and ho-ly, cra-dle of no-ble heros . . ."

"What is it?" Proudfit whispered."Don't know. Marquis answered

"It's their National Anthem!" someone said.

". . . Ne'er may in-vad-ers

tram-ple thy sa-cred shore. . ." the girls continued.

"Ev-er with-in in thy skys and through the clouds

And o'er thy hills and sea, do we be-hold

de ra-deance, feel de throb of glo-reous lib-er-ty!

Thy ban-ner dear to all our hearts

Its sun and stars a-light

Oh. . .nev-er shall its shin-ing field

be dimmed by ty-rants might!

Beau-te-ful land of love,oh land

. . of. . . light, In thine embrace

'tis cap-ture to lie

But, it is glo-ry ev-er, when thy art

wronged , For us . . . thy sons

to suf-fer and die!"

The girls finished their National Anthem,then began again as Mucci's men gained their composure and entered Platero .

"God bless Amleereka

Land dat I love

Stand beside her. . ."

The choral welcome was only the beginning for the Rangers who soon discovered that the entire Barrio was preparing a feast in their honor.

Meanwhile, Joson and Pajota's men circled Platero with a perimeter of defense so tight that not even a lizard could pass through unnoticed.

Groups of two to six Americans were assigned separate homes for dinner. While disbursement was organized, a tremendous noise of squealing pigs and squawking chickens cut through the singing and laughter. The Rangers were, again, impressed and moved. The Filipinos, who they knew were short of food, were killing their prize livestock for the evening meal. It would do no good to try and refuse the generous hospitality.. Custom dictated that the very best in food be given a visitor, even if the gesture resulted in the host doing without.

PFC Bill Proudfit was in for another unusual reception. On the way to his assigned"home" he was confronted by an elderly white man who promptly introduced himself as"Mister Bill Beedle . . . formerly of the United States Army!"

Shocked to find an American in the little Barrio so far from a major city, Proudfit, naturally, had a number of questions. Mr. Beedle, he learned, was a veteran of the Spanish-American War had married a Filipino and settled down in Platero"over forty years ago to raise a family". He had escaped the Japanese round up of American civilians after the 1941 invasion and explained,"at age sixty-one, I couldn't do the Japs no harm, anyway"

The two men were thrilled to discover that both were from Iowa. They would have much to discuss the next day, before the raid.

Proudfit then entered the home of Genaro Bernardo and Loureana Saulo where he was treated at a"table with silverware and all."

Next, another surprise.

The family rolled out an old upright piano which they had hidden behind bamboo mats since the Japanese invasion.

"We have been waiting for the Americans to return," Bernardo said."Our country can have music again!"

The family's two daughters took turns at the piano and even knew a few of Proudfit's special requests.

It was almost 9 P.M. when PFC Proudfit entered a stable and carefully picked a spot to sit down a safe distance from the bamboo shed's only other occupant. . . a mild mannered carabao.

Proudfit cradled his MI rifle in his lap and reached for his trench knife . He felt the edge with his thumb and stretched his arm, pointing the blade towards the entrance.

There, standing as silent as a shadow in the moonlight, was a small girl about seven years old. He quickly lowered the weapon.

"Hello!" Proudfit said.

"My name is Mercy . I speak English!" the little girl proudly replied.

"So I see."

Mercy boldly entered the stable."Does the American have choco late?"

The Ranger's honest Iowa face broke into a smile. He reached into his pocket and produced a thick bar of tropical chocolate. With his knife, he shaved off a strip and handed it to the child. In a moment, as silently as she appeared, she was gone in the darkness.

Not far away, in another home, Staff Sergeant Clifton Harris continued to study the glass jar on the table from which his Filipino hosts occasionally poured some liquid onto heaping piles of rice.

"Look at them long green things in that jar! Reckon them's pickles?" Harris whispered to his buddy.

"They sure are funny looking pickles!" his friend replied.

"Hell! I know pickles when I see em. I haven't had a pickle in three years. I love pickles. . .I don't forget that easy!"

The host passed the jar to Harris who reached in with his fingers and held the green"pickle" up to admire. Then, he tossed it into his mouth and began to chew. Suddenly, Harris started to choke and grabbed for his canteen to drown the terrible burning sensation with gulps of water.

His buddy bent forward, gasping with laughter.

"Bet them's ain't pickles . . .Bet them's some kind of pepper!"

"Bet you better shut your fat mouth!" Harris said between coughs.

PFC Thomas A. Grace gazed at the photo of his wife and child he had covered with plastic before he left New Guinea and carried with him for many months. It was his favorite photo, of the baby kissing the mother on the cheek.

PFC Grace carefully returned the picture to his fatigue jacket breast pocket and glanced over at his friend, PFC Eugene Dykes, who was curled up in the corner of the chicken coop, sound asleep.

"What the hell you looking for, Dave?" Grace spoke to his other bed mate, Staff Sergeant David M. Hey, who was crawling about the ground on his hands and knees.

"First it was these damned lice eating on me. . .now, I've lost my wedding ring!" Hey replied.

"How did you lose it?"

"It was on the stem of my pipe . I always carried it there . Now its gone!"

"You'll never find it in this straw in the dark . Let's get some sleep and we'll comb the place in the daylight."

David Hey never found his ring.

Sergeant"Father" Francis Schille and his big pal, PFC Roy Sweezy also found themselves bedded down for the night in a chicken coop.

It was"just like home" to them and they had no trouble getting to sleep.

Corporal Marvin"Pop" Kinder was a little more fortunate than most of the Rangers. He was assigned the lower level of one of the homes where he did not have to share his bed with either chickens or a carabao.

Sergeant Joe Youngblood, on the other hand, had a hard time fighting with several healthy pigs for a comfortable spot in their pen.

PFC John V. Pearson made himself comfortable against a concrete block wall which surrounded the Platero school yard.

Staff Sergeant Richard A. Moore had just settled down in a shed when who should poke his head in, but Colonel Mucci!

"Want a shot of stateside scotch?" Mucci asked the startled Sergeant.

"Sure thing!" Moore responded without stopping to think where the Colonel got the whiskey.

"Just one swig!" Colonel Mucci instructed as he handed the Ranger a bottle of John Walker 'Black Label'."Its got to make the rounds."

Joanquin Alas, the Barrio Lieutenant (Mayor) had given Colonel Mucci the precious whiskey which had been hidden since the Japanese invasion."I have saved it for the Americans," Alas explained."I knew the Americans would return!"

Before the night was over, Mucci managed somehow, to find every man in their unusual quarters and offered them each a sip.

At 0100 hours (1 A.M.) January 30th, Lieutenants Tom Rounsaville and Bill Nellist met with their liaison, John Dove in Platero. A few minutes later they and Lieutenant Tombo with several of Pajota's men, slipped out of the barrio, crossed the Pampanga River and crawled towards the main road and the POW camp.

By 0300 (3 A.M.) they were back in Platero and reported to Captain Prince and Colonel Mucci. There was no change in the enemy activity. Japanese troops were still moving along the road in small units . But, no new units had entered the POW camp.

* * * *

At 0600 (6A.M.) the tall barbed wire gates of POW Camp Cabanatun swung open to allow a small contingent of Imperial soldiers to enter.

These men, mostly clerical personnel released by Naotake from Cabanatuan City, were the last of the Kinpeidan Unit. Their arrival brought the total number of headquarter personnel in the camp's transient area to two hundred and ten.

With them they carried the final movement orders for the entire Kinpeidan Unit. Tonight, no later than 8 P.M., they must pull out of the stockade, clear Cabu Bridge and proceed north to Bongabon.

As soon as their unit cleared the bridge, Commander Oyabu's Battalion Dokuho 359 would know it was time to move to Cabanatuan City.

The full Japanese Division which departed San Leonardo on the 28th had filtered through Cabanatuan City on the 29th and was now well past the Cabu River. By 8 A.M. they would be at Bongabon some eighteen miles to the northeast.

Naotake planned no further troop dispatchments out of Cabanatuan for the 30th. Every soldier remaining there must prepare for the city's defense while they waited for Oyabu and Dokuho 359.

* * * *

Mucci's men were treated to another royal meal as breakfast of eggs , pork, coffee and fresh fruits were prepared by the Filipinos in Platero shortly after daybreak on the 30th.

At 0930 (9:30 A.M.), Colonel Mucci held an"officers call", including Captains Joson and Pajota and some of their staff. The purpose of this meeting was to outline to the Alamo Scouts the exact information the Rangers needed to complete their plan.

"I want to know," Mucci began,"just how many Japs are in that camp . . .where they are and what they're doing! What buildings are holding the tanks . . .what's the distance from the front gate to those tank sheds! How is the main gate secured? How many gates are there? Are all the guard towers occupied? I don't care how you get all this dope . . . but, we must have it this afternoon!"

Mucci then turned to Captain Pajota."Captain. . . I want your men to tell me exactly how many Japs are at that Cabu River. And, you can show Captain Prince the best approach to the camp. As far as you are concerned, there is no change in the original plan. Your men will hold the bridge. . .Captain Joson will hold the road to the south!"

By 0915 hours the Alamo Scouts with Lieutenant Tombo had left Platero. Captain Pajota invited the other officers to join him at a barrio home where they could continue their planning away from the curious eyes of the villagers.

The place Pajota selected for the meeting was a large nipa house constructed mostly of thatched grass, bamboo and wood.

As Captain Bob Prince climbed the wooden steps and entered the home he noticed that the floor was made of strips of bamboo, spaced about an eighth of an inch apart, and nailed to its wooden frame.

Sitting upon a blanket on the floor, in one corner, was an attractive young mother peacefully nursing her child. The girl smiled widely and nodded welcome to her unusual visitors.

The two American Company Commanders, Captain Prince and First Lieutenant John Murphy, unaccustomed to seeing bare breast, modestly turned their heads and blushed.

Sensing something may be wrong , the mother spoke to Captain De La Cruz in Tagalog. A fast exchange in the Filipino language followed between De La Cruz and Pajota. The girl raised one hand to cover her loud giggle.

143

"What did you tell her?" Lieutenant Murphy, his face still brilliant red, asked Captain De La Cruz.

The Filipino smiled."I told her that in America, babies are fed the milk of a cow. . .from bottles. She thinks that is very funny. She is embarrassed that she did not know such a thing!"

A meeting to plan death. . .and life, began with the backs of the Americans turned to the mother and child.

CHAPTER 9

If any Japs pass, it will be over our dead bodies. We will all be dead!"

Captain Juan Pajota; January 30,1945

It was past noon on January 3Oth. Though Captain Pajota's scouts had reported hourly on the enemy activity near Cabu Bridge, nothing had been heard from Lieutenants Nellist and Rounsaville and the Alamo Scouts. However, Mucci was not worried . He knew he had given them an almost impossible assignment and did not expect a report for another hour or so.

While Colonel Mucci's officers and high ranking NCO's continued to discuss various assault ideas, the Rangers cat napped in the shade, cleaned their weapons, or amused themselves by talking with those Filipinos who spoke English.

First Sergeant Bosard even found time to enter a few lines in his small diary..."Jan. 29-30 '45. Filipinos so happy to see us. They sang God Bless America and touched us to see what Americans feel like. Marched 29 miles so far."

On the Barrios perimeter, Sergeant Patrick Marquis chatted with several guerrilla soldiers and attempted to learn some Tagalog. One young Filipino remained unusually silent, his eyes fixed on the three Army.45 pistols which hung in brown leather holsters from Marquis' web belt.

The Sergeant finally confronted the young man.

"What's your name? Do you speak English?"

"Private Godofredo Monsod Junior, sir...of Lieutenant Quitive's Squadron 200!" The Filipino answered in almost flawless English.

"How old are you, Monsod?"

"Eighteen, sir!"

"You don't have a weapon... a gun?"

"No, sir. I will kill the Japanese with my bolo! My father was Provincial Commander of the Constabulary in Cabanatuan City. The Japanese made him acting Governor of Nueva Ecija. But... they discovered he supported the Americans and took him to Fort Santiago at Manila. No one returns from that place. My father did not return. The Japanese executed my father!"

Marquis slowly unhooked two holsters containing the heavy pistols."Here...now you can settle the score on a more even basis!" he said as he handed the weapons to Private Monsod.

Captain Juan Pajota and the men of his command had received generous and expert medical attention during their thirty-two month campaign against the Japanese from numerous brave doctors of Cabanatuan City who had risked their lives to treat the guerrillas. Five of these daring men were Antanio De Guzman, Nicholas De Guzman, Pedro Jimenez, Eli Ballesteros, and Juan Lazaro. In most cases, the wives or other members of the family were either physicians or qualified nurses. Each would have been shot or beheaded by the Japanese, had their activities been discovered.

Late in the campaign, on December lst, 1944, Pajota's"General Order Number 42" enlisted another doctor, Carlos Nuguid Layug, and assigned him"Commanding Officer, Medical Company".

Doctor Layug was a large man for a Filipino, well over six feet tall. In fact, when the Rangers met him in Platero the evening of January 29th, they first thought he was Chinese.

But Layug was pure Filipino, graduating from the University of Santo Tomas in 1937. After training at Camp Murphy Medical Field Service School, he enlisted in the USAFFE Medical Corps in 1941. That move took him to Bataan. He survived the Death March and Camp O'Donnell. Then, assisted by his wife, Julita, he set up a medical practice in Manila. Before long, the Japanese told Layug that he was to be the"official doctor" at a sugar plantation where alcohol was manufactured.

Considering this appointment to be"collaboration" with the enemy, Carlos Layug and his family fled to the Central Plains of Luzon and eventually settled in the Balangkare-Platero area to wait out the war while doing what they could for local villagers with limited medicines and equipment.

Naturally, Captain James Fisher was ecstatic when he and Doctor Layug met and began to discuss combat field surgery. Layug was especially appreciative and thrilled with the gifts of extra surgical tools Jimmy Fisher turned over to him.

They began the necessary plans for establishing a temporary field hospital to be ready for any casualties resulting from the raid.

Carlos Layug suggested the Barrio school house would be ideal. During the day of the 30th, the doctors, assisted by Fisher's Medical Corpsmen and several Filipinos, converted the one level wood building into an"emergency hospital".

Blankets were nailed over the windows so treatment could be performed without the light attracting unwanted attention. Oil lanterns were hung and placed in strategic places, and heavy wooden desks were arranged to serve as"operating tables". Next clean sheets and blankets, donated by Platero's citizens were stacked and bandages, blood plasma canisters, medicines and surgical instruments were neatly laid out. By mid afternoon the hospital was ready for patients everyone prayed would never arrive.

Then there was time for Jimmy Fisher and Carlos Layug to discuss the future. Once the war was over, Doctor Fisher promised, Layug would have more medicines and equipment than he could possibly dream of. Sixth Army Medical Sections would see to that, Fisher assured.

While the doctors were occupied with their emergency field hospital, Captain Pajota summoned Lieutenant San Pedro and instructed him to disseminate the fifty land mines. All would be issued, for the guerrilla leader was concerned about the functional condition of the explosives. In the tropics, mildew and corrosion often left such mechanical explosives undependable.

Twenty mines were given to Lieutenant Bobila and ten to Lieutenant Quitives for use on the main road near the point Mucci had designated for Captain Joson 's road block.

Twenty mines were to be saved for Pajota's road block at Cabu Bridge.

Now, Pajota turned his attention to logistical problems. Runners were dispatched to see how the men were coming with their assignment to have carabao carts in position along the Pampanga River.

Second Lieutenant San Pedro and part of Squadron 201A were given the job of guiding the Rangers from the Pampanga to the camp and several guerrilla NCO's were placed in charge of the preparation of food in Platero to be ready for the liberated POW's and Rangers during the withdraw.

By 1400 hours (2 P.M.) the Alamo Scouts still had not reported back to Platero. Colonel Mucci was becoming impatient and concerned. Less than five hours remained until dark. Every minute of that time was needed by Captain Prince to work out his final plan of attack and review it with the men.

Less than three miles away, the Scouts were very busy. They had circled the camp several times, crawling and creeping through the grassy fields which surrounded the stockade. Darting from tree to tree, bush to bush, from gully to bamboo grove, they had investigated the entire area from the camp, northeast to Cabu Bridge, southwest a mile and the flat rice land from the highway in front of the stockade, to the banks of the Pampanga.

Nonetheless, the Scout team leaders felt that no one had been near enough to the camp to determine with certainty all the information Mucci needed. There was only one way to obtain that data. Someone must get close to the front gate without being detected by the Japanese guards.

Alamo Scout Team Leader, First Lieutenant Bill Nellist was not a foolish individual driven by dramatic psychological motivations. Like all the Scouts, he was a soldier well trained to do a special job in the Army...a job which often required him to take more chances than the average man.

Before noon on the 30th, Nellist discussed an idea with Lieutenant Tom Rounsaville. There was a small nipa hut in the field directly in front of the POW Camp's front gate, less than four hundred yards northwest of the highway. Apparently the house was abandoned.

Lieutenant Nellist proposed that if someone could position himself in that hut, he would have an excellent vantage point from which to study the front of the camp, traffic on the road, and the field to the rear of the hut through which the Rangers must travel and ready themselves for the attack. Bill Nellist volunteered to try his idea and so did Filipino-American PFC Rufo Vacquilar. This sort of job was just what Vacquilar had been craving . Lieutenant Rounsaville agreed to release him from his team for Nellist's use.

Now the problem was how to get to the nipa hut without attracting the attention of the Japanese. Vacquilar had the solution. Runners were sent back to Platero with a peculiar request. They needed two Filipino straw Buri hats, two colorful shirts and two pairs of trousers. One outfit must be the largest size in the Barrio.

When a runner returned with the clothing, he received a special reward. Vacquilar traded his MIAI Carbine for the man's.45 pistol.

As Rufo Vacquilar slipped the native clothes over his fatigues and replaced his soft cap with the straw Buri, he crammed both his own.45 and the new pistol into his belt, under the shirt. "Now I am comfortable," he said to Nellist."I feel like I am back home in California!"

Lieutenant Nellist also struggled into the clothes and discovered that, by some miracle, the straw hat fit perfectly. Inside his shirt, he placed the aerial photograph of the camp area and a notebook. He managed to slip his MI rifle under the clothes with the barrel extending down along one leg. It would cause him to walk with a limp, but the trick should work.

The two Scouts in their disguise entered the highway some 600 yards southeast of the camp and then began to walk northeast, Vacquilar one hundred yards ahead of Nellist. In this manner, from a distance, the enemy guards at the camp would be unable to recognize the drastic difference in size between the Filipino and Nellist's huge six foot, two hundred pound frame.

As Nellist came to the south edge of the stockard fence, he turned northwest, stepped into the highway drainage ditch and began to cross the field to the hut. Vacquilar continued along the road until he was almost even with the camp's front gate. Then he too, turned and crossed the field. Once inside the empty home, the two men congratulated each other. Thus far the plan had worked.

Bill Nellist removed his rifle and set the barrel on the bamboo frame of an open window facing the stockade. To be an expert shot one must be equally proficient at judging distances and Nellist still held the record for being one of the best marksmen in the Scouts. Placing his cheek next to the rifle stock he aimed through its"peep" sight, moved the elevation adjustment up...then back to the usual battle sight setting of 250 yards.

"I would say I am exactly 350 yards from the gate," he said to Vacquilar.

Next, Nellist removed the 8x12 inch aerial photograph of the camp and, with a pencil, began to mark or circle different areas on the photo.

"Number one is definitely the tank shed. It's the metal building but, I don't see any tanks. It must be a 300 yard run from the gate to the shed."

Nellist then drew a diagram of the camp to correspond with the photo and listed the numbers he had made with a comment for each on a sheet of paper. He even suggested correct firing elevations for the nipa barracks containing the enemy troops.

Within a few minutes, PFC Franklin Fox climbed into the nipa hut, soon to be followed by PFC Gilbert Cox and Sergeant Harold Hard. They had crawled all the way from the Pampanga River to approach the rear of the hut.

"What the hell you guys think this is, a convention?!"Nellist whispered,"Where are the rest of the fellows?"

"We are all spread out about 300 yards up and down the road," Fox answered."Some are checking out the crossing at the Pampanga."

"Well, here!" Nellist said,"Make yourselves useful. Get these notes back to Mucci before he blows a fuse...and, you guys get lost! This place is too crowded. The Japs will see us sure as hell!"

F Company Commander First Lieutenant John F. Murphy was a likeable young officer but not exactly what anyone would classify as a typical"military type". Although an excellent marksman, the men often noticed that Murphy carried his MI about as if it were a toy. Lieutenant Murphy had been a football star at Notre Dame during his college years and, as with most of the men, was in the Rangers only because he wanted to serve his country in the most effective way possible.

"A dream of a man,"as one of his NCO's later described him, Murphy did not need to"order" people."Men just did things for him because they knew it must be done, and, because they loved him."

"What's up?" Murphy asked with the usual friendly college boy grin spread on his long face as he entered the house in Platero. Captain Prince was beginning another Officers Call.

"We have the first complete report back from the Scouts," Prince answered."It's 1430 (2: 30 P.M.). We don't have much time, so let's get started."

The Scout report confirmed some of the things already known from the aerial photo and topography map. The stockade sat on practically level ground, though its rear section was somewhat elevated above the front. The front of the camp ran 600 yards east and west along the highway and its depth was approximately 800 yards. All the Allied POW's were contained in a section on the northeast corner along the highway and were separated from the rest of the stockade by a single barbed wire fence, six feet high.

Additional details now available from the Alamo Scouts and Pajota's men provided what was basically needed by Prince.

The entire stockade was enclosed with three rows of barbed wire fence, four feet apart, standing some eight to ten feet tall. A dirt road ran perpendicular from the highway and front gate to a seldom used rear gate.

"There are three guard towers about twelve feet in height, here. .. here and here." Prince pointed to his diagram and watched as each officer marked points at the main gate, the northeast corner and the southeast corner of their sketch."There are normally two Jap sentries in each tower with a machine gun... but, the southeast tower is empty now. Don't take any chances ! It may not be empty after dark."

"What about the front gate?" Platoon Commander First Lieutenant Melville R. Schmidt asked.

"The front gate is barbed wire on a wood frame eight feet tall. It splits open from the middle...either inward or outward .   Must be about twenty feet if fully opened.

It's secured by one heavy padlock,three and a half feet from...the...ground. Now, how in the hell did they know that?" Prince puzzled as he read those last few words of Nellist's report. Then he continued.

"The gate is guarded by a sentry who stands in a well protected shelter, at the inside, right of the gate...just next to a wooden guard house. There are at least two Japs in the guard house."

"Where is the tank shed and communications center located?" Platoon Commander First Lieutenant William J. O'Connell asked.

"Here...and here." Prince pointed to the right center of the camp where Nellist had marked number"1" and number"4" on his sketch."A single row barbed wire fence about six feet in height separates different areas inside the stockade and runs down the center road. The rear guard quarters are these buildings between the southeast corner and the rear gate, next to the center road. There are two pillboxes along this east fence running north and south...just outside of the fence. They are elevated and protected by sandbags and logs. Each has three occupants with a machine gun. The Jap enlisted men's quarters are in the southeast section...and directly across from them...across the camps center road, are the Jap transient quarters. These buildings up near the front gate... near the communication section and tank shed hold officers and men of the main guard body... "

"How about those tanks... how many?" Lieutenant O'Connell asked.

"That's a good question. Apparently, the Scouts haven't seen any tanks around the shed...but, they may be concealed. There's suppose to be two, maybe, four in there somewhere. There are two large trucks partly concealed by another metal shed, though.. ." Prince paused to get his breath."There are between 200 and 275 Japs in the compound! Traffic has been light along the main road...so, this may be a lucky break. It's obvious, gentlemen...we'll need to isolate the POW section by hitting the Jap quarters and tank shed...and, hold the Japs in the rear of the camp. If any of the Japs fight their way forward, they'll catch us before we evacuate the POW's. Now... all of your fire should be effective. The buildings are nipa...bamboo and wood.Our fire should tear right through that stuff!"

While Captain Prince continued his meeting with his staff in Platero, Lieutenant Bill Nellist and PFC Rufo Vacquilar were becoming concerned that their position in the nipa hut across from the POW camp may be discovered.

At 1600 hours (4 P.M.) Nellist turned away from the open window to rest his eyes from the strain of staring at the stockade.

Vacquilar suddenly pulled at his sleeve."Look!" the Filipino whispered as he pointed to the southwest corner of the camp. In the center of the highway, shuffling in wooden sandals towards the main gate, was a young Filipino lady dressed in typical Barrio clothes. She seemed to be in no rush.

"I thought the guerrillas told all the civilians to stay off this road today!" Lieutenant Nellist said as he joined Vacquilar at the window."What's she doing out there?"

"Don't know."

The girl stopped at the gate and began to talk with a guard. The conversation lasted three or four minutes. The Japanese soldier handed the girl something which she shoved inside her blouse and then she turned and continued casually up the road towards Cabu.

"What do you suppose that's all about?" Nellist asked."Would it be normal for a young gal to walk up to a Jap, today?"

"I do not think so," Vacquilar replied.

The two Scouts stared at one another, each with the same question written on their face. Had the girl told the Japanese soldier something important?

Why would a Filipino gamble her safety to confront a Japanese soldier?

Did the soldier hand her money for information?

PFC Vacquilar moved toward the open rear door of the nipa hut.

"Where are you going?" Lieutenant Nellist barked.

"I will go to the gate, myself! If the Japs are tipped off, there will be lots of action in that place by now. If not... everything will be peaceful."

"I can't cover you...if they go for you, I can't shoot. You know that! I could pick off the God damned Nips in the tower and several at the gate. But, if I fire, it'll blow the whole mission." Nellist knew Vacquilar was well aware of the consequences, but he had to give the man a chance to change his mind.

The Filipino smiled."Do not worry my friend. Rufo Vacquilar knows how to do this. If they grab me they will think only that I am a guerrilla. They cannot know I am an American. And..." Vacquilar pulled up his shirt, exposing the handles of his two pistols,"ten or twelve of them will not live long to think anything!"

With that remark, Vacquilar jumped to the ground and began his walk to the camp, moving in a wide arc to the south, then up to the highway.

Lieutenant Nellist braced his MI on the window frame. Beads of perspiration formed on his forehead and trickled in small streams down his cheeks.. The question continued to race through his mind... would he... could he allow himself to fire on the Japanese if they discovered Vacquilar's true identity?

Vacquilar, meanwhile, began a walk up the highway to the front gate, his hands clasped nonchalantly behind his back, the two big automatics hidden beneath the bright colored shirt. As he neared the gate, he turned and stared into the face of the Japanese sentry, raised one hand to tip his hat, then bowed slightly while his eyes searched as far as he could see beyond the enemy soldier.

The guard frowned at Vacquilar with a puzzled look, but said nothing.

Vacquilar then continued up the road until well out of sight of the camp, turned left to cross the field to the nipa hut."I do not know what the girl said to them," he reported calmly to Nellist,"but, everything seems normal in that place."

Lieutenant Nellist let out a deep sigh of relief.

In a minute, PFC Franklin Fox was back with them in the hut. "What on earth are you guys doing?" he asked."We thought Rufo had decided to tackle the camp by himself!"

"Never mind!" Nellist responded."Get back to Mucci and tell him everything is quiet up here. We 're going to stay in this spot until after dark. If there's any change...one of us will report.Otherwise, we'll see them when they get here!"

The Scouts never learned the truth about the girl who caused them so much concern. Actually, she was helping the guerrillas. A former vendor of fruit to the stockade guards, she, like Vacquilar, had approached the gate to get, not give, information. The girl promised to bring the sentry some fresh fruit for a deposit of cash. Instead of returning, she reported directly to Pajota's men.

* * * *

It is not easy to ride a carabao. Their girth of body is so great that the strain on one's thighs is painful and at every stride the whole skin seems to slide about as if it were detachable from the flesh. The huge round body affords no opportunity for any hand grip and the only way a rider can maintain his position is to balance himself in some rhythm with the motion of the beast.

A few years of constant practice had developed the necessary skill for Pascual and Aquilar. By the age of eleven, the two boys had mastered the art of riding the carabaos and with their short legs and a touch of the hand, could command the peaceful animal in any way they desired.

On dry land or in shallow rice paddies the carabao is really no problem for such experienced riders. But approach a pond or stream and that presents a different situation. Carabaos are, after all, water buffalo and the sight of water would lead them straight for a long swim regardless of the desires of the rider.

On the afternoon of the 3Oth, Pascual and Aquilar were no ordinary farm boys. They were now guerrillas serving directly under Captain Pajota in the"intelligence section".

They, like most young boys riding carabaos in and out of the barrios, along the roads and past the rows of fence around POW Camp Cabanatuan, were familiar sights to both the Japanese guards and the POW's. The Japanese usually ignored them until a playful game of tossing stones to the POW's got out of hand. Then the boys were driven off by shouts and threats.

That afternoon, the stone game began near the east fence. As a small group of POW's picked up the rocks to toss them they noticed something unusual. Some of the stones were wrapped with pieces of paper, tied tightly with strands of grass.

The POW's removed the paper and turned to toss the rocks back across the fence. But, the boys had moved on towards the highway, waving to the guards in the east corner tower.

Once inside their barracks, the POW's unfolded the paper.

"Listen to this," one man whispered."It says,'be ready to go out anytime'!"

"Yeah! Mine says the same thing. Wonder what it means?"

"Probably just something the kids dreamed up!"

"I don't think so," another argued."Mine says, 'Be alert for... ' I can't make out the last word."

The notes were torn into tiny bits and distributed equally to four men. Once outside, the pieces were scattered and covered carefully with dirt. The messages were discounted as having no important meaning.

Meanwhile, Pascual and Aquilar had proceeded down the highway a few hundred yards and stopped to rest while their animals grazed.

Then, they mounted and started back up the road, passing in front of the camp until they reached the Cabu River. From there they followed the south bank until the point where it fed into the Pampanga, crossed, and proceeded directly into Barrio Platero.

Their report to Pajota confirmed what the Alamo Scouts had said. One guard tower, the southeast one in the rear of the camp, was unoccupied.

It was now 1620 hours (4:20 P.M.) and everything at the stockade seemed quiet.

* * * *

Shortly before Captain Pajota's young carabao riders reported to their commander, Captain Bob Prince had worked out the last details for his plan of attack on the POW camp.

In their final meeting, all noncommissioned officers were brought in to be sure each understood their assignment completely. Prince, after first outlining the plan, had left the organization of particular phases to each junior officer. Now, it was time to review the attack plan in its entirety, giving everyone the opportunity to question anything he did not understand. Colonel Mucci had reviewed the plan and, making a few comments and changes of his own design, issued his approval. The raid was to begin shortly after 1930 hours (7:30 P.M.). Everyone was expected to be in position for attack at 1930, sharp!

Above all, the element of surprise was stressed. Exact timing would yield that advantage.

Captain Joson was told, again, that he would be given a six man bazooka team under the command of Staff Sergeant James O. White of F Company. Joson's men must form a wedge shaped road block 800 yards southwest of the camp along the highway. They, along with the bazooka team and several other Rangers from F Company must stop all enemy traffic at this safe point south of the camp,beginning at 1930 hours.

The extra bazookas (under Ranger control),Colonel Mucci believed, were essential at the Joson position since this point may take the brunt of a large Japanese force moving out of Cabanatuan City. If the raid and evacuation of POW's required a full thirty minutes, as expected, enemy troops would easily have time to muster in the city and charge down those three miles of open road to reinforce the stockade.

Still unknown to Mucci, Pajota's Squadrons 200 and 202 with a combined strength of almost two hundred armed men were already in position some four hundred yards north of the road behind the point where Joson would make his stand. Squadrons 200 and 202 would be ready to move to help Joson, or swing northeast to assist Pajota...whoever most needed their fire power.

Captain Pajota's orders, likewise, remained unchanged. He was to engage the enemy camped on the northeast side of the Cabu River, and keep them from crossing the bridge to reinforce the guards at the stockade,or, attacking the Rangers as they withdrew. In order to accomplish this, Pajota must gain complete surprise on the Japanese and hold until the Rangers and POW's were safely across the Pampanga River. His signal to disengage would be a second red flare fired in the air by Captain Prince. The first flare would indicate that the Rangers were to withdraw from the camp.

Once that second red flare was fired, Pajota could withdraw southeast to lure the Japanese in the opposite direction of the retreating Allied column. He believed that there was no need to reveal that his Squadrons had four machine guns. The Rangers would have no use for the heavy weapons during the assault on the camp but the guerrillas certainly needed them. For, even though the strength of the Japanese at Cabu Bridge was now well known, Pajota had been given only one bazooka. He planned to use a combined force of less than 200 men to hold the river front and bridge. If the automatic weapons and bazooka did not stop the enemy...if the land mines failed, then the combat could quickly become hand to hand.

Colonel Mucci emphasized that he wanted all phone lines cut along the highway both northeast and southwest of the camp. Pajota instructed Lieutenant Regino Bobila to cut the wire at a telephone pole at 1800 hours (6 P.M.) near a trail which led from the highway to Bangad. Since this spot was over 1,000 yards southwest of the camp, the Japanese would not suspicion that the action had anything to do with an assault on their stockade. The guerrillas were always cutting the lines anyway, just to annoy the enemy.

However, at 1915 hours, only a few minutes before the raid was to begin, lst Lieutenant Carlos Tombo would cut the phone line at the south, but this time the sabotage must be closer to the camp ... one hundred and fifty yards from the southwest corner of the stockade. Lieutenant R. Mendoza and Sergeant Circaco Matias would cut the lines, about the same time, one hundred fifty yards to the north of the camp.

Pajota was not the only commander concerned about his assignment at Cabu Bridge. Colonel Mucci worried just how well a guerrilla army, acustom to hit and run attacks, could stand in a prolonged direct engagement with an enemy force superior in number.

What would be the course of action if Pajota's men were over powered at the bridge or, if his men broke and fled to the hills?

Mucci, at one point in the meeting, revealed those thoughts... " Captain Pajota, you must hold at that bridge!"

Pajota responded without hesitation,"We will hold, sir. If any Japs pass, it will be over our dead bodies. We will all be dead!"

On that solemn note, the meeting continued.

"Murphy," Captain Prince addressed First Lieutenant John Murphy, "your men understand their assignment?"

"Completely, sir," Murphy replied.

First Lieutenant Murphy's men, less those assigned to assist Captain Joson at the road block, were given the mission of liquidating the enemy guards at the rear entrance to the camp and preventing the Japanese from moving up into the POW section. The second Platoon of F Company must move along the east side of the camp leaving squads to destroy the guard tower at the highway (northeast corner), the two pillboxes along the east fence, and the (supposedly) unoccupied guard tower at the southeast corner. The men must also cut a large hole in the east fence near the rear of the camp for an emergency escape route if needed by C Company, who would enter by the front gate.

"We should have good cover with the help of that creek bed which runs along the east side," Murphy said."At least, until we get to the back corner. Circling behind the fence will be the most critical move. It will take the longest time."

"Now!" Prince went on,"everyone understands that the signal for the attack to begin will come from Murphy's men at the rear of the stockade! When they begin firing, we'll launch our attack through the front gate! This goes for you, also, Captain Pajota." Prince glanced at the guerrilla commander."No one is to fire a shot until Lieutenant Murphy's men open up!"

Pajota nodded. He understood.

"When Murphy's men commence firing, I'll shoot up a flare. I hope its not necessary. Everyone should be too busy to see it, but I'll fire it, anyway."

Then Prince began to review the plans for the main assault... the break into the camp. With F Company taking care of the northeast corner guard tower, pillboxes, and rear guard tower, the concentration of activity for C Company would be the main gate and POW section.

Using the concept of Ranger tactics Prince planned C Company's assault in two waves of attack. The first wave would be launched by the First Platoon's three sections. The second, by the Second Platoon's three sections.

The First Platoon, under First Lieutenant William J. O'Connell would attack the main gate, using its two Assault Sections and its Special Weapons Section.

The First Assault Section, led by Staff Sergeant Preston W. Jensen, would rush the main gate and break in as its members killed the gate guards and gate tower guards. As they jumped into action, the Second Assault Section under Sergeant Homer E. Britzuis would move quickly across the highway and fire through the right front fence to cover the entry of the First Section and the Special Weapons Section who would follow at the heels of the First Section. Just as soon as the First Section and Weapons Section were inside, the Second Section would lift its fire, move into the camp behind the Weapons Section and open fire, again, on the enemy on the right side to keep them pinned down and away from the POW's on the left side. By this time, the First Section and Weapons Section with the bazookas were expected to be at the middle of the camp, firing on the tank sheds and enemy troops on the right center and right rear area.

After the entire First Platoon had passed through the gate, the Second Platoon under Lieutenant Melville H. Schmidt would move in. Their assignment was to open the POW area, start the prisoners out, and set up supporting fire towards the left, rear of the camp.

To accomplish this, Lieutenant Schmidt's First Assault Section under Staff Sergeant Clifton R. Harris would charge through the open gate and force entry through the POW gate. Some of the Rangers would move rapidly to the rear of the POW area and open fire on the Japanese already under fire from F Company, positioned outside the fence.

The Second Platoon's Second Assault Section under Staff Sergeant William R. Butler would move in the camp, down the center road, and thwart any enemy attempt to reach the POW's.

The Weapons Section under Staff Sergeant August T. Stern would be held in reserve in or behind the ditch across the highway from the camp. Remaining there with them would be medics, Alamo Scouts, the Combat Photo men (whose cameras were useless in the dark) and a number of Filipino guerrillas. These "reserve" men would assist and direct the rescued POW's through the main gate to the waiting carabao carts at the Pampanga River .

When all the POW' s were clear of the stockade, Captain Prince would fire another red flare as a signal for the Rangers to withdraw. Just as soon as everyone had reached the Pampanga River and crossed, Prince would fire the last flare for Pajota to disengage at the bridge and withdraw southeast. Once certain he had out distanced the Japanese, Pajota's forces were to double back to protect the retreating Allied column's rear.

Captain Pajota, now, had another suggestion. He told Colonel Mucci it had been the observation of his men during the last few weeks that whenever American planes flew over the camp the Japanese became terribly upset and nervous, keeping their eyes on the sky sometimes for several minutes after the planes passed.

"Ask your planes to fly over," Pajota recommended."No shoot...no bombs. Just fly over a few minutes before your attack!"

Mucci considered the idea a few minutes. It was time to notify 6th Army that he would need air cover by daybreak, anyway. Perhaps, Pajota's idea had some merit and might present needed distraction those final minutes before the assault.

Sergeant Norton Most had his radio ready near the school house"hospital". It was 1635 hours (4:35 P.M.). The Rangers would leave for the raid in twenty-five minutes. Sergeant Most doubted seriously, considering Army red tape, if any plane could be scrambled and reach the camp before dark.

* * * *

In Barrio Pangatian, nine year old Florenico Santiago stood on the bamboo steps of the small nipa hut he called home and stared in the direction of the narrow bridge which crossed the Cabu River.

Somewhere on the opposite side of the Cabu, he knew Japanese soldiers were camped waiting until after dark to move along the highway as they had done each night during the last month.

But, there must be something special about tonight. Why would Pajota's men send word for the villagers to evacuate into the mountains? Was Pajota going to actually attack those Japanese? Surely not! There were too many Japanese there and Pajota had no tanks.

Florencio heard his mother call. It was time to join his parents and his brother for the long walk east to the mountains.

He turned and looked in the opposite direction of Cabu Bridge and could see the top of one of the guard towers at the POW camp some four hundred yards away. Then his thoughts raced to the Americans in that stockade. He and the other children of his barrio had often given food to those prisoners... whenever the Japanese guards would allow. He had even learned a few words of American slang during the last year and a half.

The Americans were always happy to see him. Now, he wondered if they would still be there to joke with him when everyone returned from the mountains.

"Hurry, Florencio! We go now!" he heard his mother call again. And, he joined his family to begin the two mile journey to the Sierra Madre.

* * * *

It was 1645 hours (4:45 P.M.) when Captain Pajota called his staff together in Platero for their last meeting.

"Are the machine guns in place and well camouflaged?" the guerrilla commander asked as the men gathered around him and squatted down on their haunches.

"As you ordered, sir," Squadron 201's Commander First Lieutenant Jose Hipolito assured.

"Excellent! We will not place the mines in the road until later. .. the same with the bomb on the bridge."

"The Japs still have no guards on the bridge," Second Lieutenant Ervie advised.

"Good," Pajota nodded."Our scouts have all reported and the Americans are ready. I will now tell you my alternate plan, should our frontal attack fail. We must remember that the objective is to hold the Japs until all the POW's and Rangers have safely crossed the Pampanga..."

"Sir," one officer interrupted."The Japs still have their tanks hidden less than a kilometer from the bridge. Do the Americans expect us to stop tanks with machine guns, rifles and grenades?"

Pajota glared with squinting eyes."If the bomb on the bridge fails...there are still the land mines in the highway. The tanks must stay on the road to cross the bridge. They cannot climb the high sandy banks of the river on our side."

"So what!" The officer persisted,"The tanks may cross the bridge... and then?"

"We will stop them with our bodies if necessary!" Pajota replied.

"What do the Americans care? We are only Filipinos...isn't it?"

"We are soldiers, Lieutenant!" Pajota snapped."The Americans have given us what we need! Colonel Mucci has given us a bazooka. The bazooka is assigned to Headquarters Company next to the left side of the road, near the bridge. The bazooka will stop tanks. Now...enough! Pay attention to the alternate plan!"

Pajota's eyes studied the faces of each man for a moment. Then he smiled reassuringly and began to explain his plan."If the Japs manage to cross the bridge before the Rangers complete their job, our entire force will move from the left flank" He began to draw lines in the dirt, lines representing the highway, the river and Cabu Bridge."...across the road to the right flank by a series of rushes...starting with Headquarters Company. At the same time, I will send runners. One will go to Squadrons 203 and 204 which are waiting north at Manacnac. Squadrons 203 and 204 will move south and attack the Japs at the rear. These Squadrons should hit the rear of the Japs in five minutes from the time the runner arrives with the order to move!"

Pajota spoke with his usual softness of voice, but with a steady, positive tone and paused long enough for only glances into the faces of each officer. It was as if he was taking their pulse.

"And then," he continued,"the other runner will have reached Squadrons 200 and 202, already...who are in reserve behind Captain Joson's roadblock at the south. Lieutenant Quitives and Lieutenant Bobila...you will then move your Squadrons 200 and 202 northeast along the highway to serve as rear guard for the Rangers. The Americans will be moving northwest out of our battle area. The Japs following me southeast will be pinched on all flanks...203 and 204 from the north, 200 and 202 from the south. Our Headquarters Company and Squadron 201A will turn about and fire on the Japs from the east. Squadron 201 and 211 will cross the highway and attack from the west.

And then..." Pajota erased the lines in the dirt with a sweep of his hand."And then we will have the Japs encircled!"

The Captain stood up slowly."Any questions?"

There was a moment of silence, but he could read the expression of excitement on all of them. It was time to make the most of their enthusiasm.

"Due to the importance of this mission, I have elected to commit our entire force. Our fire power is good. We have plans for all contingencies. We will destroy the Japs at the bridge!"

169

"If the alternate plan is not necessary," one Lieutenant spoke, "does Squadron 203 and 204 attack the Japs retreating from the bridge, past Manacnac?"

"No!" Pajota replied. "They are to move only if my message arrives for them to attack with the alternate plan. Now, remember these things...we must gain complete surprise! Once the battle begins you must stay in position until I give the order to withdraw. The Japanese are noisy fighters. They yell to increase morale. In the position they are now...they do not know the area...they will use only one method of fighting. The Americans call it 'Right down the alley'! The Japs will come across that bridge and they will keep coming until they run us over, regardless of how many we kill...unless we kill them all. I have told the American Colonel Mucci that no Japs will pass. When the night is finished...there will be no more Jap force at Cabu Bridge. We will annihilate them!"

* * * *

The freedom granted the 547th Night Fighter Squadron by higher headquarters combined with the Squadrons willingness to cooperate with non-Air Corps units was about to pay off handsomely. Thanks to that liberty, the barriers of normal military channels could be bypassed as 6th Army Intelligence received the relayed radio request for help from Colonel Mucci's Rangers. A call was, in turn, placed directly to the headquarters of the 547th, Captain Robert Wolfston, Squadron A2, had a brief discussion with his assistant, First Lieutenant Reuben E. Nieves.

"Better get Keyser or the 'Old Man', quick! It's almost 1700,Captain Wolfston said.

The"Old Man", Squadron Commander Lieutenant Colonel William C. Odell and his Executive Officer, Major Francis M. Keyser listened carefully to the report of the Ranger request.

"Tell Operations this should be a max effort!" Colonel Odell instructed."Dispatch as many as we can get air borne!"

At 1705 hours (5:05 P.M.) Captains Wayne E. Coyle and William C. Behnke studied the request and then began to move with cool precision.

"Who's next on the alert roster?" Captain Behnke asked.

"Lieutenant Schrieber," replied Coyle.

"OK. Good! Tell him we have a special mission. There will be an Army officer here from 6th Army H.Q. in a few minutes, so Schrieber will have a passenger."

There was nothing special about the selection of Schrieber as the pilot for the mission. Those P6I's scheduled for routine missions on January 30, 1945, were either already airborne or were preparing for take off. Lieutenant Kenneth Schrieber was simply the first name on the"stand-by" pilots list for any emergency that night.

But, if there was nothing special about the method of selection the pilots and crew were, indeed, a special breed of men.

Twenty-six year old Kenneth Schrieber, for example, had a proven reputation as a skilled, careful pilot and being an alert, inquisitive man with a good sense of humor. His P61 Black Widow was officially known as number"390." Schrieber and his Radar Observer (RO), Second Lieutenant Bonnie Rucks, had nicknamed their plane the"Hard to Get" and a friend in the Seabees painted a reclining voluptuous nude blonde on the fighter's nose.

What made the"Hard to Get" a perfect plane to carry a passenger was the fact that the P61 had only her four 20mm cannons and lacked the usual.50 caliber machine gun turret on her top. The raised seat normally occupied by the craft's gunner, just behind the pilot, offered good visibility for any observer.

Captain Behnke sat at his field table in the Operations Office studying a map of Central Luzon when Lieutenants Schrieber and Rucks reported for the instructions. It was 1713 hours (5:13 P.M.) and Schrieber was already dressed in his flight boots with the khaki trousers tucked inside. Both men were armed with a.45caliber automatic in holsters strapped across their chests.

"What do you have for us, sir?" Lieutenant Schrieber asked as he saluted the Captain.

"Sixth Army's got something a little different going on tonight," Captain Behnke replied."The Rangers are assaulting a Jap POW camp in the Cabanatuan, Cabu area of Nueva Ecija. The camp should be about... here!" The Operations Officer pointed to a spot on the map along a road connecting two towns. "Sixth Army H.Q. is furnishing a Captain who is suppose to know the exact location. He'll ride with you and help you find it. Now... you actually have two assignments. The Rangers' raid should begin shortly after dark, about 1930 hours. The Ranger C.O. seems to think that if you could make a couple of low level passes at sunset, it might divert the Jap guards' attention from the ground to the sky. That' s the first assignment. Second, the guerrillas have assured us that all civilians in the area will be cleared from the highways.

Anything that moves on a main road, other than right in front of that Jap stockade... even a donkey cart... should be considered the enemy. Strafe anything that moves on those roads! If the raid is successful, our boys will be returning to our lines by back trails. It's up to you to give them cover in that camp area. I'll divert as many others as I can to back you up. Any questions?"

Lieutenant Schrieber rubbed his heavy moustache with a forefinger and glanced up at the tall, slender RO."How about you, Bonnie?"

Lieutenant Rucks shook his head, no.

"Will we have radio contact with the Rangers?" Schrieber asked.

"Negative... just with our base, if you need it."

Lieutenant Schrieber's face broke into a smile."OK, sir. We're ready!"

"Good luck," Captain Behnke said as the crew of the"Hard to Get" saluted and turned to leave.

At 1725 hours (5:25 P.M.), P61 number 390, the"Hard to Get", her two man crew and an Army passenger rolled down the pierced steel runway, lifted into the evening sky over Lingayen Gulf, turned and headed east. In a few minutes, she would be over Nueva Ecija Province.

In the meantime, the Operations Office became alive with excitement as Captains Coyle and Behnke set the plans of backup cover for the"Hard to Get" into motion. All available Black Widows in the 547th were turned loose.

Two P61's on defense patrol near Lingayen were radioed and Captain Cecil A. Littlefield and Captain Edwin A. Annis vectored away from their orbit points and rushed towards Nueva Ecija.

At the base, considerable scrambling continued as First Lieutenant Richard B. Peterson climbed with his crew mate into their Night Fighter and took off.

A few minutes later, several more followed and by 1745 hours (5:45 P.M.) the sky over Central Luzon was filled with at least ten Black Widows seeking their prey.

The night sky over a particular area can become crowded in short order and even with radar, the speeds at which the P61's were traveling made navigation extremely dangerous.

But, the 547th had perfected a system for such events. While the "Hard to Get" closed in on her target at POW Camp Cabanatuan the other aircraft would remain in divided sectors nearby, ready to replace her should she expend her ammunition or encounter any difficulties.

Every possible avenue to or from Cabanatuan City and its POW he camp would now be covered from the air. No Japanese mechanized equipment in the sky or along the roads would be safe from detection and attack by the deadly Black Widows.

* * * *

At 1700 hours (5 P.M.), January 30, 1945, the force of Army Rangers, Filipino guerrillas, Alamo Scouts and Unit F's Combat Photographers marched out of Barrio Platero leaving Sergeant Norton Most and his radio crew guarded by several armed villagers. The little army, at this time, totaled almost three hundred and seventy-five men. Many of Pajota's Squadrons were already in position.

In single file, they follow Pajota's"scouts" southwest down a narrow dirt trail, which wound its way for one half mile through tall cogan grass and bamboo groves to a steep bank at the Pampanga River. There, several guerrillas split from the group and disappeared into the grass. Captain Luis De La Cruz and Lieutenant Padama would direct their men in organizing the carabao carts which must wait on both sides of the river.

The Filipinos knew where to cross the river at its shallowest point near a long, flat sand bar which split the waters in mid-stream. The River was narrow, here, and only knee deep but everyone was warned that it ran waist deep in other areas.

As the Rangers and their guides approached the water, the group split into three units. On the left, Captain Pajota and his squadrons moved up stream a hundred yards, crossed the river, and proceeded in a southeast direction for the Cabu area. On the right, Captain Joson's eighty men, accompanied by Staff Sergeant James White's six man bazooka team and several other F Company Rangers, moved down stream a hundred yards, crossed the river, and started in a south direction for the point on the higway where the road block would be established.

In the center, the Rangers waded single file into the warm, shallow water and after fifteen to twenty yards, splashed upon the sand bar. They crossed the twenty-five yards of dark sand, and then waded another twenty-five yards to the opposite, sloping bank. There, they entered more cogan grass and even higher "Talahib" grass.

The men were now well prepared with the knowledge that their map was incorrect. As Captain Prince had noted from the aerial photograph, the next two miles to the stockade would be mostly flat grass land breaking off into rice fields and shallow ponds with knee-high dikes. For this first three-fourths mile, though, it would be safe for the men to walk. The high grass would conceal them from view.

Staff Sergeant John W. Nelson, a six foot, one hundred seventy pound Medical Corpsman, was heavily weighted by the blood plasma canisters, carbine,.45 pistol and other medical supplies he carried. But, this did not worry him. He had become accustomed to being both a medic and rifleman with the Rangers long ago. His friend and Medical Detachment Commander, Captain Jimmy Fisher was just behind him and the doctor, though in excellent physical condition, was not a combat soldier.

Regardless of Colonel Mucci's fussing and the pleading of all the medics, Jimny Fisher could not be convinced to stay in Platero. He was going to be with his men.

John Nelson was the First Sergeant of the Medics and concerned with the responsibility of all his men. But, he knew they could take care of themselves very well under fire. Captain Fisher was another matter. Sergeant Nelson reached for the handle of his.45 pistol. A photograph of his wife was under the grips of the automatic. And, Nelson began to think how he would stand close to Jimmy Fisher during the raid. He would keep the Japanese away from the doctor with his carbine and then with that pistol, if necessary.

For that first one half mile all the Rangers were in excellent spirits, like a team marching onto a football field for the big important game. To most of them, the full impact of the danger which lay ahead had not yet hit.

F Company's First Sergeant, Charles Bosard, could only think of how thrilled and proud he was of his men."These are my boys," he whispered to himself over and over again."They'll do a good job. I trained them. They'll do just fine...I know it!"

Captain Robert Prince glanced over his shoulder and noticed Colonel Mucci, as usual, was moving up and down the line, chatting with his Rangers. For a brief moment, Captain Prince realized the pain from his blistered feet, but then his thoughts changed quickly to the critical minutes ahead. He prayed that his plan of attack would work.

Some of the men were teasing Sergeant Lester "Twister" Malone again. He joked back by reminding a married Ranger that there was not much time.."Twister" still needed the man's address to"go visit his wife".

PFC Bill Proudfit joined in the fun with a few men in his squad. They were complaining that Colonel Mucci had not given them enough time to become"familiar" with all those young girls who sang "God Bless America". Again, the spirit of the march seemed to Proud-fit as if they were heading for a "Sunday school picnic". He heard the BAR man behind him say,"I don't hate the God damned Japs! We just got to kill'em, not hate 'em... don' t we?"

Another Ranger responded,"Yeah! If you'd been in that camp up there for three years, you'd hate 'em. You'd better shoot that BAR like you hate'em!"

"Damned! This thing is getting heavy!" A Ranger next to Corporal James Herrick complained as he continued to shift the BAR from hand to hand.

"Give it to me! I'll lug it for awhile," Herrick offered and the the men exchanged weapons.

It was 1800 hours (6 P.M.). Twilight...and the air was warm and still, filled with the fresh, sweet smell of rice hay. The Rangers had covered a mile since leaving the banks of the Pampanga. Before them, stretching to the highway, was nothing but rice fields. Some ponds were completely dry, some muddy, many half filled with dark, stagnant water. There were no trees, no shrubbery, only a single nipa hut scarcely visible on the horizon a mile away.

Captain Prince gave a waving hand signal. Lieutenant John Murphy with his men of 2nd Platoon, F Company (less the men with Captain Joson) split away from the group and began heading east. Within another one-half mile, before they hit the highway, F Company would be in position to enter the creek bed which crossed under the road and ran along the east side of the camp.

Bob Prince moved his arms, giving another signal, and Lieutenant William J. O'Connell's First Platoon took the front line position followed by rows of Lieutenant Melville H. Schmidt's Second Platoon. Now, the Rangers began to spread apart, their lines moving with a front some thirty to forty yards wide. It would be necessary for them to stay reasonably close together to insure that each squad arrived in time at the highway. If one man was out of place the moment the attack began, the entire plan could fail.

The Rangers walked another five hundred yards, but there was no more conversation among the troops. The guard towers of POW Camp Cabanatuan were now visible on the horizon.

Corporal James Herrick shifted the heavy BAR he carried for his buddy and his right hand crossed, to grasp at the jacket pocket. His New Testament Bible was still there, over his heart. Herrick marched on, content with the thought that he had read the Bible for an hour before they left Platero.

Captain Prince glanced at Colonel Mucci who was staring at the outline of the stockade. Mucci turned to face Prince, then nodded . The Captain gave another hand signal and the Rangers began to drop to their knees. The men must crawl the rest of the way to the highway...almost a mile away.

Captain Juan Pajota's men, with far less distance to travel, began to reach the southwest bank of the Cabu River. Squadrons systematically dropped off into positions as the force moved towards the highway and Cabu Bridge.

Near the intersection of the Cabu River and the Pampanga, First Lieutenant Jose Hipolito and Squadron 201 entered a grove of bamboo and set up one.30 caliber, watercooled machine gun. Next to them, Squadron 211 under Lieutenant Toribio Paulino also set up a.30 caliber machine gun. These two Squadrons could easily cover the river and the remains of the old"temporary bridge" from their point. This was important because the banks, here, were not steep. They had been worn down by carabao carts crossing the shallow waters and afforded an easy path for the Japanese to use.

Then, part of Squadron 201A under First Lieutenant Bernardo, dropped off and set up a BAR on a tripod and a.30 caliber machine gun.

Before the remaining force reached the highway, Headquarters Company established their position with two BAR's and the bazooka. From this point, they could easily cover the river and Cabu Bridge. An excellent cross fire range would be effected with Lieutenant Ervie's men on the right side of the highway. The intersecting point of the cross fire was the bridge, but they also had clear vision up the highway some two hundred yards. Most of Squadron 201A and part of Squadron 204, all under Second Lieutenant Ervie, had moved into positions on the southeast side of the highway from another staging area and set up defenses on the right side of the bridge. With two BAR's, one.30 caliber machine gun and several Thompson sub-machine guns, these men were in the best position to rain fire upon the bridge.

Captain Pajota, accompanied by Lieutenant Abad, Corporal Andasan and Private Slayao started to inspect each position. The guerrillas were approaching a small mound of earth which stretched from the Pampanga to the highway. Pajota would make sure that all his automatic weapons were In front where they could swing freely from flank to flank and furnish the most effective range of fire. The men armed with rifles and carbines or pistols were positioned behind the automatic weapons. In the next rank were men armed with bolos and his medical corpsmen who carried long bamboo poles. The poles were part of a "stretcher". A blanket or large cloth was tied at the center section of the pole thus forming a baglike carrier in which a wounded man was placed. Two men, one on each end of the pole would then raise the bamboo to their shoulders and be on their way. Perhaps the system appeared awkward to western armies familiar with a flat stretcher with four handles, but actually the ancient method used by the Filipinos was quite effective. The pole, with a casualty in the bag, was easy to manage and light to carry. It also granted each "medic" one free hand to swing a bolo or fire a weapon.

For some unknown reason, the Japanese Commander Oyabu failed to post any guards on either end of Cabu Bridge. It was a mistake which would cost him dearly. Members of Squadrons 201A and 204, who were traveling with Pajota, easily slipped unnoticed across the highway. Others managed to place twenty land mines in the highway southwest of the bridge. The guerrillas had also succeeded in fastening a"time bomb" under the bridge on the northeast (Japanese) end an hour earlier. Pajota's"time bomb", one of several delivered by the U.S. submarine, was set to detonate between 7:40 and 7:50 P.M. Since the Rangers planned to be in position at 7:30 and begin their assault on the stockade shortly thereafter, Pajota hoped his bomb would catch the enemy on the bridge and destroy them with the structure.

Every guerrilla knew Dokuho Battalion 359 was across the river. They had spied on the Japanese all day, and now they could easily hear the voices of Imperial Soldiers as they talked around small camp fires. The Filipinos also knew the fires would be extinguished very soon...before complete darkness settled in. But during those last few minutes of light, the Japanese were enjoying a meal.

Pajota had correctly anticipated the Japanese reaction to a sudden surprise attack. Though Imperial Army strategy usually called for a Battalion Commander like Oyabu to fix a point on a front and launch rapid encircling attacks, this tactic was primarily effective when the terrain was known. Normally, the encirclement was conducted in the form of a number of attacks at one time, the first coming in a small circle, then, finally, a frontal attack with the whole Battalion weight thrown at that selected point.

The legend of Japanese courage, Pajota fully appreciated, was no myth. It may have been fanatical, blind courage, but it could not be discounted. The Imperial Soldier had been trained and skilled in teamwork, but if that broke down the soldier could become highly nervous and emotional. He was not trained to think as an individual. Without his leaders, the individual soldier's only remaining tactic was suicidal.

For night fighting, the Japanese were specially accustomed to procuring all possible information by carefully reconnoitering the area. If they could not do this, then they usually deliberately exposed men to draw fire, thereby learning of their enemy's whereabouts.

Battalion Commander Oyabu had not reconnoitered the Cabu area. Pajota's men knew he had not. After all, Oyabu and Dokuho 359 had no idea they may engage enemy forces until they reached Cabanatuan City. Oyabu could not employ the encircling tactic because his forces would be attacked from across a river.

181

Pajota, therefore, was safe with his calculation that the Japanese at Cabu Bridge would lack a battle plan. There was only one tactic remaining for them. The Japanese would charge upon the bridge and fanatically throw wave upon wave at the Filipinos (as Pajota had assured his men the enemy would do) .

But, the Cabu Bridge was less than one hundred feet long. The shallow river, in spots, was narrower than that, for a lack of rain had left the Cabu dry in some areas. The true test would come when the Japanese Battalion, recovering from a surprise attack, launched their full force upon the bridge or through the river basin. Either way, if the Japanece succeeded in crossing, only the land mines, a few bazooka rockets and the"alternate plan" could save Pajota...and the Americans.

It was now 1825 hours (6:25 P.M.). It would be another hour before Pajota, satisfied his men were ready, assumed a position directly behind Squadron 201A and Headquarters Company. It would be another hour and five minutes, he knew, before the Americans were ready outside the POW camp.

In the flat rice fields across the highway from the POW camp, the Rangers continued to crawl and snake their way over dikes which formed the rice ponds into almost perfect squares. They had less than one half mile to crawl.

"CLANG, CLANG... CLANG, CLANG..!"

Suddenly, a strange metallic noise came from somewhere in the POW camp.

The sound repeated..."CLANG, CLANG... CLANG, CLANG..." . Safeties released as the Rangers shoved their weapons forward, ready to fire. Everyone froze. On each face was etched the same expression. Had they been detected?

"Give me back that damn BAR! Corporal Herrick heard his buddy whisper. "This is stupid! You've got my BAR and I've got the ammunition"

The two men quickly exchanged weapons.

"CLANG, CLANG... CLANG, CLANG !"

Then, as fast as the noise began...it ceased. Everyone's eyes fixed on the area they knew was the front gate. If that sound was an alarm, Japanese soldiers would pour out of the camp and charge the field any minute.

Captain Prince, rolled over on his back to look at his watch in the faint evening light. It was 6:30. Where was F Company? Had they been spotted by the enemy in the towers? Bob Prince, his heart pounding, turned over and placed the sights of his MI rifle on the front gate of the stockade.

CHAPTER 10

"It's OK! We're Yanks!... Get the hell out of here!" 6th U.S. Army Ranger, POW
Camp Cabanatuan

January 30, 1945

In the POW compound section of Camp Cabanatuan one of the prisoners, a U.S. Navy man, dropped a two foot long pipe from his bony hand. The hunk of iron dangled silently from a leather thong which connected it to a triangle shaped gong.

"Is it 1830 or 1900 hours?" The POW asked his buddy.

"How in hell should I know? It's not dark yet...must be 1830 . What difference does it make?"

"Difference, mate? Dammit, it makes a lot of difference! Did I sound five bells or six?" The POW shouted.

"I don't remember. Six, I think."

"Well, then, I'm wrong! I should have struck five bells for 1830, not six. Don't you remember anything, mate? Five bells for 6:30 and six bells for 7 P.M. I've messed up again!"

"You sure it ain't the other way around?" The debate between the two Navy POW's was practically a daily occurrence but generally ignored by the other POW's. At 6:30 P.M. that night most of the prisoners were wandering about their compound yard or preparing to bed down for the night. When some of the Navy POW's first erected their"bell" during the middle of 1944 and began to strike out the typical half hour"period of watch", their experience did, for awhile, generate curosity.

But, none of the prisoners actually ever"stood watch" and by January 30th, 1945, even the originators of the system had lost enthusiasm.

In the rice fields one half mile from the front of the stockade the Rangers were still prone, weapons ready, and unaware that the clanging sound was not an alarm but two U. S. Navy men attempting to hold to a small memory of their days aboard ship.

Captain Prince turned to his side and squinted his eyes to read the watch...1835 hours (6:35 P.M.). Less than an hour remained for everyone to be in position. A full five minutes had passed since the last clanging sound. Prince could wait no longer. He raised his arm, palm forward, and swung it down. The Rangers resumed their crawl towards the stockade.

At 1840 hours (6:40 P.M.) Alamo Scout Lieutenant Bill Nellist stood at the back door of his nipa hut in the rice field, three hundred and fifty yards from the highway and the POW camp's front gate. He had been watching the Rangers crawl towards his position for the last fifteen minutes.

The faint sound of an airplane in the distance caught Nellist's attention and he turned to look north. The plane's silhouette was easy to recognize. It was an American P61 Black Widow.

"What's that fly boy doing over here?" Lieutenant Nellist whispered to PFC Vacquilar."I thought this mission was top secret. We're suppose to get air cover on the way back...not now. That guy may think we're Japs and cut loose on us!"

Vacquilar hunched his shoulders."Don't know. Perhaps we should go to the field and join the Rangers before they think we are Japs."

The two Scouts shed their Filipino clothes, leaped out the back of the hut, and began to crawl to the first small rice pond dike . There they lay motionless and watched unnoticed until more than half of the rangers had passed. Then, they turned and began to crawl with Mucci's men towards the highway.

"Hey! Where'd you guys come from?" a Ranger spoke to Nellist.

"We've been waiting for you and Mucci."

* * * *

Second Lieutenant Bonnie Rucks' eyes shifted from his radar instrument to the canopy assuring that the sky was free of enemy planes. The crew of the P61,"Hard to Get", knew there were only a few Japanese planes left on Luzon, but it would take but one to jeopardize their special mission.

"It's 1845 (6:45 P.M.)...getting dark out there, Chubby. Where in hell is that camp?" Rucks spoke into the radio to his pilot, Lieutenant Kenneth Schrieber.

"Don't know for sure. We should be close. You got anything to eat? I'm getting hungry." Schrieber replied with a slight laugh, knowing his Radar Observer loved to tease him about his insatiable appetite.

"I thought so!" came Rucks' reply.

"How about it, Captain?" Kenneth Schrieber leaned back and glanced over his shoulder to the"gunner's" position where the Army Captain sat, a topography map spread across his lap.

None of them knew exactly where to look for the camp. The"Hard to Get" had been moving in a large circle, west over Talavera, north to Bongabon and east to the Sierra Madre Mountain chain for several minutes. Gradually, Lieutenant Schrieber lowered the altitude and tightened his circle, using Bongabon as a vortex.

"We'll find it this round," the Captain assured."If that's Bongabon we're over. Let's follow the highway. If we're heading southwest we should approach our target."

"We're heading southwest," Schrieber said."If we were higher you could probably see Lingayen Gulf far off our right wing on a clear day."

"Good! What's our altitude? Can we take her down a little for a closer look?"

"We're at 1,500 now. How low you want?" Schrieber asked.

"As low as we can get."

"OK...here we go! Keep your eyes peeled, Bonnie!"

"Roger...", the RO responded.

"1,000...800...600...400...200 feet. Leveling off at 200, boys!" Lieutenant Schrieber calmly announced.

"All clear," Bonnie Rucks called into the intercom."There's a river up ahead and... a bridge."

"That's got to be the Cabu. We're on target!" the Captain interrupted.

The big Black Widow roared at tree top level over Cabu Bridge, startling the bivouacked Japanese. Suddenly, the"Hard to Get" was over Cabanatuan POW Camp, the plane's wing scarcely one hundred and fifty feet above the northeast guard tower.

"My God, there she is!" Lieutenant Rucks cried into the microphone... off our left wing!"

"I can see our boys deploying in the field across the highway... over on our right! They must be almost ready to attack!" The Captain yelled.

In seconds the Black Widow was a mile down the road and Lieutenant Schrieber throttled back to slow his fighter. Did we blow their cover?" he called with a concerned tone.

"Negative! Quite the contrary. We really got the Nips' attention. Let's go back...a little slower. We'll take another look," the Captain said.

Lieutenant Schrieber put the"Hard to Get in a wide, sweeping turn to the west and climbed to 1,000 feet. Then, he turned again near Bongabon to head southwest. At 1850 hours (6:50 PM) Schrieber lowered his altitude to five hundred feet and slowed the big ship to eighty-five miles per hour. In a moment they buzzed over Cabu Bridge for a second time and turned left gradually to pass directly over the stockade.

"There are the guard towers," Lieutenant Rucks spoke first. "Look at the Japs duck! Too bad we can't cut loose on'em. If our boys weren't there, we could blow the whole place to hell!"

188

"You can see the prisoners out in the yard!" Lieutenant Schrieber stated.

"Yeah! I see 'em," the Captain acknowledged.

Lieutenant Kenneth Schrieber fed more rich fuel to the"Hard To Get's" big engines and banked her into another sweeping turn. "We got to be sure these roads stay clear," he said.

* * * *

Inside the POW camp, a tremendous amount of excitement had been generated by the Black Widow's sudden appearance.

"I tell you that plane was ours!" Sergeant Abie Abraham insisted, "I saw American writing on her nose. I could have hit it with a rock!"

"We don't have no plane like that!" another POW argued. "Why would anyone paint a plane black?"

"To fly at night, stupid!"

"It was ours! How long has it been since you saw a Jap plane around here? The slope heads couldn't build anything like that baby. She 's American!"

As darkness enveloped the camp, the arguments diminished and the POW's broke into small groups to return to their quarters.

Doctor Merle McNeal Musselman sat down on the wooden steps to the camp's dispensary and leaned back, staring dreamily into the darkening sky."Think I'll just sit here awhile and watch the stars come

189

out" he said to a medic sitting next to him. "Tell me some more about the constellations, Sergeant."

The man with Musselman was an authority on the stars and the two POW's often engaged in conversations on philosophy and the heavens.

Not far away, on the steps of his barracks, Sergeant Abie Abraham, started to relate another experience from his days of Army service in Panama to his friend, Bill. "It was a long time ago," Abraham began, "before my assignment to Luzon. The jungles are hot and steamy in Panama...even at night. Not like these mild evenings here in the Central Plains..."

Twenty-seven year old PFC Eugene Evers had been on duty at the Hospital Ward all day and the medic was completely exhausted. He left the group of friends who were still debating the identity of the strange black plane, and returned to his barracks. There he decided to play some scratched phonograph records as long as his arm had strength to turn the mechanical crank or, until sleep ended his day.

By 1915 hours (7:15 P.M.) Captain Prince and C Company's lst Platoon had reached the drainage ditch directly across the highway from the front of the stockade. It was dark but, the glow of the rising full moon yielded light for Prince to see his men of the 2nd Platoon at their position in another shallow ditch, ten yards behind. Lying in the field ten yards behind the 2nd Platoon was his "reserve", third line of troops consisting of Combat Photographers, medics, several Filipino guerrillas and Alamo Scouts. In fifteen minutes, 1930 hours, F Company was expected to be in position at the rear of the stockade. Prince was convinced that, thus far, none of them had been seen by the enemy. C Company was now ready for that first shot from F Company which would signal the start of the raid.

While C Company waited at the front of the camp, F Company, 2nd Platoon, made their way cautiously into a muddy creek bed and through a six foot diameter drainage pipe which passed under the highway. They emerged on the camp's side of the road still concealed in the five foot deep creek bed, but they knew that the ditch would become shallower within two hundred yards. Those who must travel all the way to the rear of the camp would resort to crawling again at that point. Lieutenant Murphy was leading the first three squads through the ditch. They would be the ones who had the greatest distance to travel... along the east fence, then turn right and crawl to the rear gate area of the camp.

Staff Sergeant Richard Moore, Sergeant Patrick Marquis, PFC John Pearson and PFC Gerhard Tiede were in one of the front squads. As they passed the first (northeast) guard tower, they heard a voice cry out in Japanese. Every Ranger in the ditch froze. From their position, heads peeking over the edge of the creek bank, they could see the enemy sentries in the twelve foot tower. It was less than fifty yards away. One Japanese soldier had his back turned to the Rangers and was looking out over the POW section. The other guard was staring directly at Moore's squad. The Japanese slowly raised his rifle, as if not certain what he had seen.

"He's pointing that son of a bitch at us!" Sergeant Marquis whispered.

"Ssh! He's wearing eye glasses. Maybe he can't see us." Staff Sergeant Moore replied.

"We'd better blast him while we can!" Marquis suggested.

"NO! Don't fire!" Moore ordered."We got a long way to go, don't shoot! We can't fire until Murf gives the signal. Keep low. .. keep moving!"

191

The squad of Rangers crouched lower in the ditch, hugged the right bank and continued on. The tower sentry, apparently convinced he had seen nothing,lowered his rifle.

Staff Sergeant David M. Hey's squad was one of the last of F Company. They took a position on the creek bank with their weapons aimed at the two northeast tower sentries... and waited.

As the rest of F Company continued along the creek bed, another squad was left at a point only twenty-five yards from the first enemy"pillbox". They could see three Japanese standing in the"box" next to a machine gun which was pointing at the creek bed. The sentries seemed to be engaged in a casual conversation.

Further along the fence, less than one hundred and fifty yards from the stockade's southeast corner, Sergeant Joe Youngblood's squad was left for the second"pillbox". Their assignment would be to destroy that machine gun nest, cut a hole in the camp's three fence rows for C Company's emergency escape route, and keep the enemy quarters in the stockade rear sections under fire.

PFC Bill Proudfit crawled up next to Sergeant Yowngblood, set his MI sights on the"pillbox", and glanced around. They were on a small bank of earth which could permit a parallel range of fire to the enemy. Like himself, three other Rangers aimed their MI's and were silently joined by a man with a carbine and one with a BAR. The last man carried a Thompson submachine gun. With all of that fire power plus their grenades, Proudfit sensed a slight feeling of enthusiasm. They should easily pulverize the pillbox and rip apart the nipa barracks less than a hundred yards away. PFC Proudfit turned to look at the southeast guard tower.

"You think it's really empty?" Proudfit whispered to Sergeant Youngblood.

"I don't see anyone up there, but we'll blow it apart anyway." The Sergeant replied,"I'm sure Murf and the boys back there have the same idea."

Youngblood attached a grenade launcher to the barrel of his MI, placed four rifle and four hand grenades in front of him... and waited.

At 1925 hours (7:25 P.M.), Lieutenant Murphy, with the remaining squads of F Company, reached their positions at the rear of the camp. There, concealed by a ditch which ran along a seldom used dirt road, the Rangers began to take aim on selected targets inside the stockade. As Sergeant Youngblood suspicioned, Lieutenant Murphy was concerned with that "empty" southeast guard tower. Murphy instructed one BAR man and three armed with MI's to prepare to"riddle it" with bullets.

Tech 5 Bernard Haynes, the medic assigned to accompany the men to the back of the camp, aimed his automatic carbine at the rear gate pillbox and began to mumble to himself,"...I hope to hell this works...I hope to hell this works..."

Further west, along the ditch the last squad prepared for action. It would be their job to maintain the heaviest fire into the barracks at the rear of the camp. Staff Sergeant David Hey crawled through the ditch, checking the positions of his men.

"Dave, I can see the Japs in the barrack's windows! See there!?" Tech 5 Francis"Father" Schilli pointed his MI in the direction of one nipa building .

"They're sitting in there in their underwear!" Corporal Roy Sweezy noted as he released the safety on his M1.

193

Tech 5 Patrick Marquis balanced his rifle on a bank of earth and reached back to open the flap of his pistol holster. It was then that he remembered he had given two 45's to the young Filipino guerrilla. He had only one left.

"Say! What's that? Pat Marquis whispered to PFC Gerhard Tiede, "What's that sound?"

"I don't hear nothing", Tiede replied."What kind of sound?"

"I'm not sure. It's...," Marquis began to chuckle before he finished his statement.

"What's so God dammed funmy at a time like this? I'm scared silly!"

"Me too!" Marquis confessed,"That sound..."

"Yeah?" said Tiede.

"It's my teeth chattering!"

Total darkness had now settled on the area, dim yellow lights were glowing in the barracks near the rear of the stockade. Occasionally, the red glow of a cigarette could be seen in the darkened buildings. The enemy soldiers in that rear area were relaxing, their voices and laughter cutting the still evening air.

1930 hours (7:30 P.M.). Lieutenant John Murphy's men were in position and ready for the attack. All waited for Murphy to fire that first shot. But, Lieutenant Murphy was cautious and uneasy. Pajota's men had assured him that the buildings outside of the stockade, behind F Company's positions, were unoccupied. Murphy wanted to be sure of that. He also wanted to be certain that all his men were exactly where they were supposed to be. He dispatched two men to quickly check on the outside buildings and PFC Peter P. Superak to retrace their approach route and check squad positions. John Murphy would allow fifteen more minutes before firing that first shot.

PFC Superak crawled cautiously around the southeast corner of the camp and began making his way towards the creek bed while his eyes shifted from the ground to the guard tower and back again. It was much too dark to tell if anyone had climbed into the tower. Superak crawled another fifty yards and was beginning to wonder just what had become of the rest of F Company as he entered the creek bed. The gully was only a foot or so deep at this point. As he inched his way along something in front of him moved. His heart seemed to leap into his throat. He was staring into the barrels of four rifles.

"Who is it?" someone whispered..

"Superak!"

"Damn! You scared the hell out of us, Pete! What are you doing sneaking around like that? What's holding up the works?"

"Murf"

"Why? It's past 7:30."

"Yeah", PFC Superak said."Murf wants to be sure everyone is in position."

"Well... go back and tell the Lieutenant everybody's ready but him!"

Superak turned to begin his crawl to the rear of the camp.

* * * *

Eight hundred yards southwest of the stockade, along the highway, PFC Thomas Grace and PFC Eugene Dykes of F Company contemplated an idea as they waited with the others in Captain Joson's road block formation. All of Joson's men were positioned in ditches on the north side of the highway. Staff Sergeant James White's bazooka team was on the south side, as were several other F Company Rangers. They had set up their road block in a"V" alignment with the open end towards Cabanatuan City. Thus, an approaching enemy could be sucked into a tighter wedge of fire. Everyone with Joson was ready.

What had Grace and Dykes' attention, though, was the row of twenty foot tall telephone poles and the sagging wires connecting them along the south side of the highway. PFC Grace stretched his arm and tried to hook one wire with the front sight of his rifle. He could not reach it. Then, jumping as high as possible, he tried again. The wire was still inches from the tip of his barrel. Disgusted with his effort, he turned to Dykes.

"You reckon anyone thought to cut these wires?" he stated.

"I'm sure Mucci wouldn't forget something like that", Dykes replied.

"Yeah... but, suppose he didn't know these lines were here."

"Well... let's cut' em."

Eugene Dykes sat his rifle down and"shinnied" up the pole.

"Careful!" Grace warned."They might not be phone lines. They may be hot!"

196

PFC Dykes produced a pair of wire cutters from his pocket, snipped the two lines and dropped to the ground.

"Boy! It's really getting dark. The moon will be coming up in a few minutes. Wonder what's holding up the attack?" PFC Grace puzzled.

What Grace and Dykes did not know was that First Lieutenant Carlos Tombo had already cut the phone lines one hundred and fifty yards south of the stockade and Lieutenant Mendoza and Sergeant Matias had severed the lines one hundred and fifty yards from the stockade's northeast corner, all along the same highway. The Japanese in POW Camp Cabanatuan had been isolated for eighteen minutes. The enemy had not yet realized they were without communication with both Cabanatuan City and Bongabon.

* * * *

1940 hours (7:40 P.M.). Captain Pajota was standing calmly in the rice field about two hundred yards northwest of the highway and one hundred yards behind his Squadron 201A. Directly in front of him was Private Sulayao and Lieutenant Abad. To his left stood Corporal Andasan. From this slightly elevated area in the terrain the guerrilla commander could see past the positions of his men of Headquarters Company, to Cabu Bridge.

Across the river, the Japanese had extinguished their campfires but their voices still echoed through the narrow river valley.

Pajota raised his fatigue cap and placed it further back on his head. His men were now ready for their most important battle of the war. Pajota was content with the thought that, at long last, he would have that one great stand against the hated enemy of his people.

* * * *

At the rear of the stockade PFC Peter Superak completed his dangerous assignment by reporting back to Lieutenant John Murphy. All the men of F Company were in correct positions and waiting for the signal to begin the attack.

The minutes crept by, but still John Murphy did not fire the signal shot. He glanced at his watch...1944 hours (7:44 P.M.). There was a coincidence about that next minute. What difference would one more minute make? It was January 30, 1945... 1945 hours was, indeed, a special time.

At exactly 1945 hours, Lieutenant John Murphy raised his MI rifle, aimed it at an open window in the nearest ememy barrack, and squeezed the trigger. In the next few seconds, complete pandemonium engulfed the area. The raid on Cabanatuan had begun.

* * * *

At the same instant Lieutenant Murphy fired, volleys of rifle, BAR, carbine and Tommygun fire erupted along the dirt road at the rear of the stockade. In a split second, the Japanese sentries in the"pillbox" at the rear gate were dead. Several men near the camp's southeast corner turned their weapons on the "empty" guard tower and cut loose with continual bursts.

"Give'em hell, boys!" Sergeant Joe Youngblood yelled and the Rangers with him along the stockade's east fence blasted away at the"pillbox" only thirty-six feet to their front. Then, they too turned their weapons to the"empty" tower.

The bamboo box at the top of the tower splintered into large pieces which flew wildly into the air. It was a good thing F Company did not ignore the tower. One lone enemy soldier, killed instantly in a hail of bullets, toppled head first and smashed to the ground with a heavy "thump."

As Youngblood's squad concentrated their fire on the barracks inside the stockade, the Sergeant jerked the safety pin free from a hand grenade and tossed it towards the pillbox. The moment the grenade left his hand, he pulled the pin on a second and tossed it at the same target. With a deafening noise, the first grenade exploded just in front of the pillbox. The second one landed inside the"box" and exploded with a muffled sound, ripping to pieces the bodies of its occupants. They had been killed in the first barrage of the Rangers fire before returning a single shot.

Then, Youngblood's squad held its fire as five men rushed the fences. A gaping hole some fifteen feet wide was quickly cut through all three fence rows. As the wire cutters rushed back to their gully, orange flashes developed at the windows of one large nipa barrack. Bullets began to snap over the Rangers' heads and kicked up bits of dirt at their feet. The squad now trained their fire on that building and in seconds the orange flashes ceased.

As the steady popping squnds from the MI carbines, the cracking of MI rifles, the booming of BAR and the ear shattering chatter of Tommyguns continued all along the stockade's east and rear fences, Sergeant Youngblood began to launch his rifle grenades. They exploded well inside the camp tearing large sections from the walls of nipa barracks.

Further up the creek bed, towards the highway, the other "pillbox" was destroyed in the same moment and manner as the first. Their occupants never had the opportunity to return a single shot. And, at the northeast corner of the stockade, near the highway, Staff Sergeant David Hey and a smaller squad, blasted away at the two silhouetes in their corner guard tower. One enemy soldier collapsed to the floor, the sentry with the eye glasses "spun completely around" and draped over the rail, his rifle falling to the ground. The Rangers continued to fire into the tower and hunks of wood splintered away from its structure. Automatic weapons fire sliced into the limp form of the Japanese on the rail,"ripping him apart at the middle".

Both halves of the body finally fell from the tower.

Sergeant Hey's squad, their mission complete, moved towards the highway and headed for the front gate.

The moment F Company's first shots were heard by Captain Robert Prince, waiting in the ditch across from the front of the stockade, he raised his"Very" pistol and jerked the trigger. The flare went high into the evening sky and burst with a brilliant red glow, illuminating the area for several seconds. As Prince predicted, few Rangers noticed the flare. Everyone had sprung into action when Lieutenant Murphy fired.

Staff Sergeant James V. Millican aimed his BAR at the enemy sentry standing in the waist-high pillbox at the front gate, and squeezed the trigger. Through his sights, Millican could see the top half of the guard"disintegrate". Practically every soldier in the ditch had joined the Sergeant in firing on that lone Japanese. Millican then turned his automatic rifle on the guard shack, located just inside the gate, and began to fire rapid bursts through its wooden walls. At the same moment, other Rangers opened up with heavy fire directed into the main gate guard tower. Two Japanese soldiers toppled from the tower and fell to the highway near the gate.

Meanwhile, PFC Joseph Lombardo, with deadly accuracy, had tossed a hand grenade across the highway. It sailed through the fence and into the open window of the guard shack. As it exploded Lombardo pulled the pin on another grenade and threw it like a football directly into the cloud of smoke which was once the shack. Following the second explosion, bits of wood and bamboo began to rain down upon the highway.

Less than thirty seconds had elapsed since F Company fired the first shots. All the guard towers, guard shacks and"pillboxes" were now neutralized. C Company moved into action.

Staff Sergeant Theodore R. Richardson's job was to open the stockade's front entrance. While others were firing into the guard house and towers, Richardson, Tommygun in hand, charged across the highway and up to the main gate. Using the butt of the submachine gun, he began to frantically smash at the large padlock. In a few seconds, he realized his efforts would be unsuccessful. He drew his.45 automatic pistol and started to point it at the stubborn lock. Next, one of those strange "impossible" events which sometime occurs in combat, rapidly began to develop.

PFC Leland A. Provencher, carrying a BAR was directly behind Sergeant Richardson when both Rangers saw a Japanese guard appear on the road inside the camp only thirty feet away. The enemy soldier had his rifle at his shoulder and fired. The bullet missed Richardson, but struck his pistol, knocking it from his hand. PFC Provencher cut loose with his BAR at the same instant Richardson fired his Tommy gun from the left hip. The guards' arms flew up and he fell backward, killed instantly. Somehow, Richardson managed to quickly recover his pistol and fired one shot at the lock. It shattered with the impact of the.45 slug.

But, before the two men could push the gate open, another figure appeared in the road near the body of the guard.

"What the hell is going on here!?" the man inside the camp called out in English.

For a moment, Richardson and Provencher held their fire, fearing the man may be a POW. Then the figure turned towards the nipa barracks and began to shout in Japanese. He had revealed his true identity. Both Rangers fired another burst from their automatic weapons. The man jerked backward as bullets tore through his body, and he crumpled to the ground.

In the ditch, just as Lieutenant William J. O'Connell was about to wave his lst Assault Section into action, he heard the Ranger next to him exclaim with disgust,"Damn! My rifle's jammed." The Lieutenant tossed the man his own Ml and pulled his.45 pistol from its holster. The gates were open.

"NOW!" Lieutenant O'Connell shouted to Staff Sergeant Preston Jensen. The Sergeant and his men sprang from the ditch and rushed for the open gate.

At the same moment, less than twenty-five yards to the right of Jensen's squad, Sergeant Homer Britzius and the 2nd Assault Section dashed across the highway and opened up with their covering fire as the lst Section entered the stockade. Behind the lst Section, the Weapons Section of the lst Platoon prepared to start their charge into the camp. It was 1945:50 hours. The raid had been underway only fifty seconds.

Staff Sergeant Manton Stewart of C Company's Weapons Section cradled his bazooka under his right arm while the grasp of the left hand tightened on his Ml rifle. His thoughts raced to his little Baptist Church in Texas. He could feel the words come to his lips,"Trust in the Lord..."

Up from the ditch Stewart leaped, followed by other members of the Weapons Section.

"Trust in the Lord... three hundred yards to go... go... GO!

Out of the corner of his eye he could see bodies of dead Japanese as he charged through the gate."Stay to the right of the road," he mumbled to himself. Seconds ticked by. Everything counted on his Section's bazookas destroying that corrugated metal tank shed before the enemy armor could move against them.

As the Rangers with Stewart entered the stockade, the 2nd Assault Section at the highway fence lifted their fire, rapidly shifted to the left like the backfield of a football team, and charged in. Fifty yards inside the camp, Sergeant Homer Britzius signaled for his 2nd Section to leave the road and move to the right. They had passed a large drainage pond and spread out to begin spraying the enemy officers' quarters with a continual hail of bullets.

"100 yards... 100 yards...", Manton Stewart, running up the center road, repeated to himself,"200 to go...200 to go! Got to get those tanks!"

Bullets were ricocheting and pinging all around the   Weapons Section as they continued their charge up the camp's center road. Now, they could see the orange and red flashes from F Company shooting from outside the fences. Stewart's Section was racing time through a cross fire from their own men and the Japanese!

"200 yards!" Stewart puffed,"100 to go...100 to go! 250... 250...almost there... 50 more to go...Lord...Lord!" Everywhere was the noise of battle, rifles cracking, BAR's pounding and the burping bark of Tommy guns. But, at the moment, the sounds seemed far away, as if he were running desperately in a dream.

"Twenty-five yards to go!" Suddenly, there on his right he could see the metal buildings... the corrugated iron sheds.

Less than two minutes had elapsed since the Weapons Section left the highway. Sergeant Stewart's heart was pounding. He gasped for breath as he dropped to one knee and raised the five foot bazooka tube to his shoulder. Men were behind him and beside him, firing in several directions, yet his thoughts fixed only on his target. He could feel his legs trembling, not from fear, but from the exhaustive dash.

Now he had the first shed in the sights of his bazooka. He blinked his eyes to clear them of the small rivers of perspiration which flooded from his forehead. The sheds seemed only in outline form. He could not see them clearly, but he knew they must be the target. He was certain he had run three hundred yards and they were the only metal buildings in the area.

Then the Sergeant had his confirmation. Two large trucks, loaded with Japanese soldiers, were preparing to pull away from the sheds. But, where were the tanks? They must be in the shed, he thought. Aim for the shed, his brain commanded.

"Range... fifty yards! READY! Sergeant Stewart shouted.

The Ranger behind him shoved the first rocket into the bazooka tube and slapped Stewart on the head . "READY!" the loader replied.

Stewart squeezed the trigger and a bright flame burst from both ends of the tube as the rocket sped towards the target. In less than two seconds, the rocket penetrated the thin metal wall of the building and a tremendous explosion shook the area. The first blast was followed by a secondary explosion and hunks of metal began to rain to the ground with funny clanking sounds. Stewart's first rocket had hit something... Some type of vehicle inside the shed.

204

He felt the slap on his head again, turned the bazooka to the next shed and fired. In a second, the building erupted with a blinding flash. Now, one of the enemy trucks was on fire. The Japanese were spilling out of the vehicles, flames of burning gasoline leaping from some figures as they dove earthwards. Other Japanese escaping the inferno, but illuminated by the holocaust, fell before they could run a few yards. The deadly marksmanship of the Rangers was exterminating most of the Imperial Headquarters Unit before they could fire a shot.

Sergeant Menton Stewart had the second truck in his sights when he felt the slap on his head. For a third time, he squeezed the bazooka's trigger. The front half of the truck disintergrated in the rocket's blast.

The sheds, and whatever they contained, were nothing but a smoldering mass of twisted metal. Both trucks, likewise, were an indistinguishable pile of junk, surrounded by dead or dying Imperial Soldiers of Kinpeidan Unit.

Only thirty seconds had elapsed between the first and third rocket blast. The Weapons Section had accomplished their mission in less than four minutes from the start of the raid.

Manton Stewart set aside his bazooka, raised his MI rifle, and began to fire at anything that moved in front of him.

* * * *

At Cabu Bridge, a mile northeast of the stockade,"All hell had broken loose" the moment Captain Juan Pajota and his guerrillas heard the first shots fired by F Company.

Along the southwest bank of the Cabu, Pajota's squadrons opened fire with a continual barrage directed at the Japanese bivouac area less than three hundred yards away. Pajota had succeeded in gaining the element of complete surprise his forces needed.

At the same moment the firing began, a tremendous explosion erupted with a cloud of dust and smoke at the north end of the bridge. The"time bomb" had been detonated. In seconds a light breeze carried the cloud away and the guerrillas nearest the bridge noticed that something had gone wrong. Only the northern one fourth of the bridge was destroyed by the explosion. The remaining seventy-five feet on the Filipinos' side was still very much intact.

In a minute a runner from Squadron 204 brought the news to Pajota. The guerrilla commander smiled."Tell Lieutenant Ervie to aim his weapons just above the damaged area! The Japs will still charge the bridge from the highway. Tell him not to worry. It is now impossible for the tanks to cross the bridge!"

Pajota's eyes narrowed and his smile spread across his face. A smell that excited him had reached his nose...the odor of burning gun powder.

Suddenly, above the constant chatter of Pajota's four machine guns and the staccato cracking of hundreds of rifles, the shouts of the Japanese could be heard. They were now organizing and returning fire. Four minutes into the battle, the first squad of Imperial soldiers emerged from the woods, formed on the highway and started for the bridge at a fast trot. It was not until they reached the river bank that they realized the north bridge section was gone. Nothing but a gaping hole filled with broken timbers awaited them and, a hail of bullets from the guerrillas.

The Japanese shouted as they attempted to leap across the hole. Then they were silent. All had been killed.

But, in less than a minute, a second squad appeared in the road. With, screams of"BANZAI", they charged the bridge. Before they reached the hole, all were dead. It seemed as if the murderous fire from Pajota's squadrons may not discourage the Japanese. Behind the second squad, another appeared, and, behind them, yet another. All met the same fate. None succeeded in crossing the destroyed section of the bridge.

Now, screams and shouts from the Japanese developed all along their side of the river. The Filipinos answered by remaining silent and turning their weapons in the direction of their noisy enemy. At the bridge, shouts of"BANZAI" always began somewhere up the highway and became louder as squads of Oyabu's Dokuho 359 Battalion reached the river. Bodies of Japanese soldiers, falling to ferocious gun fire, began to stack up as they fell upon one another at the bridge. The battle had become a slaughter. In the first bloody minutes Pajota's men had not used one hand grenade or suffered a single casualty."Everyone was too busy firing at the Japanese to even think of using grenades."

For some reason, Imperial Army Commander Oyabu had not yet ordered his precious tanks into action. Perhaps he was waiting to learn the true strength of his enemy across the river and their positions. Perhaps he had no intentions of wasting them by approaching a bridge he could no longer cross. Whatever, by the fifth minute of the battle, the tanks still remained concealed in a mango grove less than three hundred yards up the highway. But, his truck loaded with sixteen troops and a mounted machine gun did pull onto the highway, turned, and started for the bridge.

Twenty-five yards short of the bridge a blinding explosion completely demolished the truck and it burst into flames. The first bazooka rocket fired by Pajota's Headquarters Company had found its mark. The few Imperial soldiers who survived the blast leaped clear of the burning wreckage, but were quickly liquidated by guerrilla small arms fire.

Now, Pajota's bazooka squad aimed their weapon at the tanks, which were clearly visible in the light from the burning truck. A second and a third rocket sped toward the mango grove and the entire area erupted in an orange fireball. The tanks were out of action before firing a shot. Squadrons 201A and 204, on the right flank of Pajota's line of defense, raised the elevation of their automatic weapons and began to rake the illuminated mango grove with heavy fire.

* * * *

At POW Camp Cabanatuan the raid was now into its fourth minute. F Company continued to fire through the east and south fences, receiving only scattered light return fire from the Japanese.

The lst Platoon of C Company, lst and 2nd Assault Sections and the Weapons Section had their enemy pinned down in the stockades right-front area. Three Ranger squads were already directing fire towards the rear of the camp, trapping the Japanese in that area in a deadly cross fire with F Company.

The Rangers had achieved complete surprise with their assault. Thus far, the Japanese had been unable to establish any organized resistance. By the end of the fourth minute, there were no American casualties.

PFC Leland Provencher reached for his ammo pouch and then slammed another magazine into his BAR. Just as he raised the weapon to fire into a small shed in front of him, the door to the building flew open and a voice called from inside,"Don't shoot! Don't shoot... I'm an American!"

"What the hell you doing on this side of the camp? Provencher shouted."I thought all you fellows were on the other side!"

A frail figure shuffled up to PFC Provencher."I had a premonition", the POW panted,"that something was going to happen tonight. I'm a generator operator. I got permission to go to that generator shed...pretended to work on the equipment. Look at this old magazine I was reading!" The POW held up the tattered pages of a"Life" magazine. There was a bullet hole through it."Just missed me a moment ago!" he added.

Provencher nodded."Head for the main gate! QUICK!

The first Allied POW had been liberated. C Company's 2nd Platoon, led by Lieutenant Melville Schmidt, had moved into action with its 2nd Assault Section rushing up the camp's center road. This Section, with Staff Sergeant William Butler leading the way, joined the Rangers of the Ist Platoon by aiming their fire at both the rear and right (southwest) side of the stockade.

The Ist Assault Section of the 2nd Platoon, led by Staff Sergeant Clifton Harris, dashed up the camp road, then turned to break into the POW compound area.

Staff Sergeant "Twister" Malone was the first to reach the gate to the POW area."YA WHO!", he yelled as he placed the barrel of his MI against the lock and pulled the trigger. The padlock shattered with the impact of the.30 caliber bullet. The big Cowboy shoved the gate open.

The moon was up, now, and in its full cycle, bathing the area in a bright glow. A few yards inside, Twister encountered his first POW. A skeleton of a man stood in the moonlight, his mouth wide open, his sunken eyes staring at Twister.

"It's OK...We're Yanks! Get the hell out of here!" Sergeant Twister Malone barked at the POW.

"I can't leave yet", the bewildered man replied."I 've got records hidden. I must take them with me."

"No time! Come on... assemble at the main gate!"

Behind Twister, the rest of the 2nd Platoon's lst Assault Section charged into the POW compound.

Ward Medic PFC Eugene Evers was sitting on his bamboo bunk, inside the POW camp barracks, listening to his old phonograph records when he heard the first shots fired by F Company. His immediate thought was that the Japanese had begun to execute his fellow POW's. Evers dove, head first, for the floor.

As the battle continued to rage, the concussion from exploding grenades caused the phonograph needle to jump and skip about the record. Evers had no intention on moving to attempt to stop the machine. Then, the form of a big man, carrying a strange looking weapon, appeared in the open doorway of the barrack. PFC Evers and the other POW' s huddled around him let out a gasp. They were sure they had but seconds to live.

"Take it easy, fellows The Yanks are here!" the big man assured. "Assemble at the main gate...you're going home!"

"My God!" Evers exclaimed,"You're not in khaki! We thought you were a Jap!"

"We're Rangers!"

"A what? You're a what?"

Suddenly, several bullets zinged through the nipa wall just inches from the man in the doorway. The Ranger turned and, from a half crouch, fired a rapid burst across the camp road."Come on! Let's get out of here!"

Still trying to recover from their shock, Eugene Evers and his roommates followed the Ranger out of the compound and on to the center road. In their empty barrack, the phonograph needle became stuck in a final record groove and it turned with a whining sound until the mechanism finally became unwound.

In the nipa barracks next to the one occupied by PFC Evers, four American POW's fell to their knees and began praying the moment the shooting started. They, too, were sure the Japanese had begun a mass execution. Above the sounds of battle they could hear the shouts from men dashing about the compound.

"Did you fellows hear that?" one of the POW's whispered. "Some-one out there said, God damn son-of-a bitch!"

"God forgive him", another POW answered as he crossed himself with a trembling hand.

"NO... NO! That's English... That's English! Those must be Americans out there, not Japs! Those are our boys!"

Before any of the POW's could say another word two men leaped in the open door. One was carrying a BAR, the other and M1.

"Come on, fellows...you're free! Assemble at the main gate!" one of the Rangers shouted.

"Hello Yank, glad to see ya!" a POW responded."Where's your helmets?"

"Left them at home, pop! They're too heavy."

Only seconds before F Company started the raid, Sergeant Abie Abraham and his Navy buddy,"Bill" were still sitting on the wooden steps to their barracks in the compound exchanging wild stories of by-gone days.

"Well," Sergeant Abraham said, "looks like we lived another day. . ." The first sounds of F Company's shots abruptly cut their conversation.

"The Japs!" Bill Shouted, "Oh my God! They're coming to kill us! Hide...Quick!" He scampered into his hut and joined other POW' s who were already hugging the floor.

Sergeant Abraham stood up. The entire stockade seemed to have erupted in rifle and automatic weapons fire.

"Not me!" The Sergeant shouted,"Not after all this. I won't die on my knees!"

Abraham fell to the ground, crawled under the barrack and dug into the soft dirt with his hands until he found a club he had carved from Narra wood and hidden months ago. He then scampered back to the steps and entered his barrack with only one thought on his mind. He would strike and kill the first Japanese soldier that came through the door. He would take one of the enemy with him when his time came to die.

"Please don't kill me!" Bill pleaded as Sergeant Abraham entered.

"It's me...Abie! Your pal Abie. Take it easy."

It was then that the voices of Rangers caught Abraham's ear and he turned to see a man with a Tommy gun racing towards his barracks.

"We're Americans!" The Ranger was shouting," Tell everyone to assemble at the main gate!" The Ranger reached the foot of the steps."Can you walk, Mac?" he asked Abraham.

Sergeant Abie Abraham felt the tears begin to flood his eyes. "Yes. I can walk. You'd better give these other boys a hand. They' re real sick. I walked out of Bataan. I reckon I can walk out of this place", he choked.

Lieutenant, Merle McNeal Musselman, M.D., and his friend were still engaged in their conversation about the stars while sitting on the Camp Dispensary steps when the raid began.

Lieutenant Musselman leaped to his feet. Like most of the others, his first thought was that the Japanese had begun a systematic execution of POW's. Then his thoughts were on his patients in the Surgical Ward a good two hundred yards away.

He ran as fast as he could to the Surgical hut and climbed in. All the beds were empty. A chill ran through his entire body. How could over one hundred bed patients disappear so fast? He turned, jumped to the ground and headed towards the front of the compound.

Bullets were whizzing everywhere. It was obvious to the Doctor that something more than an"execution" was underway...but what? He had covered fifty yards. Suddenly, he was confronted by two large men in strange, muddy green uniforms. One man shoved a rifle barrel into Musselman's stomach.

"Who are you?" The man with the rifle demanded.

"I'm Doctor Musselman! Who are you fellows?"

"We're Rangers..."

"What?"

"Rangers! Yanks! Come on...we got this place, pal!"

POW Colonel James Duckworth, M.D. was in a deep sleep when the raid began. Even the explosions and weapons fire did not wake him. But, when the first Ranger burst into the hut, the Colonel sat up quickly.

"Assemble at the main gate!" The Ranger yelled into the dark room.

"Don't anyone move until I find out what's going on here!" Duckworth ordered.

"Who are you?" the startled Ranger asked.

"I'm Colonel Duckworth!"

"Well...Colonel, get your ass out of here! I'll apologize tomorrow."

POW Edwin Rose was asleep in his barracks when the first shots were fired. The years of confinement at Cabanatuan had all but finished the life of this sixty year old Englishman. Weakened by beriberi, dysentery and malnutrition and eye sight failing, Rose was nothing but a shell of a man. His sense of hearing was practically nonexistent. As the battle reached a crescendo, he swung from his bamboo bunk and stared into the face of one of his buddies.

"What is that noise?" Rose asked."I thought I heard shots."

"My God, man", his friend replied,"they are coming to kill us!"

"Who?"

"The bloody Japs! They are shooting up the place."

Rose shuffled towards the open door of the nipa hut.

"Where are you going, Rose?"

"To the latrine... dysentery, you know."

"At this time? We'll bloody well be dead in a minute and you're going to the latrine!"

"Ah,what?"

"Dammit, Rose, they are going to kill us!" his friend screamed.

"Then... I am going to die comfortable. The Japs must wait until I am done or, kill me there! Cheerio!"

Edwin Rose hobbled down the wooden step, turned and disappeared into the night. In a few moments his friends in the hut heard the voices of Rangers.

"All Americans...head for the main gate!"

The POW's shouted back,"We're not Americans...but, we're coming too! Rose! Rose! Dammit, Rose... come back! The Yanks are here!"

Edwin Rose did not answer.

1954 hours...nine minutes into the raid... At the rear of the camp and along the east fences, the men of F Company continued to fire into the Japanese quarters. The enemy's return fire, which remained light from the beginning, now began to dwindle . Staff Sergeant David Hays' squad had completed their withdraw to the highway and started circling to the front of the camp to assist with the evacuation of POW's.

Inside the POW compound area the men of C Company's 2nd Platoon were well underway with the organizing of bewildered, frightened and sick prisoners.

Corporal Marvin"Pop" Kinder had one POW by the arm, attempting to help him to the camp's center road. The man pulled back.

"What's wrong?" Kinder asked.

"I've got to get my papers!"

"No time", Kinder replied."We got to keep moving."

"You don't understand", the POW insisted."A man ate my cat...and officer's cat! I Court Martialed him for that. She was a beautiful cat..." The POW began to cry... Corporal Kinder gently picked him up to carry him towards the gate.

Corporal James Herrick slung his Ml over his shoulder and leaned forward to speak to the POW laying on the bamboo bunk.

"Come on trooper, we got to go now", Herrick spoke softly to the man."I'll carry you. I've got a Bible. You can read it on the way home... but, we got to get out while we can!"

"No... I'm going to die", the POW replied between short breaths."Leave me... help the others! I'm going to die anyway. Save yourself!"

Corporal Herrick picked up the man by placing him on his back, grasping the POW's arms in front of his chest, piggyback style. They moved out into the compound yard and through the gate to the center road. About halfway to the main gate, the POW suddenly gasped and became limp. Herrick at first feared the man may have been hit by a stray bullet and quickly, but gently, sat him on the ground next to a fence post. The Ranger checked the man's pulse. There was no beat. The POW was dead, apparently from a heart attack...fifty feet short of the front gate, and freedom.

1955 hours...the raid had been under way ten minutes. PFC Rufo Vaquilar waited impatiently with the other Alamo Scouts in the ditch across from the front gate for the first POW's. With the Scouts were several Filipino guerrillas, the Combat Photo men, a few medics and the"reserve" Weapons Section of C Company.

The full moon, crossed occasionally by clouds, continued to bath the stockade with its bright glow. Far down the camp's center road the first POW's, accompanied by a few Rangers, were finally visible to the men waiting in the ditch. Rufo Vaquilar could wait no longer. Drawing both .45's from his belt, he leaped to the road and dashed through the open gateway. Three hundred yards to his front, the lst and 2nd Assault Sections with the bazooka Weapons Section were still firing on the Japanese in the rear area. He would go join them and then help with the POW evacuation later.

At a full run, one hundred and fifty yards into the stockade, Vacquilar began to pass the silent buildings on his right which once housed the enemy officers. Rufo Vacquilar stopped and turned to face one large nipa structure. From the corner of his eye he had caught a glimpse of something moving in its doorway. A Japanese soldier, his face dripping with blood from a head wound, staggered onto the porch and started to raise his rifle. He pointed it directly at the Alamo Scout.

"MABUHAY!" PFC Vacquilar yelled, and he fired both pistols simultaneously. The recoil of the guns jerked the small Filipino's arms to his nose. Two .45 caliber slugs slammed into the chest of the enemy sending him sprawling off the porch. Rufo Vacquilar then turned to assist the Rangers with the POW's.

1957 hours...twelve minutes into the raid and still there were no casualties among the Americans. POW's, some walking, some being carried by Rangers, were now emerging from the stockade.

Sergeant John Nelson, to this point had succeeded in maintaining a watchful eye on his friend Captain Jimmy Fisher. But the excitement and desire to join in the evacuation was too much for Fisher.

"Hold on, Jimmy! Stay down for awhile until they cross the highway", Sergeant Nelson cautioned.

"Let's spread out", Captain Fisher replied."Move off to my left a little."

Sergeant Nelson reluctantly obeyed and began to jog northeast along the highway until he reached a point about fifty yards from Fisher.

Suddenly, a blinding explosion erupted in the center of the highway near the front gate. Three seconds later another explosion a few yards from the first...and then a third blast some twenty feet from the second left a small round hole in the road.

"Man down! Man down!" Shouts sprang up along the ditch and highway. Several men were caught by the explosions and had collapsed.

"Medic! Over here...man down!"

Somehow, within the far southwest corner of the stockade, at least one Japanese soldier had escaped the murderous fire of the Rangers and made it to a shallow zigzag trench. From there a light mortar had been quickly set up. Three rounds were fired with pinpoint accuracy towards the front gate, almost six hundred yards away. In the process, the enemy's effort was cut short. The distinctive dull "thump" sound of the mortar rounds leaving their launch tubes attracted the attention of the Rangers outside the rear fence. Every member of F Company' s squad with Tec 5 Francis"Father" Schilli and Corporal Roy Sweezy turned their weapons in the direction of the mortar sounds and began firing. The mortar fell silent, but its first three round had been extremely effective.

On the highway, at the front of the stockade, the good fortune of the Allies had run out. Alamo Scout Alfred"Opu" Alfonso lay near the edge of the road, bleeding profusely from a shell fragment wound in his groin. Corporal Marvin"Pop" Kinder had just turned a POW over to a Filipino and started to go back into the camp for another when the mortars exploded. Kinder was knocked sideways from the concussion but not hit. As he struggled to regain his senses, he noticed Staff Sergeant David Hey reaching for his back.

"What's wrong?" Kinder shouted.

"Pop! I think I'm hit. Look at my back! Touch it... it's wet!" Hey replied.

Staff Sergeant Hey's back had been pierced by several flakes of road gravel kicked up by the blast, but his wounds were minor.

Corporal Martin T. Estensen had been hit by a small shell fragment. But, Estensen was a medic. He ignored his own wound and rushed to administer a shot of morphine to Private Alfonso and bandage the Scout.

Alamo Scout Lieutenant's Tom Rounsaville and Bill Nellist were on the highway when one of the mortar shells exploded behind them. Nellist miraculously was unhurt. He saw Rounsaville crumple forward, then rise to his knees.

"Where are you hit?" Lieutenant Nellist yelled as he reached Rounsaville's side.

"In the butt! I'm bleeding..." Lieutenant Rounsaville had received a shell fragment wound in his buttock.

"Lay down... lay down!" Nellist commanded. Bill Nellist quickly drew his large trench knife and sliced a bloody rip in the seat of Rounsaville's fatigue trousers."I can see a hunk of shrapnel sticking out," Nellist said.

220

"What the hell are you doing?" Rounsaville barked.

"I'm going to cut it out!"

"Not with that God damned knife, you're not!"

"Hold still, Tom! Dammit, hold still!"

Lieutenant Nellist pulled a pair of small wire cutters from his pocket and grasped the protruding metal fragment with the tool. With a quick jerk, he had the fragment removed.

"OUCH! Damn you, Nellist" Tom Rounsaville screamed.

"It's all over with, pal...I think you're gonna live. When we get back they can pin the Purple Heart on your ass!"

First Sergeant Charles Bosard shoved his way through the crowd of men on the highway. Most of the wounded were already being carried into the field towards the Pampanga River. Bosard felt a man grab his arm and turned to Captain Bob Prince.

"You OK?" the captain asked.

"Yes, Sir!"

"How many did we lose ?" Prince was calm, but the expression of concern on his dusty, sweat lined face was clearly visible in the moonlight.

"Five or six wounded...none killed," Bosard reported.

Sergeant Bosard started to enter the ditch, then froze momentarily. A Ranger was lying on his back in the ditch, with bloody hands clasped at his abdomen.

"Man down... here!" Bosard shouted."Medic...medic! Man down!"

Charles Bosard turned to the wounded Ranger."Where are you hit?" he asked.

"Stomach!" came a weak reply.

Three Rangers rushed up to Bosard.

"Find Captain Fisher...Quick! This man is hit bad!" Bosard yelled at the figures beside him.

The wounded man raised one hand."This is Captain Fisher!" he managed to say.

"Jimmy! My God!... What kind of medicine can we give you? "Sergeant Bosard asked as he dropped to his knees."

"None! There's no medicine... for this wound."

Captain James Fisher had just started onto the highway and was heading for the gate to assist the POW's when one of the mortar rounds exploded in front of him. The concussion had lifted the Battalion Surgeon into the air and slammed him into the ditch. A large hunk of the mortar shell had penetrated deep into his stomach area. James Fisher, of course, knew his wound was critical.

Sergeant Bosard gave the doctor a shot of morphine and together with PFC Leroy Myerhoff and two Filipinos, carried him two miles to the bank of the Pampanga.

222

"Stay with him!" Bosard ordered the others when they finally reached the river."No matter what happens...stay with him and get him to Platero!" Bosard turned and started back to the stockade.

* * * *

2000 hours (8 P.M.). The men at Captain Joson's road block continued to glance back up the highway towards the stockade. For fifteen minutes the sounds of the battle at the camp, accompanied by flashes from grenade and rocket explosions had frustrated the road block troops. They wanted desperately to be in that battle.

"I guess if the Nips are coming from Cabanatuan City they should be on this road soon. They must have heard all that shooting by now." PFC Eugene Dykes said.

The brilliant full moon illuminated the highway and the men could see almost a mile in all directions. Suddenly, PFC Thomas Grace pointed his M1 south at Cabanatuan City and began to shout ,"Come on you sons-of-bitches...come on! We're ready for ya!"

"Are you kidding?" Dykes laughed,"There are over 7,000 Japs in that city! If they come up this road all at once, they'll run right over us! We'd better pray they decide to stay home!"

The road block troops waited and wondered... when would the Japanese rush out of the city to reinforce their comrades.

* * * *

2005 hours (8:05 P.M.). Approximately twelve miles west of Cabanatuan City, above the Rizal Road, a P61 Black Widow from the 547th Night Fighter Squadron turned slowly at 5,000 feet. The pilot began to lower his altitude for a pass along the highway so his Radar Observer could verify what he thought was below.

The RO spoke into the fighter's intercom."I was right! Sure as hell...looks like six trucks...no, could be five trucks and a tank."

"Roger..." the pilot answered."Cannon magazines ready!"

The early fears of Imperial Army Command Naotake at Cabanatuan City had just materialized. Their Inoue Battalion, which evacuated San Jose to return to the Capital City's defense had been spotted by the Black Widow's crew.

The RO scanned the moonlit sky in all directions for enemy planes."No bandits anywhere!" he reported."You're safe... all clear for the approach. Ready...left a little! OK...hold her steady! Might as well follow the road...steady...steady..."

The big plane dropped lower and lower. The pilot, now had the opportunity to try his"night binoculars" which were mounted on a track above his head and slightly to the left. This recent technological development gave him a visual range five times that which the human eye could see. And, with its optical gun sight, accurate cannon fire was assured. The pilot swung the binoculars into position in front of his face and lock them in place. He began to align the dots in the instrument with the vehicles on the highway.

"Contact! I've got my eyes on them now! You're right... trucks and a tank! Stand by...we're closing in...closer now..."

The Black Widow leveled in flight at five hundred feet above the highway, her big engines roaring at full throttle. The pilot's hand moved slowly to the twin gun button switches on his control wheel. Then, before the Japanese convoy saw the fighter, devastating fire from the four 20 mm cannons converged on the vehicles. Immediately, three trucks exploded in flames. The P61 passed over the inferno, banked and turned for another pass.

"We missed a few. The tank's still moving!" The RO called.

"We'll get'em this time!" The pilot assured.

The pilot did not need his binoculars in the second pass. The burning enemy trucks had illuminated the countryside. Again, cannon shells raked the highway, ripping flesh and metal into tangled fragments. Dark smoke bellowed from the engine of the tank. Flames now leaped from all the vehicles.

"We'll make one more pass... just to be sure," The pilot of the Black Widow announced."Let's see if we can get some of the infantry!"

The Japanese convoy would never reach Cabanatuan City. The Inoue Battalion had ceased to exist. Now, Naotake could only hope that the Oyabu Dokuho 359 Battalion would arrive from the Cabu River before dawn. The Imperial Command at Cabanatuan City did not know that Dokuho 359 Battalion was rapidly being liquidated at Cabu Bridge. With communication lines down, Naotake did not even know that their Prisoner of War camp, four miles away at Barrio Pangatian, was under attack. The men with Captain Joson at the road block had nothing to worry about. There would be no Japanese reinforcements charging up the highway to challenge them.

* * * *

2008 hours (8:08 P.M.). Twenty-three minutes into the raid, at Cabu Bridge, the slaughter of Dokuho 359 continued. No more Japanese squads rushed at the damaged bridge. Now, they only trotted down to the remains of their truck and attempted to return fire at the guerrillas. As fast as one squad was annihilated, another appeared in the highway.

But, Captain Pajota had detected something even more reassuring. His enemy seemed to be in a state of total confusion. Not only could the guerrillas hear the shouts of"BANZAI" from the charging squads along the highway, they could also hear considerable shouting and yelling amongst the Japanese all up and down the river. There was one logical conclusion to draw. Most, or all, of the enemy officers must be dead.

Captain Pajota sent Lieutenant Abad forward to check their ammunition supply and casualties. In a few minutes, Abad returned, his face beaming with excitement.

"Sir," the Lieutenant reported,"many Japs dead on the highway at the bridge. Their bodies are three deep!"

Suddenly, two mortar rounds exploded in the field a good hundred yards behind Pajota. He did not turn, but continued to stare at the battle scene on the other side of the bridge. Several more mortar rounds exploded safely behind them.

"And... our casualties. How many?" Pajota asked.

"None, Sir!"

"None?" Pajota's lips parted in a slight smile.

"None, Sir!" Abad repeated.

"And wounded... how many serious?"

"None, Sir! Only some scratches."

"Our ammunition?"

"The men have plenty, Sir!"

Juan Pajota's eyes shifted from the dead and dying Japanese at the truck to the mango grove where one tank was still burning.

Could all the tanks be destroyed? Why were they not turning their cannons on his men? These questions raced through the mind of the guerrilla commander. Apparently, either the tanks were destroyed or else in such damaged condition that they could not be turned to fire across the river.

All the tanks had been facing the highway and not the bridge when the attack began. If they were damaged, then the cannons and machine guns were pointing in the wrong direction, completely useless against the Filipinos.

Lieutenant Abad stared into Pajota's calm face and then asked, "How long will the Jap commander permit his men to die this way?"

"They are only human," Pajota replied. "But, they will keep coming. They know no other way. They believe death is where eternal life begins."

"The same with we Christians, isn't it?"

"The same," Pajota acknowledged, his eyes still fixed on the battle.

"Then... Mabuhay!" Abad shouted.

Pajota smiled and nodded, "Mabuhay!"

By 2008 hours the Rangers at the stockade had evacuated more than three fourths of the some five hundred POW's.

Sergeant Joe Youngblood's squad had withdrawn from their position on the knoll across from the silent"pillbox" and were now at the highway, helping with the evacuation. The only men of F Company firing were those at the far southeast corner and along the dirt road at the rear of the camp. They were still receiving light, scattered fire from the few Japanese alive inside the wire fences.

Most of the POW's had to be carried the two miles through the rice fields and high grass to the Pampanga. There at the river, waiting carabao carts were filled with human cargo for movement to Platero.

Staff Sergeant August Stern, his BAR slung over his shoulder was carrying one POW"piggyback" from the highway. He had traveled only a few yards through the muddy terrain when the odor from the area revealed his location. He was wading through the camp's sewerage drainage ditch. Stern tripped and toppled forward to his knees in the slime but managed to balance his POW without dropping him. The Sergeant staggered to his feet, a flood of profanity pouring from his lips.

"Son," the man on his back said,"I'm Chaplain Kennedy! I'm a Catholic priest!"

"I'm sorry, Father," Sergeant Stern replied.

"That's OK... I understand. There's a time and place for everything. I guess this is it!"

At the Pampanga River, most of the loaded carabao carts had crossed to the opposite bank. The remaining POW's must be carried

228

across and placed in empty carts returning from Platero. But, many of the Rangers approaching the Pampanga without Filipino guides found themselves wading in knee to waist deep, fast moving water. They had missed the sand bar area, used earlier, by over one hundred yards.

Corporal James B. Herrick and PFC Melvin P. Shearer removed their fatigue jackets and buttoned them over their MI rifles, quickly improvising a stretcher.

"What are you doing?" the POW with them asked."Why don't you leave me? I can make it now!"

"We're making a stretcher. We're going to carry you across," Herrick replied.

"Boy! You fellows sure are tough!"

"Na," Shearer said,"we ain't tough...just tired, that's all."

2015 hours (8:15 P.M.). Thirty minutes into the raid. Thus far, the Americans had suffered no deaths from the battle at the POW camp. Captain Bob Prince accompanied by POW Lieutenant Herb Ott completed their second search of the POW compound area of the stockade, convincing themseves that all Allied Prisoners had been safely evacuated. Prince removed another flare from a canvas pouch, loaded his"Very" pistol and fired it into the air. The flare burst and burned for several seconds with a brilliant red glow as it floated to the ground. This was the signal for all the Rangers to withdraw from the camp and head for the Pampanga."All the POW' s" were safely on their way to Platero. But, unknown to Lieutenant Colonel Mucci, Captain Prince or anyone else, there was still one POW somewhere in the camp. Prince has searched the barracks but not, of course, every shadow of the compound.

Various Rangers and Alamo Scouts were to recall that during the entire raid Captain Robert Prince had performed with the cool precision of a well oiled machine, like a"perfect leader". Yet in these final minutes a matter of great concern ate at the young Captain. One squad of F Company, at the far rear of the camp, had not returned to the highway. Captain Prince and at least twenty-five other Rangers would wait for them.

At the road block, eight hundred yards southwest of the stockade, the Rangers of F Company's Weapons Section and Captain Joson's men saw the red flare signal. A few of the Filipinos under Joson were released to return to Platero. Others were assigned to cross the rice fields to the fording area at the Pampanga to assist with any remaining POW's and carabao carts there. The Americans moved up the highway and joined with their comrades who were in the final rescue phase near the front gate. The remainder of Joson's command was to stay in position until the second flare was fired.

One mile northeast of the stockade at Cabu Bridge, Captain Juan Pajota's men were still heavily engaged with Japanese Battalion Dokuho 359, or rather, what was left of the unit. For thirty one minutes the Japanese had showed no sign of giving up with their suicidal efforts to cross the Cabu.

Private Sulayao, standing near Pajota, pointed to the southern sky. Captain Pajota turned, glancing for a moment at the red flare signal and then the battle captured his attention again. That first flare made little difference to his squadron's situation. They were to hold until Captain Prince fired the second flare, indicating that all the Rangers and POW's were safely across the Pampanga.

Off to the left Pajota noticed his men of Squadron 211 and 201 suddenly shift their fire to an area across the river near the point where the Cabu intersects the Pampanga. There, twelve Japanese soldiers, clearly visible in the bright moonlight, were dashing from the Pampanga bank towards the Cabu, apparently attempting a flank attack.

The guerrillas' machine guns began a constant chatter and rifles cracked in heavy volleys. Four of the enemy dropped twenty-five yards short of the river bank, the others charged on through a hail of bullets. Five more toppled over like toy soldiers, their screams masked by the sounds of automatic weapons fire. The last three almost reached the river before they fell.

Captain Pajota's squadrons, to this point, had not suffered one fatal casualty.

The last squad of Lieutenant John Murphy's F Company, which was still at the rear of the stockade, saw Captain Prince's flare and began to withdraw. First, they moved slowly east along the rear fence rows, then turned the corner to proceed some eight hundred yards to the highway. To this point they had received no enemy fire from inside the stockade. In fact, for almost four minutes prior to the flare signal, not one shot had been fired at them.

F Company had carried out their assignment with perfection. Apparently all the Japanese along the east and rear fences and inside the rear of the camp were either dead or too seriously wounded to offer any further resistance. During the thirty minute raid there had really been very little effective resistance from the enemy and none of that was organized. Except for those Allies wounded by the three mortar rounds and a few others with minor scratches, there were no other American casualties.

Now, six Rangers, the last squad of F Company began to trot along the east fence rows of the stockade. They had covered about four hundred yards when suddenly, bullets began to"pop" over their heads, rip through the grass, and ricochet from numerous spots on the ground. The six men immediately"hit the dirt", clutching their rifles and looking for targets as they fell.

"Where in the hell is it coming from?" one Ranger shouted.

"Must be stray shots from that battle up at the bridge!" some- one answered.

"Get moving! Head for the highway...keep low!

"OK!... Let's move out... Go!"

The members of the squad leaped up, one at a time, and con- tinued to jog towards the highway. They were moving parallel to the east fence rows, about twenty yards from the wire. The full moon was covered now by heavy clouds and total darkness gripped the area. Before they had covered another hundred yards, rifles began to"crack" from somewhere inside the camp near the fences. There were still a few Japanese alive. The two Rangers ahead of the others picked up speed, turning sideways as they ran to fire at the gun flashes inside the camp. In seconds, they were out of sight of their buddies.

Tech 5 Bernard Haynes, the medic assigned to the rear area squads, fired a burst from his carbine but continued to run for the highway. Tec 5 Patrick Marquis fired his MI until the dull clank sound of the ejected clip told him the weapon was empty. He reloaded while following Haynes. The shots from inside the camp ceased but bul- lets from the battle at Cabu Bridge were still zipping around them.

"There's the creek bed!" Marquis shouted."Head for the creek bed, Barney!"

Bernard Haynes and Patrick Marquis started to dash for the safety of the ravine through which they had traveled to reach the rear of the camp less than an hour before. Both men dove head first into the chest high ditch.

"Dammit to hell!" Marquis muttered as he sat up and examined his Ml."My rifle barrel's full of mud!"

In a moment Tec 5 Francis"Father" Schilli dove in with them. Bullets were still snapping over their heads.

"Where's Sweezy?" Marquis asked.

"He's coming," Schilli replied as he raised his head slightly to look for his big friend."He was right behind me."

Corporal Roy Sweezy was"lumbering along" at a steady trot, his head leaning slightly forward. Suddenly, another rifle shot was fired from inside the camp. Sweezy turned as if to fire his Ml from his hip. Then, there was a short burst of automatic weapon fire from somewhere near or in the camp. Roy Sweezy's rifle flew from his hands, he jerked and fell backward into the ditch. Two bullets had struck him in the chest, passing clean through his body.

Tec 5 Bernard Haynes leaped to Sweezy's side and ripped open the wounded man's fatigue jacket."Sucking chest wound!" Haynes instinctively yelled as he reached for a foil covered bandage in his medical aid satchel.

Francis Schilli crawled to his friend. Corporal Sweezy, his eyes wide in a blank stare began to gasp his final words.

"God! I... got hit... by my OWN...men! My God, my own men... Shot me!"

Tec 5 Schilli shook his head violently. "No, Roy!...No.. . cross fire! The Japs..." Francis Schilli reached for his canteen and unscrewed the cap. Slowly, he allowed a few drops of water to splatter upon his friend's forehead. Then, he spoke with a firm tone. "I baptize you, Corporal Roy Sweezy ...In the name of the Father, and of the Son... and the Holy Ghost... Amen!"

"Amen!" the others repeated.

Roy Sweezy had stopped gasping for breath.

"He never really bothered nobody, God!" Schilli angrily added. "He was just doing his duty!"

It was 2025 hours (8:25) until that last F Company Squad reached the highway, but there were still several Rangers there waiting for them.

"Where in the hell have you guys been?" 1st Sergeant Bosard snapped at the last squad."Everyone's accounted for but you guys! Most everyone is at the river!"

The last three men were completely out of breath.

"Roy Sweezy's dead, Sarg!" Tec 5 Patrick Marquis reported.

Charles Bosard stared at the three for a moment, unable to respond. The Rangers had lost one man, but that man had been a member of the Sergeant's company... and a friend.

By 2030 hours, forty-five minutes after the raid began, practically all the Americans with their liberated POW's were either at the Pampanga or in the field heading for the river. They all could easily hear the sounds of the battle raging at Cabu Bridge and they began to wonder if the Filipinos could hold the Japanese until everyone was across the Pampanga. Pajota must hold a few more minutes, then Captain Prince would be ready to fire the final flare.

234

But, an eerie silence had fallen over POW Camp Cabanatuan. The clouds had passed the moon and once again the area was bathed with a bright glow. Small streams of dark smoke still spiraled upward from the smoldering ruins of the camp's motor pool section. In the stockade, in the"pillboxes" and under the guard towers, over two hundred and seventy Japanese Imperial Soldiers lay dead.

Their seriously wounded would die before dawn. The contingent of Imperial POW camp guards and the Kinpeidan Headquarters Unit had ceased to exist. One American was dead, but over five hundred Allied POW's were free.

CHAPTER 11

"Luck . . . on the way out!"

Captain James C. Fisher Balangkare

January 31, 1945

At the south bank of the Pampanga River, across from the long sand bar, Captain Bob Prince watched as the last carabao cart rolled into knee deep water and started for Platero. It was 2040 hours (8:40 P.M.).

For another twenty minutes a number of Rangers waded back and forth through the river, carrying the POW'S and loaded them carefully into carts waiting on the Platero side. When everyone was finally across, Captain Prince held a short meeting with Lieutenants Tom Rounsaville, John Dove, and Bill Nellist. The Alamo Scouts were asked to establish an ambush on the north bank, adjacent to the sand bar, and prepare to hold off any pursuing Japanese. From concealed positions on that bank, they would have an excellent open field of fire over the river and into the grass lands on the south side. With PFC Alfred "Opu" Alfonso under surgery in Platero, the Scouts were down to thirteen men, counting Lieutenant Dove.

At 2045 hours, one hour after the raid began, Captain Prince loaded his "Very" pistol, held it up and fired a red flare. It was the signal indicating all Rangers and POW's were safely across the river. Captains Pajota and Joson could now withdraw.

Eight hundred yards southwest of the stockade, Captain Edwardo Joson saw the red flare and immediately ordered his few remaining men to pull out to Platero. Once in the Barrio, his forces were to divide again. Half would form a second line of defense around Platero in case the Alamo Scouts waiting at the Pampanga were overrun by pursuing Japanese. The other half would form a flank guard for the Allied column moving from Platero to Balangkare. By 2050 hours (8:50 P.M.) the highway south of POW Camp Cabanatuan was completely deserted.

A mile north of the stockade, at Cabu Bridge, Captain Juan Pajota also noticed the red flare signal. He could now disengage, but the battle was still raging. For a full hour squads of Dokuho 359 Battalion had charged down the highway only to be slaughtered before reaching the remains of the bridge. The northeast banks of the Cabu, the highway and the underbrush were littered with hundreds of dead Japanese soldiers.

Yet, the Imperial Army upheld their reputation as brave fighters. The wild enthusiasm of the remaining Japanese fully indicated to Pajota that he could not disengage. If he did, his enemy may not only pursue him southeast but some may turn northwest and accidentally stumble into the retreating Allied column.

Pajota's squadrons had still not suffered a single fatal casualty and his ammunition supply was more than sufficient. It would be wise, he concluded, to destroy his enemy's capabilities of pursuing anyone.

* * * *

Edwin Rose did not know how long he had been sitting on the open box latrine inside the prison compound at POW Camp Cabanatuan. In fact, he wasn't even sure if he may have drifted off to sleep. It had happened before. He had no way of knowing he had been asleep for over an hour. It was 2100 hours (9 P.M.). When he left his nipa barrack for the latrine, he heard the noise of the battle. Well, a little of it anyway. Once, he saw the flashes of guns and even

237

thought he detected voices of men rushing past the latrine area on both sides of the barbed wire fences. But, Edwin Rose was convinced it was all part of one of his fevered dreams.

Now, Rose was fully awake. He began to make his way back to the barracks. Everything seemed unusually quiet, but the world had not offered much sound to Rose in a long time. He entered his nipa quarters and found it completely empty. Had the Japanese taken everyone away for execution? He sat down on his bamboo bunk and thought for awhile . Then he got up and wandered back outside to check some of the other barracks. Everyone had vanished!

Rose walked slowly to the compound gate and finding it open, strolled out onto the camp's center road. After shuffling along for a few yards, he suddenly stumbled over something . A chill rippled through him. He was sprawled across the body of a Japanese soldier. Edwin Rose was puzzled. Some strange events must have developed while he was at that latrine. All the POW's were gone. He had been left behind, and there were dead Japanese everywhere. More important though, the gates of his hell were standing open and no one was there to stop him from leaving.

Rose returned to his hut, selected the best clothing he could find, and redressed himself. He placed his few personal belongings on a patched blanket and folded it all into a neat bundle. But, no self-respecting Englishman could depart for a trip without looking his very best . With some cold water, coconut oil and a homemade razor he began to shave a week's growth of whiskers. After several minutes, he was ready for his journey. Out through the compound gate and down the camp's center road he shuffled. He paused only a moment at the front gate to decide which way to turn on the main highway. He decided to turn right towards Cabu Bridge. By now it was almost 1 A.M., January 3lst.

With new strength and energy brought with that wonderful feeling of freedom, Rose traveled about three hundred yards and elected to turn on a dirt trail which led southeast. He did not know where he was going, but common sense told him he must leave that open highway as soon as possible.

For almost an hour, he shuffled along the path, pausing now and then to get his wind. He reached a fork in the trail and stopped for a longer period of rest to make another decision. . which way was safe to travel? At that moment, there was movement in the underbrush on both sides of the trail. A score of men carrying rifles stepped out into the moonlight. Rose was completely surrounded.

"Hello! What have we here?" Rose exclaimed with typical British composure.

No one answered, but a man, his rifle aimed at Rose's head, came forward.

"Americano?" the man with the rifle asked.

"Ah, what?"

"You. . . American?" The man lowered the rifle slightly.

"My word. . .no! I'm British!"

Edwin Rose was now in the hands of one of Captain Pajota's rear guard units.

* * * *

Long before Edwin Rose prepared to leave Camp Cabanatuan, Barrio Platero had become a scene of massive commotion. It was

2100 hours (9 P.M.) and the villagers were already distributing water and food to more than six hundred POW's, Rangers and guerrilla soldiers. Other civilians were busy organizing the carabao carts into a single file for departure to Barrio Balangkare. Many of the POW's who could walk were given little time to recover from their confusion and shock but were raining questions upon the busy Rangers.

"What are Rangers?"

"Who's from Texas?"

"Any you fellows from Pennsylvania?"

"What the hell is that thing?"

"A carbine!"

"Carbine! Looks like a BB gun!"

"What's your name?"

"First Sergeant Bosard!"

"By golly, Sarg. . .you're one man I'll never forget!"

"The first thing I want when we get back is a hamburger. I've dreamed of hamburgers and Cracker Jacks for almost three years!"

Other POW's were either too sick or bewildered to comprehend what had happened or appreciate all the excitement.

Staff Sergeant Norton Most, waiting at his radio, would never forget the shock which gripped him when the first gaunt POW's entered the barrio in their tattered and patched clothing. He was not sure how he expected men held captive so many months to appear. But, the sight of his fellow Americans moving like shuffling zombies left him appalled. When the seriously ill arrived in carabao carts and on the backs of Rangers, Norton Most and the other radio crewmen were overcome with emotion.

Doctor Merle Musselman had been free a little over an hour, but was already back on duty as a physician. Surgery was underway in the Platero schoolhouse on those wounded by the mortar shell blast. By the time he arrived, the "hospital" was bustling with activity. Filipino nurses were rushing in and out, bringing fresh sheets and boiling water. The Rangers' medical corpsmen were busy aiding with the surgery.

PFC Alfred Alfonso was the first serious casualty brought to the "hospital". Doctor Carlos Layug immediately went to work on the Alamo Scout's nasty groin wound, removed the shell fragment and cleaned the damaged area. Alfonso would live, but needed additional treatment in a better equipped operating room as soon as possible.

A few minutes later the most serious of all the Allied casualties arrived. Doctor Layug's eyes turned saucer-like above the white surgical mask as he crossed the room to the desk where the wounded Ranger had just been placed. Captain Jimmy Fisher, the man who worked and dreamed of the future with the Filipino surgeon earlier that day, now was prepared for surgery in the hospital he had helped create.

A plasma needle was inserted into Fisher's arm. During the rough three mile trip from the stockade to Platero he had lost a dangerous amount of blood.

Now, the skilled hands of Doctor Musselman and Doctor Layug began the surgery. Colonel James Duckworth could serve only as a frustrated "consultant". He had fallen somewhere between the stockade and the Pampanga and fractured his arm. As the doctors began their work, it was obvious that James Fisher's condition was extremely critical. The mortar shell fragment had done tremendous damage to his abdominal cavity.

"Perforated intestines. . .massive bleeding from the liver..." One doctor muttered his statement in calm monotone as the delicate work proceeded.

There was no antiseptic. Only morphine to kill the pain, and Captain Fisher remained awake during most of the operation.

"More light! More light . . . get another lantern over here!"

Staff Sergeant John Nelson, assisting the doctors, studied the face of Jimmy Fisher with growing concern.

"Hold on, Jimmy! How's the pain?" Nelson asked.

"It's OK. . .", Fisher replied.

"The fellows are collecting their morphine, Jimmy. We'll have more morphine in here in a few minutes."

Fisher forced a smile. "Tell them thanks. . .but, save the morphine for someone who may need it more than I", he answered. "It's a long way back . . . anything can happen." He tried to turn his head to Nelson. "Did we get them all? Did we get all. . . the POW's?"

"Every swinging one of em," Nelson assured . "Prince is bringing up the rear. The last of them will be here soon."

Fisher drifted into unconsciousness, but in a few moments was awake again. "Did we lose any of our boys ?" He asked.

"Everyone's OK . . . a few minor wounds, that's all!" Nelson replied, unaware of Corporal Sweezy's death.

"Who's got O positive? . . .Who's got O positive blood!" one of the doctors called out.

Medical Corpsman Tec 5 Bernard Haynes was near the "operating table" and quickly responded, "I'm O positive. Let me know when you need me. I'll check outside for others."

Sergeant Haynes walked out of the schoolhouse and into the crowd of Rangers and Filipinos who were busy organizing the column of carabao carts. The Corpsman began to compile a list of men with the needed blood type. As he returned to the school yard, Haynes was confronted by former POW, Father Hugh Kennedy.

"How are they doing in there?" Chaplain Kennedy inquired.

"I think everyone is going to be OK but Captain Fisher. He's in bad shape!"

"The Filipinos say the battle is still going on up at the highway bridge, " Lieutenant Kennedy advised. "They suggest we pull out of here as soon as possible in case the Japanese break through."

"If they break through, Father, we have an ambush waiting at the river. Don't worry. That will slow them down."

"Are you a Catholic, son?" Father Kennedy looked Bernie Haynes in the eye.

"Well. . . I guess I'm a half way Catholic, Father."

"Would you like me to hear your confession?"

"Now? " Haynes responded , "I . . . don't know . . . It's not a very good time, Father."

"Don't you think this may be the best time," Father Kennedy convincingly replied.

The two men slipped into a vacant nipa hut and remained there a minute or two while the Ranger gave his confession.

At 2140 hours (9:40 P.M.) Captain Robert Prince arrived at Platero along with twenty-five carabao carts loaded with POW'S. Now, everyone, except the Alamo Scouts at their ambush point, had cleared the river area and were in the barrio.

Lieutentant Colonel Mucci had already issued orders for the column to start moving to Balangkare, beginning with twenty Rangers and those POW's who could walk. But, Captain James Fisher was still under surgery and at least another hour may be required to get the carts properly organized and underway.

Mucci and Prince knew that Captain Fisher must be left in the hands of the doctors. To move the wounded man now would surely mean death. But, who would stay with Fisher? Runners were bringing in word from Cabu Bridge. Pajota's men were still engaged with the Japanese. The battle was going well for the guerrillas. Pajota was holding. Nonetheless, Colonel Mucci could not risk the chance that his slow moving column be caught by even one squad of Japanese soldiers.

Captain Prince returned to the Pampanga with instructions for the Alamo Scouts. As soon as the last of the column pulled out of Platero, the Scouts could withdraw from their ambush position, but must serve as guards for Fisher and the medical team. Pajota and his men would set up the rear guard defense at the Pampanga as soon as he was able to disengage at Cabu Bridge.

"Get to Balangkare as soon as you can," Captain Prince said to Alamo Scout Lieutenant Bill Nellist. "See if your men and the Filipinos can clean an area for an airstrip near that barrio. We'll try and get a plane to come for Fisher!"

In a few minutes, Prince was back in Platero and faced a task he hated to perform. Father Hugh Kennedy and the medics had volunteered to remain in Platero with Fisher until they could move with the Scouts to Balangkare. Prince entered the "hospital" to confront Doctor Musselman.

"How is he?" Bob Prince inquired as the two officers stepped away from the "operating table" and into the shadows cast from the yellow light of oil lanterns upon the schoolhouse walls.

"Not good!" Musselman reported. "I hear you fellows are pulling out. We can't move him yet. I 'm not even sure if he'll make it at all!"

"I'm sorry I must ask this," Captain Prince began, "after all you have been through in that camp . . . "

"You want me to stay back here with him? "

"You don't have to, you know," Prince quickly added. "We came here to free you men. . ."

"I'll stay." Musselman replied calmly. "Lieutenant Ott is a veterinarian but often assisted the medics in the camp. He has already volunteered to stay."

The serious natured Captain Bob Prince smiled one of his rare but sincere smiles.

245

"Now. . .don't worry, doctor. We're leaving some men with you. There will be thirteen Alamo Scouts and the guerrillas..."

"Thirteen! My God!" Musselman exclaimed.

"They are the best! Don't worry. They'll get you out. Our lines are not far away."

* * * *

At Cabu Bridge Captain Juan Pajota finally had a chance to glance at his Lord Elgin wristwatch. It was 2200 hours (10 P.M.). His forces had been engaged with the Japanese for over two hours. But now, a full five minutes had passed without so much as a single shot being fired by the enemy. The Japanese offensive had lost its momentum some fifteen minutes earlier. In their unsuccessful attempts to reach the opposite end of the bridge or cross the Cabu River, Commander Oyabu had apparently sacrificed the bulk of his Dokuho 359 Battalion.

As incredible as it seems, Pajota's squadrons had not suffered a single serious casualty. The element of surprise, combined with excellent planning and massive accurate fire power had produced an impressive victory for the guerrilla commander. Most of all, the enemy had been held from reinforcing the Imperial Troops at POW Camp Cabanatuan. The bloody battle at Cabu Bridge was over.   Yet, the guerrillas continued to rake the enemy area with rifle and automatic weapon fire.

Captain Pajota moved forward to his Headquarters Company and gave orders to "cease fire" and begin the withdraw in "leapfrog" fashion across the highway. In keeping with Lieutenant Colonel Mucci's orders, all the squadrons would move first towards the southeast. Headquarters Company Commander, lst Lieutenant

Florencio Bernardo was next to Captain Pajota as they neared the highway. Suddenly, a single rifle shot from the Japanese side of the river broke the silence. Bernardo instinctively dove to the ground.

"By gum, Lieutenant," Captain Pajota said, "you fight the Japs for two hours and now, for only one shot, you fall!" He reached down to help his friend to his feet and both men began to laugh.

It would require almost three hours for Pajota's squadrons to circle southeast and swing up to the Pampanga River. Once there, they would establish the last rear guard lines to assure that no Japanese crossed the river or jeopardized Mucci's retreating column in any way.

At 2230 hours (10:30 P.M.) the first of the retreating column of Rangers and POW's reached Barrio Balangkare and began to regroup. Here, fifteen more carabao carts were added, bringing the total number to forty. But, at this time, some carts were still in Platero and at least twenty were rolling along the two and one half mile dirt road between the two barrios.

Pajota's Lieutenants were doing their best to keep the strange looking convoy under control. The mild mannered carabao, understandably excited with the unusual fast pace, required constant attention. Keeping a close eye on those liberated POW'S who were walking out of Platero and maintaining the carabao carts in orderly intervals was only part of the problem as far as Ist Sergeant Charles Bosard was concerned. The Filipino civilians helping the convoy were stopping every few hundred yards to remove their shoes. This began to both puzzle and annoy Bosard.

"Those are American shoes" , one guerrilla explained. "The submarine brought the shoes to us with all the guns. The men have saved the shoes for something special. They have never worn shoes before. Shoes fill with sand and small pebbles. The men are stopping to empty the shoes."

While the column rolled on the dirt road and regrouped in Balangkare, Staff Sergeant Norton Most sat with his SCR 694 radio in Platero and continued to tap out a message while Tec 5 George Disrud and Tec 5 William Lauver took turns at the generator's crank. They had been trying unsuccessfully for over an hour to establish contact with their Guimba Base radio station. It was now 2245 hours (10:45 P.M.). The operation on Captain James Fisher was still in process. Captain Prince anxiously waited for that radio contact so he, with the last of the Rangers, POW's and carabao carts, could pull out and catch up with Lieutenant Colonel Mucci.

* * * *

Near Guimba, Tec 4th Class James Irvine continued his vigil in the Rangers staff car equipped with the SCR 284 radio. It was now a few minutes before 2300 hours (11 P.M.). Though sleep almost conquered him several times, Irvin had succeeded in remaining awake at his radio post for fifty-seven hours.

Around 6 P.M. the large group of Army "Brass" and reporters, who had gathered about the staff car all day, broke up as a few returned to Guimba for softer quarters. The majority had stayed on, though, waiting with the sleepy radio man for some word from Mucci.

James Irvine could feel his eyes begin to roll back into their sockets again. He fought that powerful urge to sleep by stretching his cheek muscles and raising his eyebrows. Slowly, the flickering lids closed. His head nodded with the weight of sleep and the steel helmet. Thud! The helmet, with Irvine's head still inside, smashed down on the radio frame. His head snapped back . He was groggy, but awake. The "alarm clock" idea had worked. Irvine stretched his arms, yawned and began to rub his bloodshot eyes. At that moment the radio came alive and a message, broken with radio "skips", began to come through. Quickly he grabbed a pencil and scribbled the coded letters on his yellow message pad.

"BZ . . . GB . . . BZ . . . GB . . . Leaving Some With Friends . . . I"

In moments, the radio was once again producing the clicking sounds of the message, "BZ. . .GB. . .Leaving Some With Friends.I"

Irvine knew the code letters by heart. He had repeated them to himself a million times, it seemed, during the long wait. Decoded the message read, "Mission Accomplished . . . Starting Back . . . Leaving Some With Friends." Mucci and his Rangers had succeeded, but there must be casualties.

"They've done it!" Irvine shouted to the crowd around him. "They've done it!"

In Platero, Sergeant Norton Most was becoming increasingly concerned. It was now 2300 hours (11 P.M.) and he did not know if his message had been received by either Guimba's base station or the relay post at Licab.

Then, the radio key gave the acknowledgement everyone in the Barrio had been waiting for. Guimba base had received his message. Most looked at his watch and began to record the time of the acknowledgement on his note pad. But, in his excitement, he committed a very minor, human error. He recorded the time as "11:03".. In a split second he realized his mistake and wrote the correct military time as "2303" over the common "11:03" and circled it with his initials, "N.M."

The radio message acknowledgement came as a special welcome to Captain Bob Prince. The Company Commander had no objection, of course, to his assignment of "bringing up the rear". But, Lieutenant Colonel Mucci with the bulk of the column had a long head start and no one knew exactly how far they were spread apart.

Captain Prince turned to Lieutenant Nellist, "We're pulling out, now! Good Luck! We'll see you fellows soon."

"Good luck! Nellist nodded. "Tell Mucci we'll do our best to get Fisher out of this alive. Watch out for Huks! The Filipinos seem to be as concerned about them as they are the Japs."

In the last carabao cart in Platero, a lone POW lay on the straw and shivered with his sickness. He felt a cool sensation on his forehead and slowly opened his eyes. The eyes blinked and strained to focus on the figure standing beside the cart . The eyes blinked again. He was staring into the pretty round face of a Filipino girl who now wiped his cheeks with a damp cloth. His eyes, with a disbelieving gaze, fixed on her dark eyes and the raven black hair.

A smile exploded on the face.

How strange are American eyes, she thought. An interesting thing had finally been confirmed for Nurse Wilma Monsod. Now she knew the legend was true. Some Americans' eyes are truly blue.

"Hi Joe!", she said softly and raised both eyebrows simultaneously in the characteristic Filipino expression.

The POW's eyes flooded and lips quivered in an effort to speak. The nurse dabbed at the tears as they began to flow down into matted hair.

"We're moving out! Let's get rolling!" a shout came through the darkness.

As the cart jerked forward, the young girl stepped clear. The American strained to raise his head, keeping his eyes fixed on the girl. She held her arm up and with index and second finger spread, began to wave the familiar "V"

"Victory Joe! Goodby Joe. . .Victory. . .Victory! " she called as the cart pulled away.

The American's mouth opened with a weak smile and the taste of the tears met his lips. She saw his smile, dropped her arm and faded into the darkness of contrasting shadows from the moonglow and a large banana tree.

"Keep'em rolling up there! Let's go!"

Within a few minutes the last of the strange Allied column had rolled out of Platero.

Along the trail from Platero to Balangkare, Tec 4 Frank Goetz heimer, his short legs almost numb from miles of walking, welcomed a brief rest as the Allied column suddenly came to a halt. The front of the column had just reach Balangkare. Goetzheimer sat down and placed his heavy camera equipment next to him.

"Here! Take these when you get too sleepy to walk!" A Ranger stood before him and was holding out his hand.

"What is it?" Frank Goetzheimer asked.

"Some kind of pep pills the medics are issuing."

"I 'm sleepy now!" the cameraman replied as two little pills about a fourth the size of an aspirin tablet fell into his palm. "Damn!" he swore. The pills rolled from his hand and dropped to the ground. "Where in the hell did you go . . . ?" Goetzhefmer moved his equipment and began to crawl on his hands and knees feeling in the sandy soil for the Benzedrine.   He managed to find one pill, scooped it up and washed it down with a gulp of water from his canteen. The column began to move again, and he stood up.

"What were you doing crawling about the ground, soldier? Lose your film?" a voice in the darkness teased.

"No. Lost my pills . . . found one , but I think I just swallowed part of Luzon with it!"

"I saw one of your Signal Corps fellows back at the last village. Good to see men from my old Corps again," the voice said.

Goetzheimer turned to take a closer look at the skinny man beside him. "Who are you?" he asked.

"Major Paul Wing. Before I was assigned to Luzon, I was with the Training Film Production Lab at Fort Monmouth. The Japs made Cabanatuan my home for the last . . ."

"My God, Sir! I'm glad to meet you," Goetzheimer interrupted. "Do you need any help? How about the carts? Don't you want to ride?"

"No. . .no, son. I'm doing OK, so far. I'll make it now."

"You should meet Goen and Lautman. . . our other cameramen. They are up front somewhere. We are all disappointed. It was too dark to get any action shots when we stormed your camp. They got some good photos yesterday and we'll all be active just as soon as the sun comes up. I've been carrying this equipment for two days and haven't been able to take a single foot of film. Every time I'm ready to set up the Rangers are on the move again!"

Major Wing laughed. "Well, tell me about the Signal Corp' coverage. I want to hear about all our progress . . . everything!"

Shortly before 2400 bours, midnight, January 30th, the Allied columm of Rangers, guerrillas,their liberated POW'S and forty carabao carts began to pull out of Balangkare with Lieutenant Colonel Henry Mucci leading the way. In less than in hour the last of the Column rolled out with Captain Bob Prince still in command of the convoy's rear. The trail they followed would take them three and a half miles northwest to the Morcon River, then a mile north to Barrio Mataas Kahoy. Most of the POW'S who had managed to walk, from Platero to Balangkare were now too weak to continue unassisted. They were crowded into carabao carts. Mucci then requested the Filipinos send runners ahead of his column to Mataas Kahoy. They would need ten more carts and fresh water before continuing.

At 0100 (1 A.M.) January 31st, the small group of Alamo Scouts, medics and former POW's, who had volunteered to remain in Platero, were informed by the Filipinos that some of the Japanese soldiers had definitly survived the battle at Cabu Bridge. Lieutenants Nellist and Rounsaville were also concerned that enemy troops from Cabanatuan City may decide to move north and investigate the cause of their inability to contact the stockade units. If this occurred, it would be possible that the enemy may begin to comb the countryside. The trail left by the Rangers from the Pampanga to Platero would be an easy one for the Imperial Army to follow.

First Lieutenant Saturnino Coquia, of one of Pajota' s squadrons, advised that his "scouts" were reporting that the surviving Japanese at Cabu Bridge were beginning to "move about". He strongly recommended the Americans move for Balangkare as soon as possible. He and a few guerrillas would accompany them to the next Barrio. Captain Pajota was expected to arrive at the Pampanga River soon and serve as a delaying rear guard force.

The Alamo Scout team leaders met with Doctor Musselman. The operation on Captain James Fisher was complete. But, could Fisher be moved?

"I fear it will make little difference," Musselman reported. "Fisher stands only a slim chance of pulling through. But, if we move him, we'll need to be extremely careful!"

The bamboo and cloth sack type stretcher used by the guerrillas for transporting wounded was considered much too awkward to move someone in Fisher's condition the two miles to Balangkare. Something must be employed as a stretcher which would keep his body practically motionless. The Scouts came up with the answer. A wooden door was removed from one of the finer homes in the Barrio. With care, Captain Fisher was placed upon it. Six men gently lifted the door.

With Lieutenant Coquia leading, the last of the Americans marched out of Platero, carrying their dying comrade.

* * * *

It was 0200 (2 A.M.). Lieutenant Colonel Mucci and the first of the carabao cart convoy reached Mataas Kahoy. There, the Filipinos were waiting with both food and water and eleven more carabao carts. The convoy now consisted of fifty-one carts.

Colonel Mucci wasted no time. By 0230 hours the column was once again on the move. The line of carts, carabaos, guerrillas, former POW's and Rangers stretched a distance of one and one half miles. They were heading toward the Rizal Highway and their next destination, the town of General Luna. But, after traveling two miles, the column came to a halt. They now faced a new problem. The highway could still be under enemy control. For a column over a mile long to cross at any one point would take considerable time. To make matters worse, Colonel Mucci was informed by the guerrillas that it would be impossible for the carabao carts to cross the road at their front because the opposite bank was too steep. They must move down the highway a mile and then cross.

First Lieutenant William O'Connell was given the road block assignment. A bazooka team, two squads of Rangers and a few of Captain Joson's men were sent four hundred yards northeast to halt any traffic moving from the north. A similar force established their blockade 3,000 yards southwest down the road to hold any Japanese who may be moving from the south. At 0330 hours (3:30 A.M.), Lieutenant O'Connell sent word back to Mucci. The road blocks were ready. The column could begin crossing.

The men with those two road blocks "did as much praying as watching for the enemy". If a large Japanese force proceeded along the road, every Ranger realized they could hold for a few minutes, at best. It would be impossible to guarantee the safety of the vunerable column. The bulk of the Allied force with Mucci entered the highway at 0331 hours, moved one mile southwest along the road, and finally crossed at a point just north of General Luna. The crossing required an hour. The road blocks were called in at 0430 hours (4:30 A.M.).

While Colonel Mucci and his column were making their way cross-country in a northwest direction, the Alamo Scouts along with Captain Fisher, arrived in Balangkare. It was approximately 0205 hours (2:05 A.M.). The Scout Team leaders organized a work force composed of villagers and guerrillas who would assist in clearing an area to be used as an aircraft landing strip. Meanwhile, Dr. Musselman, assisted by Lieutenant Coquia and his wife, Aurolia, attended to Fisher's wounds.

By 0239 hours, a flat parcel of land was selected on the north-west edge of the Barrio and work began on the airstrip. It would take them to dawn to complete their task.

* * * *

It was daybreak when Edwin Rose and the squad of Pajota's guerrillas entered a small barrio. The Bamboo Telegraph had notified the villagers of their pending arrival. Fresh fruit, water, rice and broiled chicken was ready for the guests. While Rose enjoyed his feast, a young attractive girl, perhaps sixteen or seventeen knelt down in front of him.

"Where am I?" Rose asked.

"Barrio Macatbong," the girl replied with a big grin. "From what place are you, sir? "

"Why . . . from the prison camp!" Rose answered between heaping mouthfuls of chicken.

"Did the Americans leave you there?"

"Americans", Rose looked puzzled. "What Americans?"

The young girl turned to reply to a barrage of Tagalog, as everyone nearby seemed to jabber at once . Then, she faced Rose again. "The Americans who came to kill the Japanese last night! "

"Really? My word. . .so that's it, eh!"

"Yes, sir. My husband will be here tomorrow, " she added with a reassuring smile. "His men will accompany you to the Americans after they take Cabanatuan City from the Japs."

"Who is your husband?" Rose finally asked.

"Captain Pajota, sir."

In two more days the war would be over for Edwin Rose, the POW the Rangers accidently left behind.

* * * *

The first rays of warm sunlight cracked over the emerald island of Luzon. The Black Widows of the 547th Night Fighter Squadron were returning to their nest near Lingayen Gulf.

During the long night of January 30th and through the early hours of the 31st, the P61's accomlished their mission by keeping Nueva Ecija's roads clear of enemy traffic. The venom of the deadly Widows had destroyed a total of twelve Japanese trucks, one tank and hundreds of foot troops trapped in those vehicles or around camp fires near the roads. The only damage to the Widows was a few small holes in one aircraft from ground fire.

As the P61 crews settled down for a well earned rest, their ground personnel began their service, all proud of the fact that the 547th had never lost a single airplane due to mechanical failure. And, while the night killers rested, a squadron of sleek P51 fighers, not far away, warmed their powerful engines. Within an hour the silver planes scrambled into the sky and roared off towards the rising sun, to seek new prey.

At the Cabu River, Battalion Commander Tomeo Oyabu sat on his haunches and sucked air between his teeth as he listened to the casualty report from a bloodied noncommission officer. It was almost 0600 hours (6 A.M.) January 31st.

All his Junior Officers were dead. His truck with its machine gun was completely destroyed, his four tanks, disabled beyond repair. Except for part of his First Horino Company and Fourth Iwashiro Company, everyone else in Dokuho 359 Battalion and its attached units was dead. The bodies of over 1,000 of his men, some of the best Imperial Soldiers on Luzon, lay scattered along the Cabu River bank, throughout the underbrush and bamboo thickets, and piled and tangled on the highway at the bridge. Most had been blasted beyond recognition by the continual barrages from the enthusiastic Filipinos.

Commander Oyabu mustered Horino and Iwashiro Companies together to take a head count. The survivors of the battle totaled two hundred and fifty-five. Only two were without serious wounds. No one was in condition to proceed immediately to Cabanatuan City.

Oyabu was not even certain what army had hit his Battalion. His enemy obviously lacked tanks and artillery. Based on the firing he heard in the south during his long night's battle, he could only assume that the stockade was also hit . The unit which attacked him had withdrawn. . . disappeared in the night as quickly as it all began. He knew that only guerrillas fought with these tactics, and concluded that it would soon be safe to continue to Cabanatuan City. Oyabu withdrew the remainder of his unit a few hundred yards northwest to the banks of the Pampanga River where his men could doctor their wounds and rest.

* * * *

Shortly before reaching the Casili River, Colonel Mucci halted at a small barrio for a brief rest and to give his column a chance to close together. It was 0530 (5:30 A.M.) and Captain Prince, with about twenty-five percent of the Rangers, POW's and carabao carts was at least two miles behind.

While the column rested, Sergeant Norton most set up his radio and attempted to establish contact with James Irvine at the Guimba base. First, Sergeant Most's radio produced only static, and then it ceased to function. Immediately, the radiomen went to work on the equipment and discovered that there was really nothing wrong with the radio. Their signal was simply not getting through. But, Mucci did not wish to wait any longer and the column rolled on for another half mile.

As they approached the next small barrio , Lieutenant Toribio Paulino, one of Pajota's officers assigned to assist the Rangers, received a message from a runner. Paulino was told that the Huks had control of the next village.

"It is not safe to go through that place," Paulino warned Colonel Mucci. "The Huks have over one hundred armed men. They are waiting for us. It could be trouble."

Colonel Mucci had no desire to mingle in Filipino political squabbles. He had a mission to complete.

"Is there another road around the barrio?" he asked Lieutenant Paulino.

"None, Sir!"

"Then . . . send someone up there and tell the Huks we are coming through!" Mucci snapped.

"I will go myself, Sir," Paulino replied. "The Huks caused the death of my brother, Captain Simplicio Paulino, at Talabutab Sur exactly a month ago!"

Colonel Mucci and the column waited. In a a few minutes, Lietenant Paulino returned.

"The Huks will permit only Americans to pass , Sir." He reported, "They will not allow any USAFFE soldiers or Filipino civilians to go through that place!"

Now the Ranger Commander was in another serious situation. With Captain Prince some two miles away and the Ranger column strung out over that entire distance, it would be difficult to assemble his troops to storm the town. Of primary concern was the safety of the POW's.

"Lieutenant, go back and tell those Huks that we all are coming through. If they offer any resistance whatsoever . . . if even a dog snaps at one of my men, I'll call in artillery and level the village!"

Paulino had a worried look. "The radio, Sir . . . the men say it does not work!"

Mucci grinned. "The Huks don't know that!"

Once again, the column rolled and began to pass through the village between rows of armed Huk soldiers. Curious villagers stared at the strange sight, while the opposing Filipino groups exchanged evil looks at one another. But, none said a word. Colonel Mucci's bluff had worked.

For two more miles the column rolled west until they came to the small town of Sibul . It was 0800 (8 A.M.) . At Sibul, the Filipinos were waiting with fresh water, food and twenty additional carabao carts. Mucci's column now included a total of seventy-one carts. Another rest was called. Sergeant Norton Most set up his radio again to try and contact the Guimba base. This time he succeeded. The news they received from Guimba came most welcome. The large town of Talavera, less than twelve miles away, had fallen to the Allied forces. While the Rangers were on their mission, General Krueger 's army had advanced half the distance from Guimba to Cabanatuan.

* * * *

At Guimba, Tech 4th Class James M. Irvine tried to concentrate on his radio signals as scores of high ranking Army officers and news men crowded around the staff car. Irvine had now been awake at his radio post for over sixty-seven hours.

The message from Colonel Mucci began to come in on the radio. Irvine printed it with a pencil on his standard Army "message" pad.

"Will be at highway / BZ - VJ / about / DHE / or QXM. Have PI / need trucks to transport / JE / Also ambulances for approximately / HE / 310900/"

Decoded, the message informed 6th Army Headquarters that Mucci's Rangers would be at the National Highway in about two hours. He needed trucks to transport four hundred and twelve men and ambulances to move one hundred litter cases . The date and time was expressed as January 31, "0900" (9 A.M.). Due to the ex-citement at the staff car, it would be another fifteen minutes, 0915, before James Irvine could notarize the message with his initials. Mucci's column was now moving for the National Highway.

On the edge of Barrio Balangkare, the Alamo Scouts continued to wait for the plane to pick up Captain James Fisher. It was 1000 hours (10 A.M.) and still no sign of a plane.

In a large wood and bamboo home in the barrio, Staff Sergeant John Nelson sat at the side of his dying friend. Captain Fisher had drifted in and out of consciousness since dawn. Once more, his eyes opened and stared into the tired face of Nelson.

"How you doing, pal?" Nelson asked, "Can you hear me, Jimmy?"

Captain Fisher managed a weak smile and his lips moved slowly as he tried to answer. "Luck. . .on. . .the way out!" he said. Then his eyes closed for the last time.

Sergeant Nelson, his voice choked with emotion, replied softly, "Luck, on the way out . . .Jimmy!"

At 2:30 P.M. the small group of American soldiers gathered in a grove of trees about two hundred yards from the edge of Balangkare. Around them, almost three hundred Filipinos . . . guerrillas and civilians, stood silent while the Americans said farewell to one of their own.

Lieutenant William Nellist spoke first, as Captain Fisher's body, wrapped in a canvas, was lowered into the grave.

"Oh God! We commend to you the soul of a very brave man. . . " he began.

Afterwards, Father Hugh Kennedy conducted the formal burial service.

The Americans waited for another two hours . Still, no plane arrived. They could wait no longer. The Filipinos, thanks to the bamboo telegraph, informed them. . . Talavera was in American hands. The Alamo Scouts decided it would be best to try and reach their lines before dark. As the group of Americans passed the grove of trees where they had buried the 6th Rangers' Battalion Surgeon, they noticed a number of Filipinos on their knees, praying before a small cross . Next to the cross , on one of the trees, the citizens of

Balangkare had nailed a sign which read, "Doctor-Captain James C. Fisher Memorial Park"!

* * * *

At 1100 hours (11 A.M.), the rear of the Rangers' carabao column still was a mile from the National Highway. Captain Prince could only conclude that Lieutenant Colonel Mucci had already reached, or crossed the road.

Suddenly, at the rear of the column, the roaring hum of approaching fighter planes cut the still morning air. Everyone's eyes searched the sky.

"Oh, my God!" one Ranger shouted. "It's the Japs! Out of the carts!"

"Take cover! Get in the grass! Take cover!" came a command.

There was no time to move the slow carabaos from the road.

"No . . . oh, no !" a POW exclaimed as a Ranger helped him from the cart. "Not after all this . . .not now!" He landed on shaky legs and headed for the tall grass.

Seconds drifted by. The first plane came into the rifle sights of the Rangers.

"Suppose they are our guys?" PFC Bill Proudfit whispered to the man next to him.

"Damn! They may still strike us!" came the reply "They wouldn't know who we are!"

The first fighter was almost in rifle range now, dropping slowly. . .nose pointed at the column of carabao carts, fuselage almost level with the ground. It was in a perfect approach for a strafing run.

"He's at about five hundred feet! . . . Ready!

Fingers began their slow squeeze on triggers of a variety of weapons . But, before anyone could fire, the silver fighter lifted its nose and soared towards the heavens, revealing its wing markings.

"He's ours!" came the shouts along the column.

Up and up the fighter climbed until she was only a shiny speck near 10,000 feet. Then she flipped over and began an eighty degree dive towards the column. The scream from her powerful engine reached ear splitting proportions as she streaked earth ward. At one thousand feet, the pilot pulled out of his dive and roared over the column, tilting the wing first to the left, then to the right . . . then, back again. As the men on the ground watched, three more fighters buzzed over, each waving their wings. Cheers and shouting engulfed the column. The planes banked north, and joined each other in a tight formation.

"What kind of plane is that?"

"They're P51' s, soldier!"

Far up "on the point", several hundred yards ahead of Colonel Mucci's column, Tech 5 Patrick Marquis slung his MI rifle over one shoulder and began to sing.

"Home . . . home on the range,Where the deer and the antelope play, where seldom is heard, a discouraging word, and. . ."

"HALT!" a voice from the bushes ahead of Marquis shouted. "Advance , and be recognized!"

"Are you kidding!? " Marquis replied.

"Who are you?"

"Ranger!" Marquis shouted back, a little "high" on Benzedrine, "What do you think I am?"

Patrick Marquis had just run into a reconnaissance patrol of the United States 6th Army front lines. In less than an hour, the liberated POW's and Mucci's tired Rangers were loaded up in trucks and ambulances for a jubilant ride into Guimba. There the POW's from Cabanatuan began medical process through the 92nd Evacuation Hospital. For them, the war was over.

* * * *

As the happy welcome got underway in Guimba, the Alamo Scouts, medics, Dr. Musselman, Dr. Herb Ott and Father Kennedy were making good time on their journey northwest. About 1500 hours (3 P.M.), as they approached a small barrio where they planned to take a break, they were confronted by about twelve armed Filipinos

"Careful, Sir. They are Huks!" a guerrilla spoke quietly to Lieutenant Bill Nellist.

"They look like a bunch of bandits to me!" Nellist stated to Lieutenant Rounsaville.

"Yeah, but they could do a lot of damage, " Rounsaville replied.

The Alamo Scouts began to spread out, but continued to move forward towards the waiting Huks who were now arguing with the guerrillas. A Huk shoved one guerrilla backward and shouted something in Tagalog.

Sergeant Galen Kittleson calmly released the safety on his Thompson submachine gun." If they stay bunched up like that, I can take' em all with one burst," he whispered to Lieutenant Nellist.

Nellist was now directly in front of one Huk, who obviously had no intention of stepping aside. The huge Alamo Scout Lieutenant looked down on the little man blocking his way.

"You shall not pass!" the Huk shouted.

"Why don't you go to hell" Nellist barked .

The startled Huk moved from the trail and the Americans continued without uttering another word.

By evening the group had safely reached the Allied lines.

* * * *

Battalion Commander Tomeo Oyabu, at the Cabu River, had his orders. Dokuho 359 must assist with the defense of Cabanatuan City and delay the Americans as long as possible. Oyabu would obey those orders even if he was a day late and no longer commanded a full fighting battalion. Three of his wounded soldiers had died during the night of January 3lst and were left on the banks of the Pampanga River.

Now, Oyabu and two hundred and fifty-two Imperial Soldiers, staggered back to the highway, crossed over and continued east for three quarters of a mile to avoid the Bridge area. They tramped through the muddy Cabu River bed and cut back to the highway just north of Pangatian. Down the highway, past the deserted POW camp they marched, paying little attention to the blackbirds which circled above the stockade and dropped inside the compound to feed on the dead.

Dokuho 359 could easily hear the battle at Cabanatuan City as they marched. And, when they reached the suburbs, they ran head-on into a small unit of the United States lst Cavalry. The Americans had smashed into the city from both the west and the north.

The determined Oyabu knew his men were unable to conduct a charge . He elected, instead, to issue orders for them to take a position along the highway. They held that position through the night of February lst. By mid morning of the 2nd, Oyabu could take no more and withdrew from the battle, leaving one hundred and eighty dead members of the battalion behind .

Like wounded wolves pursued by a stronger pack, Oyabu and his remaining seventy-two men soon became easy prey for the Filipino guerrillas. Within fourteen hours , the Oyabu Dokuho 359 Battalion had ceased to exist.

THE END

EPILOGUE

"Time is the villain! it changes all; annihilates the bitterness and everything--including purpose, including love."

General Carlos P. Romulo, 1943

With the help of the Filipino guerrillas and civilians, the United States Sixth Rangers and Alamo Scouts successfully liberated five hundred and sixteen Allied prisoners of war from Camp Cabanatuan at Barrio Pangatian in Nueva Ecija Province, Luzon, that night of January 30, 1945. In the action, the American Rangers lost two soldiers killed..Captain James C. Fisher, M.D. and Corporal Roy Sweezy. Seven Americans were wounded seriously. The Filipinos, under the command of Captains Juan Pajota and Edwardo Joson, suffered even fewer casualties...twelve received superficial wounds, none were killed. All of the Allied wounded recovered.

During those same hours of combat, slightly over 1,275 Imperial Japanese Army soldiers were killed and approximately two hundred and sixty were wounded. These figures, of course, include Japanese casualties from both the POW camp assault and the battle at Cabu Bridge. The surviving Japanese soldiers from this engagement were apparently all killed during the Allied liberation of Cabanatuan City.

On January 31st, some of Captain Juan Pajota's men located the body of Corporal Roy Sweezy in the creek bed on the east side of the stockade and carried him to Barrio Balangkare. They buried Roy Sweezy next to Captain James Fisher in the "Memorial Park."

The official document listing the names of the rescued POW's was originally classified"Secret" and is known as the"Cabanatuan List." Within a few days after the raid, the families of those liberated were notified by the U. S. Military, but the complete list was never released for publication.

One POW had died at the gates of the stockade of an apparent heart attack only moments before being carried to freedom. Englishman Edwin Rose was not processed with the bulk of POW's at Guimba on January 3lst and February lst. The"Cabanatuan List" contains five hundred and fifteen names...four hundred and twenty-four U. S. Army' personnel, one Filipino civilian (the records do not indicate why this individual was in the camp), twenty-five U. S. civilians, two Norwegian civilians, one Dutch Army, nineteen British Army, two U. S. Marines, thirty-eight U. S. Navy personnel, two British Navy and one British civilian. Rose's name would bring the total number of POW's rescued to five hundred and sixteen.

By the end of February 2nd, Cabanatuan City and the Naotake Command had fallen and the city was liberated by Allied forces. Soon after, world news men, correspondents, and photographers received a briefing on the most successful mission of its type in U. S. Military history...the"Cabanatuan POW Camp Story." Even then, the details released were distorted and not complete.

The official "Press Release" issued by General Douglas Mac-Arthur immediately following the raid stated, in part,"I have awarded the Commanding Officer of the rescue mission the Distinguished Service Cross, all other officers the Silver Star and all enlisted men the Bronze Star for this heroic enterprise. No incident of the campaign has given me such personal satisfaction."

General Walter Krueger personally presented the awards on March 3rd, 1945. Actually both Colonel Henry Mucci and Captain Robert Prince received the Distinguished Service Cross. The other American officers received the Silver Star and enlisted men, the Bronze Star. In addition, all members of both C Company and the 2nd Platoon of F Company received the special"Unit Citation." Although officers in the Army, for some reason Captain Juan Pajota and Captain Edwardo Joson did not receive the Silver Star. They had to settle for the Bronze Star.

The news of the raid, the tragic Bataan Death March, and the "death camps" flashed about the world."Cabanatuan" was a front page story for a few days, but the rapid developments in a world at war soon superseded it. In less than three weeks, a place where more than one thousand Americans were dying for every mile gained became a common name... Iwo Jima.

Yet, the war in the Philippines was far from over. While the Rangers were conducting their raid on Cabanatuan, the U. S. XI Corps landed on the west coast of Luzon, north of Bataan and by February l5th the peninsula was practically secure. During the first week of February, three U. S. Divisions reached the outskirts of Manila and began a month long, house to house battle. At least 100,000 Filipino civilians were killed in the fight for the Capital. Manila cost the Americans 1000 killed and 5,500 wounded. Practically none of Rear Admiral Sanji Iwabuchi's 17,000 man defending force survived. On February 28th, MacArthur declared,"My country has kept the faith! Your Capital City, cruelly punished though it be, has regained its rightful place-- Citadel of Democracy in the East!"

Luzon was not declared"secure" until July 4th and General Tomoyuki Yamashita, with the remnants of his defending force in northern Luzon, did not surrender until September 2nd. His l4th Area Army of 450,000 troops (counting eleventh hour reinforcements) was down to about 100,000 sick and wounded men. Less than 50,000 were still with Yamashita at his surrender. As late as 1974, individual Japanese Imperial soldiers were still surrendering in remote areas of the Philippines. It is reported that a few are still holding out. In total, the liberation of the Philippines had cost the Americans over 15,000 killed and 50,000 wounded.

But, what was the major significance of the raid on Cabanatuan? From a military point of view, the assault was a perfectly cordinated effort, well planned and executed. It was the first and, to this date, the most successful mission of its type carried out by the United States Army. Yet, the basic planning involved nothing particularly revolutionary in tactics. Only the performance of each soldier involved was extraordinary. From a practical standpoint, the raid reminded a troubled world that the United States may go to great extremes to rescue a few of her citizens. But, the psychological effect was most overwhelming. The suicidal tactics of the Japanese military (the Kamikaze being only one) indicated that Japan would not surrender her mainland without a fight to the last man. The rescued POW's from Cabanatuan were living proof of the atrocities which had been committed during the Bataan Death March and in the death camps. With this knowledge, the Allied world became even more outraged. In the minds of Americans at home and on the war front, anything which might save lives in the long run must be employed. Any method, any weapon, could now be justified if it shortened the war. A brutal military power who obviously had no regard for human life must be destroyed. The indirect result was Hiroshima and Nagasaki!

On August l0th, 1945, the Japanese agreed to surrender and at 9 A.M., Sunday, September 2nd, the formal surrender documents were signed aboard the USS Missouri, anchored in Tokyo Bay. On the morning of July 4, 1946, during an official ceremony in Manila's Luneta Park, the American flag was hauled down. The flag of the new Republic of The Philippines went up. For the first time in over 400 years, the Philippines was a free and independent country.

What became of some of the individuals mentioned in this book? Imperial Army General Masaharu Homma and General Tomoyuki Yamashita, along with many other Imperial Army Officers, stood trial for"war crimes." Homma was executed for having Command responsibility during the Bataan Death March and ignoring early atrocities committed by his forces on the Islands. Yamashita was executed for having Command responsibility while Japanese atrocities continued unchecked during the Liberation. Captain Yoshio Tsuneyoshi, the first commandant of the Death Camp O'Donnell was found guilty of mistreatment of prisoners of war. On November 2lst, 1947, he was sentenced to be confined at hard labor for life. Lieutenant Colonel Shigeji Mori, Commandant of the Death Camp Cabanatuan was found guilty of mistreatment of prisoners of war. On November 7, 1947, he was sentenced to be confined at hard labor for life. Colonel Mori was not the Commandant at Cabanatuan at the time of the raid.

USAFFE General Jonathan M. Wainwright and many other high ranking U.S. POW'S were shifted from one Death Camp to another until the end of the war. They were liberated from their last camp in Manchuria by Russian troops. General Wainwright stood with General MacArthur on the USS Missouri to witness the signing of the Japanese surrender. Within a few years, all retired from the military except MacArthur, whose colorful career came to an abrupt halt during the Korean War.

Abie Abraham lived to testify against the Japanese during Post War Trials but his service in the military was not over. Within a short time after his liberation from Cabanatuan, General MacArthur personally assigned the tough little NCO a task which was unfair, considering all that Abraham had been through. He could have declined MacArthur's"requested assignment," but did not. Abie Abraham was allowed to spend a few days with his family (who had survived civilian prisons in Manila) and then returned to Bataan to carry out his duty. Abraham, with a team of Filipinos, sought the American graves along the Death March route and exhumed thousands for reburial in National Cemeteries. For more than two years after the war, Master Sergeant Abraham continued to search for the remains of his comrades until ill health finally forced him back to the U.S. He later wrote his own book, describing in detail his nine years of service in the Philippines. Of the American Guerrillas, Major Robert Lapham returned to the U.S. and retired as a Vice President of Burroughs Corporation. Today he resides in Arizona.

Captain Harry M. McKenzie, a civilian living in the Philippines before the war, returned to private business. The moment Manila fell to the Allies, Colonel Bernard Anderson rushed to Santo Tomas civilian prison to seek his fiancee. He received the heart breaking news that she had died of a ruptured appendix a few days before freedom. The Japanese had refused to operate and claimed they had no medicines for civilian prisoners. Anderson returned to the hills and continued his fight with the enemy until Japan's surrender. He remained in the Philippines as a civilian executive for many years. Now, he resides in Flordia.

At the peak of the Viet Nam War, in November, 1970, a team of United States Special Forces (Green Berets) were carried by helicopter behind enemy lines on a special mission. They launched an assault on the North Vietnamese POW camp known as Son Tay, near Hanoi. There are some interesting relations (with regard to participants) between the Raid on Cabanatuan and the raid on Son Tay, although the raids occurred in different countries and different wars, almost twenty-six years apart. As a guerrilla in Northern Luzon in 1945, Donald D. Blackburn was well posted on the situation at Cabanatuan. Twenty-six years later, Brigadier General Donald Blackburn helped organize the raid on Son Tay. Captain Arthur D. Simons, as B Company Commander of the 6th Rangers in 1945, missed out on the Cabanatuan assignment due to his earlier orders to Santiago Island. In 1970, Colonel Arthur "Bull" Simons trained his Green Beret team and led the raid on Son Tay. One of those Green

Berets on that raid, manning a helicopter machine gun, was none other than Master Sergeant Galen Kittleson. This former tommygunner with the Alamo Scouts, holds the distinction of being the only American soldier to have participated in three major assaults on enemy POW stockades. The first two were in World War II (the raid in New Guinea to free Dutch POW's, and Cabanatuan). The third was Son Tay. Colonel Simons has passed away. Kittleson retired in Iowa.

Of the other Alamo Scouts, Lieutenant Tom Rounsaville stayed with the Army and recently retired as a Colonel. Lieutenant Bill Nellist returned to civilian life in the U.S. as did most of the Scouts. At the end of the war, Nellist and Rounsaville asked Filipino-American Rufo Vacquilar what his plans were."I think I 'll just keep going down this dusty road. I'll see you guys some day," Vacquilar replied. They never saw him again. But Vacquilar had not completely disappeared. In 1976, I found him living peacefully in California surrounded by a number of grandchildren.

Huk leader Luis Taruc had a long bitter war ahead, after the Liberation. Soon the Huks began a vigorous military campaign against the government. Taruc, his first wife dead from disease and his second killed in a battle with Federal troops, finally surrendered in the mid 1950's. By 1975, he became leader of Faith Incorporated in the Philippines, working as a liaison with the Marcos government. At long last, Taruc had found a peaceful way to help the plight of his farmers and underprivileged.

General Walter Krueger retired just after the war and died a few years later.

Captain Edwardo Joson later became Governor of Nueva Ecija. Lieutenant Colonel William C. Odell, the 547th Night Fighter squadron Commander, is now a writer, having over fifty published works to his credit. Henneth R. Schrieber, the pilot of the P61 "Hard to Get," stayed in the service until 1947. In 1951, he was recalled to flight status for the Korean War and retired as a Lieutenant Colonel in 1966. Today he lives in California.

Colonel Mucci kept his promotion promise to Robert W. Prince.The Ranger C Company Commander finished the war as a major then returned to his favorite Northwest coast area to enter the apple business. Today, Bob Prince travels the world representing the Apple Growers Association in an executive capacity.

Henry A. Mucci was transferred from the 6th Rangers he had developed into such an effective fighting force, to the 6th Division to command the lst Infantry Regiment in February, 1945 which ultimately led to a 1946 medical discharge. After an unsuccessful try at politics in his native New England, Mucci joined the petroleum industry and functioned as an executive. In this capacity, he worked in Asia for fifteen years. In 1977 he announced he would retire to Flordia.

The other Rangers involved in the raid eventually returned to civilian life, pursuing a wide variety of careers. T/5 Francis "Father" Schilli, for example, returned to farm implement and violin repair. PFC Bill Proudfit returned to Iowa and is a bricklayer. In October, 1976, Bill Proudfit traveled to Leyte to attend an anniversary celebration of MacArthur 's return to the Philippines. There, Bill was presented an old American flag which the Filipinos had been saving for the first Ranger to return to that area. It was the same flag the 6th Rangers raised on Dinagat, October 8, 1945, two days before the major Allied invasion.

For Juan Pajota and his squadrons, the war continued into Northern Luzon until the Japanese surrender. By that time, Pajota had been promoted to the rank of major. After the war, he was appointed temporary Military Governor of Nueva Ecija. Then came the bitter irony. Although Pajota and many of his men were "recognized" as official members of the U.S. Armed Forces, none of Squadron 202 and most of Squadron 200 who fought at Cabu Bridge (and many battles later) were recognized. This should be appalling to the families of the five hundred and sixteen liberated POW's from Camp Cabanatuan.

The argument over"recognition" continues today. Of the more than 100,000 Filipinos still unrecognized (mostly of USAFFE and guerrilla squadrons), the majority have long since forgotten hope for U.S. Veteran benefits. They now simply desire to have their service to the United States acknowledged officially. The U.S. Military stands firm with their claims that a fair system was employed for recognition after the war. The system may have been fair but its employment left much to be desired. In 1946, most former guerrillas had returned to the farms and barrios and could not be located. Corruption on the part of some Filipinos and Americans involved in the recognition process is a matter still debated.

Juan Pajota came to America in December, 1976, to file for U.S. Citizenship. But the Citizenship for all World War II Filipino veterans had been blocked in Federal Court. A year later the case was resolved in favor of the veterans, but Major Pajota died of a heart attack a few days before he could see his lifelong dream to become an American fulfilled.

The war also did not end quickly for Unit F (Photo) of the 832nd Signal Service Battalion. Little five foot five inch T/4 Frank J. Goetzheimer, proving once again that bravery is something more than size, volunteered for the 503rd Parachute Regimental Combat Team's airborne assault on Corregidor. On February 17, 1945, he landed with the first wave of paratroopers and was later awarded the Oak Leaf Cluster for his Cabanatuan Bronze Star. Behind him, in the second wave, came Corporal Robert C. Lautman and Ist Lieutenant John W. Luddeke making their very first parachute jump ... on a small rocky island.

But, while on Luzon, luck ran out for the 832nd. PFC Wilbur B. Goen also jumped onto Corregidor with Goetzheimer in that first wave. The unit was later assigned a mission in Northern Luzon with the 37th Division. Following closely behind a tank and snapping photos with his 4 x 5 Speed Graphic, PFC Goen was struck by shell fragments and died in a field hospital four hours later.

The parents of Captain James C. Fisher moved with two basic courses of action upon learning of the death of their son. First, they made arrangements for Doctor Carlos Layug and his wife, Julita, to journey to the United States for medical post graduate studies. It was a generous move to reward one of the Filipinos who had assisted in attempting to save Jimmy Fisher. Today, in Cabanatuan City, Doctor Layug has retired from practice, but outside his medical clinic there is still a sign which reads, "James C. Fisher Memorial Clinic."

The second step for the Fishers was to find a method whereby the Filipinos would know of the appreciation for their brave assistance to the Rangers. The Fishers decided to have a memorial tablet placed on the tree marking the spot where Captain Fisher was buried. They pleaded with the Army to leave his grave at Balangkare, but the Graves Registration Service had acted swiftly. Captain Fisher had already been reburied in a military cemetery. During war time there was little bronze available, so the plaque had to wait. Some eight years later, through the help of General Carlos Romulo and many others, a monument was erected. Standing in Barrio Balangkare, Nueva Ecija is a large circular concrete apron with a stone fence and benches on its perimeter. In the center, one can walk up four steps and confront two bronze plaques set in concrete cubes some eight feet in height. The words on one plaque are in English, the other, Tagalog. They read:

"This tablet is erected to honor the humane kindness of the people of Balangkare Sur, to an American Officer, who died here and was buried under this tree January 31, 1945. Captain James Canfield Fisher, Medical Officer of the 6th United States Rangers, had gone with them on their expedition to free 516 prisoners held by the Japanese at Cabanatuan. Wounded there, he was brought back here. At the risk of their lives, the men and women of this barrio gave him shelter and protection during the last hours of his life. This act of courageous Filipino friendliness will never be forgotten by Dr. Fisher's family and by his comrades in the American Army. May the memory of dangers shared and blood they shed together, unite our peoples forever. Men die...the spirit lives."

Author's Notes

Most of the information for this story comes from those who participated. There is little printed data available on the raid , although a fair amount of published material is obtainable on the Bataan Death March and the war in the Philippines. I have listed related works in the bibliography.

My sincere thanks must surely go to those who gave freely of their time so that this story could finally be told in its entirety. Over six years of research was required to complete it. ..procuring the appropriate documents, maps and photographs and locating the key individuals who were involved . A skeleton of the story was complicated to form as it could be outlined and assembled from "after action" Reports, Unit History Reports and related documents. But, its structure was like a simple picture, leaving the scene full of empty spaces similar to a half finished jigsaw puzzle on a table. The "Declassification" of here to fore "secret" Goverment information on World War II in Luzon helped fill in a few of the spaces.

Those individuals who participated were able to complete the puzzle. Each remembered his particular assignment in often remarkable detail. Since 1945, until the time I began my research, about twenty percent of those who were involved had passed away. Another eight percent died during the research phase. The remaining were literally scattered about the world.

I was fortunate to find, and privileged to talk with, over fifty percent of those who did participate. More than five hundred people were interviewed during those six years.

The total accumulation of data filled three file cabinets and contained everything from information on the amount of ammunition used by the P61's on January 30, 1945, to the type of wristwatch that Captain Pajota was wearing. Those who helped not only gave freely of their time, but turned over for my viewing their treasured scrapbooks, snapshots, maps, personal diaries, and memorabilia. Unfortunately, there simply is not enough space to list and thank each one, but they do have my deepest appreciation.

Conversation in this book was reconstructed through the assistance of those engaged in the dialogue or, in some cases, by the memory of two other people who were present during a meeting or event. Where possible, both parties were asked to verify to the best of their ability of recollection what was said and how it was said.

My apologies go to those who may have felt for a moment that they were being interrogated rather than interviewed as we became involved in trivial detail. Also, apologies to those brave men whom I was unable to locate or to the ones whose names may not appear in the list of participants. Someone may have been overlooked. But, the records were reviewed many times and carefully compared to notes from personal interviews. War and the military paperwork, which supports or reports it often produces injustices when it comes to the recording of names, rank or position of an individual .

In some cases, especially with former POW's or Bataan Death March survivors, reminiscences were painful. Often, a delicate approach to certain subjects was necessary. The human brain can play games with us all, in particular, those who suffered much. For example, when I questioned Doctor Merle Musselman about the POW's homemade radio assembled and used at Cabanatuan, he remarked "Oh, my God! Do you know I still have nightmares about that radio! I did not want to know where it was. If the Japs knew about it, we would have been tortured and beaten until we revealed its location. To know its location could mean death. Sometimes...I dream I know the radio's location and I wake up , heart pounding... until I realize that was over forty years ago."

One area of controversy prevailed. Were there tanks in Camp Cabanatuan at the time of the raid? When the bazooka rockets hit the metal shed, the Weapons Section of C Company witnessed both a primary and secondary explosion. Yet, they did not see the tanks. The Alamo Scouts who spied on the camp all day on the 3Oth did not see tanks either enter or leave the camp. The suspicion of the existence of tanks was based on three factors. First, the U. S. Air Force had seen at least one tank in the stockade a few days earlier. Next, the guerrillas insisted that the tank had not been moved. The tanks at Cabu Bridge had come from somewhere else. And last, 6th Army G2 apparently thought they saw some indication of the tanks presence in aerial photographs. Whatever the case, Mucci and the Rangers planned correctly.

Before this story could be written I felt it necessary to study the actual terrain on which the battles were fought. I journeyed to Luzon to see Bataan and Nueva Ecija. Weeks of hiking and bouncing jeep rides produced the results I needed -- firsthand knowledge of the trails, rivers and mountains where it all occurred.

Interviews with Filipino witnesses (both civilian and military) to the Bataan Death March and the Raid yielded a colorful conclusion to my trip. Luzon, of course, is an island. The life style and customs of its inhabitants, influenced by traditions, had permitted the majority to maintain close contact with one another since the war. It is a fact that in various Provinces on Luzon life has changed little since 1945. For most former guerrillas, life has not elevated to the hectic pace as it did after the war for Americans. The Filipinos live in and around their history and their memory has not been clouded by rapid changing events of a mechanized, computerized world. That memory, and their methods of obtaining information was very helpful.

I am grateful to the Philippine Government for their gracious hospitality and assistance. My thanks go to Mr. Mario S. Garcia, former Mayor of Cabanatuan City. Likewise to the hundreds of Filipinos who made my stay in their country most fruitful and pleasant.

Special thanks to Consular Jose R. Nuguid, former Congressman of Bataan, whose"contacts" proved very valuable. Also to Robert Prince and Juan Pajota whose great memory for detail provided many missing pieces to the puzzle. It is seldom that one has the opportunity to meet men of such high caliber and dignity.

My deep appreciation to my friend, Lieutenant Colonel Chan Wysor, Special Forces, USAR, for his enthusiastic encouragement.

While on Luzon in January 1976, I stood on a dirt road in the center of a large rice field near Barrio Pangatian...the same road which once ran through the center of POW Camp Cabanatuan. To the south I could see the small chapel which the Filipinos erected just prior to World War II. It is the only thing left of what was once the POW camp.

Around me was nothing but fresh green rice fields. There were no markers, no monument, no flags. Not even a strand of barbed wire to remind one of what had once been there. In late 1945, Graves Registration of the U.S. Army exhumed those buried at the camp cemetery for reburial in other places.

Mayor Garcia and his staff in nearby Cabanatuan City had a program underway to convert the former POW camp area into a memorial park.

In 1975, the U.S. Embassy in Manila was approached with a request for a small contribution to be applied towards the cost of erecting a marker. The Filipinos would pay the balance and furnish the land. Mayor Garcia was advised that the United States had "no funds available for such a program".

At that time the United States officially rejected the opportunity to help mark the site where over 3, 000 of her young men died a slow horrible death...where over a hundred American volunteers risked their lives to snatch 517 comrades from death' s grasp.

A few years later, a monument was erected at the site. The Filipinos donated the land and furnished the labor. But, the irony of the Cabanatuan Story continued. The funds for the memorial were raised by former American POW's and veterans as a tribute to their comrades who had suffered and died before the Raid on Cabanatuan.

The following officers and enlisted men of the U.S. 6th Rangers are officially credited by Government Archives for being on the Raid on Cabanatuan. Ranks are of early 1945.

Lt. Col. Henry A. Mucci
Capt. James C. Fisher
Capt. Robert W. Prince
Ist Lt. John F. Murphy
1st Lt. William J. O'Connell
1 st Lt.Melville R. Schmidt
1 st. Lt. Clifford K. Smith
Ist Sgt. Robert G. Anderson
Charles H. Bosard
Ned A. Hedrick
T Sgt. Melvin H. Gilbert
Daniel H. Watson
Ralph C. Franks
S Sgt. John W. Nelson
Charles W. Brown
David M. Hey
James V. Millican
Richard A. Moore
Cleatus G. Norton

James O. White
Norton S. Most
Floyd S. Anderson
Lyle C. Bishop
William R. Butler
Thomas H. Frick
Clifford B. Gudmunsen
Clifton R. Harris
Preston N. Jensen
Mike Koren
Lester L. Malone
Theodore R. Richardson
August T. Stern, Jr.
Manton P. S tewart
Sgt. Claude R. Howell
Albert F. Outwater, Jr.
Vance R. Shears
James M. Tucker
Leo M. Wentland
Milo C. Mortensen
Arthur T. Williams
Harry G. Killough
Tec 4 Homer E. Britzius
Robert L. Camp
Cpl. Martin T. Estesen
Waymon E. Finley
James B. Herrick
Marvin W. Kinder
John G. Palomares
Roy F. Sweezy
Robert L. Ramsey
Tec 5 Bernard L. Haynes
Edward L. Biggs
Patrick F. Marquis
Francis R. Schilli
William A. Lawver
Robert W. White
Dalton H. Garrett

Alymer C. Jinkins
Pfc Robert C. Strube
Warren M. Bell
James W. Conley
Donald A. Adams
Carlton O. Dietzel
Eugene H. Dykes
Howard R. Fortenberry
Thomas A. Grace, Jr.
Dale F. Harris
Norman F. Higgins
Frank C. Hudoba
F. J. Hughes
Edward N. Knowles
John V. Pearson
Joseph M. Pospishil
William H. Proudfit
George H. Randall
Buford K. Spicer
Frank R. St John
Gerhard J. Tiede
Joseph O. Youngblood
Vernon Ablott
John D. Blannett
William F. Crumpton
Virgil S. Dixon
Waverly R. Duke
Edwin G. Enstrom
Mariano Garde
William H. Garrison
Paul J. Grimm
Pfc Howard J. Guillory
Clarence W. Heezen
Andrew J. Herman
Eugene J. Kocsis
Edward Littleton
Joseph Lombardo
Alfred A. Martin

287

Billy McElroy
Alfred J. McGinnis
Ralph C. Melendez
Leroy B. Myerhoff
Edward Paluck
Jack A. Peters
Roy B. Peters
Alva A. Polzine
Leland A. Provencher
Merrie K. Purtell
James M. Reynolds
John B. Richardson
Alvie E. Robbins
Edgar L. Ruble
Roy D. Sebeck
Melvin P. Shearer
Charles Q. Snyder
Conrad J. Solf
Peter P. Superak
Charles S. Swain
Russell J. Swank
Ronald R. Thomas
Alexander E. Truskowski
Jasper T. Westmoreland
Ray E. Williams

The following men of Combat Photo Unit F, 832nd Signal Service Battalion are credited for accompanying the 6th Rangers on the Raid. Ranks are of early 1945.

Ist Lt. John W. Lueddeke
Tec 4 Frank J. Goetzheimer
Pfc Wilber B. Goen
Pfc. Robert C. Lautman

The following men of the Alamo Scouts, 6th U. S. Army are credited for their involvement in the Raid. Ranks are of early 1945.

Ist Lts. Thomas Rounsaville
William Nellist
John E. Dove
Sgts. Harold Hard
 Galen Kittleson
Rufo Vaquilar
Franklin Fox
Gilbert Cox
Wilbur Wismer
Francis Laquier
Alfred Alfonso
Andy Smith
Sabas Asis
 Thomas Siason

The following roster of Allied Prisoners of War who were liberated the night of January 30, 1945, during the raid was known officially as the"Cabanatuan List." It was originally classified "Secret" and remained so for years after World War II. The list has been copied from the original which was compiled by the United States Sixth Army Headquarters at Guimba within Forty-eight hours of the raid. Names were misspelled and many ranks were incorrect. Apparently, several clerks attempted to procure necessary information from over 500 P.0.W. 's who were confused, sick or still in a state of shock. Several P.0.W.'s gave the Philippines as their home address. Most of these men lived in the Islands before the war. A few had families who were unable to evacuate during the Japanese invasion.

Colonels
Alfred Oliver (Chaplin)_____ Washington, D.C.
James Duckworth M.D._____ San Francisco, California

Commander
Lea Sartin _____ Houms, Louisiana

Lieutenant Commander

Jerry Steward _____ Los Banos, Luzon
Robert Strong, Jr. _____ Arlington, Massachusetes
Hjalalmar Erickson _____ Los Angeles. Calif.

Lieutenant Colonels
Albert Fields (or Fralds) _____ Coffeyville, Kansas
William Galos _____ none listed
Robert Johnson _____ Columbus , Georgia
Edward Kallus_____ Caldwell, Texas
Donald Sawtelle _____ Corpus Christi, Texas
Thomas Willson _____ Little Rock, Arkansas
James Green _____ Mt. Contoc, Luzon

Captains
Robert Roseveare_____ Manila, Luzon
Wilson McNeil_____ Lawton, Oklahoma
Bertram Bank _____ Tuscaloosa, Alabama
Matt Dobrinic_____ Taylor Springs, Illinois
Robert Lewis_____ Cape Elisabeth, Maine
Robert Whiteley _____ Palo Alto, California
Ben King_____ Austin, Texas
Raymond Knapp_____ San Antonio, Texas
Charles Leasum _____ Stergon Bay, Wisconsin
Robert Sly_____ Eugene, Oregon
James Trippe _____ Los Angeles, California
Dallas Vinette _____ Tarts, New Mexico
John Lucas _____ Washington, D.C.
Caryl Piccotte _____ Oakland, California
Denton Rees_____ Milwaukee, Wisconsin
Donald Robins _____ Detroit, Michigan
Homer Colman _____ Grand Junction, Colorado

First Lieutenants
Seaton Foley_____ San Rafael, California
Francis Lunnie _____ Concord, Vermont

Walter Stone _____ Chicago, Illinois
George Kane _____ Scarsdale, New York
Melvin Johnston _____ Long Beach, California
Richard Hedreck_____ Manila Luzon
William Haines _____ Waynesburg, Pennsylvania
Buerly Gibbon_____ Marshall, Michigan
George Kane _____ Atlanta, Georgia
Hugh Kennedy (Chaplin) _____ Scarsdale, New York
Merle Musselman, M.D. _____ Nebraska City, Nebraska
Herbert Ott _____ Wheaton, Illinois
Earl Baumgardner_____ Yonkers, New York
Knut Engerset_____ San Pedro, California
George Green_____ Auburn, Alabama
Isaac Lavictaire_____ Pigean, Michigan
Alma Salm _____ Oakland, California
Emmet Manson_____ Worthington, Minnesota
Eugene Okeefe_____ South Orange, New Jersey

Second Lieutenants

Frank Burgess _____ San Diego, California
Donald Miller_____ South Gate, California
Daniel Limpert_____ Albuquerque, New Mexico
Charles Fox, Sr. _____ Oakland, California
Ambrose Wangler_____ Graveport, Ohio
Jerome Triolo _____ El Paso, Texas
Edward Thomas _____ Grand Rapids, Michigan
John Temple_____ Pittsfield, Massachusetts
Willard Smith_____ Altadena, California
Melvin Johnston _____ Long Beach, California
Richard Hedreck_____ Manila, Luzon
William Haines _____ Waynesburg, Pennsylvania
Buerly Gibbon_____ Marshall, Michigan
William Gentry _____ Harrodsburg, Kentucky
William Duncan_____ Pelahatchia, Mississippi
Claude Daniel_____ Bogulusa, Louisiana
Clifton Chamberlain _____ Marlin, Texas
Robert Burke_____ Quebec, Canada
Jarry Brown_____ Brownsburg, Indiana

Raymond Bliss _____ None listed
William Romme_____ Terre Haute, Indiana
John Zimmerman _____ Lynchburg, Virginia
Jack Jennings_____ Sausalito, California
Tony Wheeler _____ Seagraves, Texas

Warrant Officers
Grover Gilbert_____ Liedlow, Illinois
James Pfeiffer_____ Mineral Point, Texas
Ralph Ellis_____ San Antonio, Texas
Eric Lundblad _____ San Francisco, California
James Shimel_____ Philadelphia, Pennsylvania

Sergeants
Stanley Bronk _____ Seattle, Washington
Dale Lawton _____ Mineral Point, Wisconsin
Marvin Laycock_____ Libertyville, Illinois
Orville Drummond_____ Clovis, New Mexico
George Clow_____ Omaha, Illinois
Damon Howard_____ Norway, Minnesota
John Batcheler _____ Ashland, Oregon
Harold Beasley _____ Timpson, Texas
Donald Bridges _____ Emeryville, California
David Chavez _____ Albuquerque, New Mexico
Nathan Cleaves _____ Portland, Maine
Earnest Clements_____ Wrens, Georgia
Richard Craycroft _____ Vine Grove, Kentucky
Fredrick Crocker_____ Sartenburg, South Carolina
George Darling _____ Deming, New Mexico
Wilber Disosway _____ Hampton, Virginia
John Kelly (Sergeant Major) ___ San Diego, California
Archibeque Esperidion _____ Albuguerque, New Mexico
Julius Farrell_____ San Diego, California
Jack Fogerson _____ Clovis, New Mexico
Virgil Ford _____ Memphis, Texas
Walter French _____ Hardy, Arkansas
Fred Gaston _____ San Francisco, California
Samuel Goldy _____ Gloucester City, New Jersey

Cecil Heflin	Lake, Mississippi
Elmer Howell	not given
Everett Keyes	Concord, New Hampshire
Joseph Knapp	Fairport Harbor, Ohio
William Lambert	Fort Meyers, Florida
Sylvester Lane	New Port, Kentucky
Burney Machovic R	Ridgefield Park, New Jersey
Lewis Taylor	Phoenix, Arizonia
Roy Smith	Pelly, Texas
Austin Rodgers	Florence, South Carolina
Hassel Short	Whitesboro, Texas
Alma Owen	Salt Lake, Utah
Charles Short	Philadelphia, Pennsylvania
Richard Neault	Adams, Massachusetts
Charles Mortimer	Crowe, Virginia
Leon Tice, Jr.	Odgenburg, Pennslvania
Harry Pinto	Mount View, California
Clifton Copeland	Indianola, Mississippi
Kenneth Miza	Beattie, Kansas
Milo Folson	none listed
Edward Witmer, Jr.	Stansburg, Pennsylvania
Gerald Wagner	Rapid City, South Dakota
Charles Walker	Springfield, Illinois
Leon Swindell	Tifton, Georgia
William Thamos	Bloomsburg, Pennsyvlania
Robert Doyle	none listed
George Dunn	Riverside, California
Abie Abraham	Manila
Ermon Addington	Harrison, Idaho
Louis Albin	San Antonia, Texas
Robert Baker	Valdosta, Georgia
Floyd Barnhardt	Chicago, Illinois
Chester Brown	Trenton, Missouri
Julian Brown	Madison, Flordia
Edward Burns	Bowman, North Dakota
Rodger Cambell	Marble, New Mexico
William Claxton	Los Angeles, California
Floyd Cooney	New Castle, Indiana

John Culp _____	State Line, Mississippi
Jacob Dusich _____	Queson, Philippines
Roy Gatewood _____	Elijah, Missouri
Leonard Gibbs _____	Willis, Texas
Clinton Goodbla _____	Long Beach, California
Robert Guice_____	West Wind. Iowa
Frederick Guth _____	Whitmore, California
George Gwin_____	Dubuque, Iowa
Almer Hannah_____	Liberty, Missouri
Arthur Harrison _____	Fresno, California
Roy Hoblet _____	Fayetteville, Arkansas
Oliver Hoover _____	Huntington Park, California
Robert Howe, Jr._____	Batavia, New York
Melvin Johnson_____	Biggs, California
Gust Katrones_____	Manila
Marcos Keithley _____	Oakford, Illinois
Walter Ruig_____	San Roque, Luzon
John Ryan_____	Baltimore, Maryland
Lavergne Ritchie_____	Trenton, Illinois
Calvin Rhoades _____	Wolfe City, Texas
Everett Reyes_____	Concord, New Hamphire
D.C. Raines _____	Bonifay, Florida
Fredrick Rabin _____	Long Beach, California
Arnold King_____	Hutchinson, Kansas
Togan Kinnison_____	Lincoln, Nebraska
William Kippen _____	Cleveland, Ohio
Charles Kyllo_____	Salt Lake city, Utah
Stanislaus Malor _____	Salem, Massachusetts
Charles Mokewen_____	Ithica, New York
Paul McKinley_____	Portland, Oregon
Eldred McPherson _____	Fortuna, California
EdwardMiller_____	Hagerstown, Maryland
Walter Miller _____	Los Angeles, California
Darwin Patrick_____	Hummelstown, Pa.
Alfred Pharr_____	Jasper, Texas
Charles Quinn_____	Dayton, Ohio
Donald Smith _____	Boulder,Colorado
Harry Staples _____	Binchamton, New York

Blake Vanlaningham _____ Crosses, Ark.
Ari Vico _____ Crockett, Calif.
Stanely Wallace _____ Sikestown, Missouri
Fredrick Walther _____ Provo, Utah
Finas Williams_____ Washington, D.C.
William Smith _____ San Diego, Calif.
Milton Englin _____ Seattle, Wash.
Eugene Commander_____ San Diego, Calif.
Harry Arnold _____ Liberty. Missouri

Corporals

Millard Basinger _____ Pomona, Calif.
Lloyd Blanchard _____ Port Arthur, Texas
William Davis _____ Medford, Oregon
Hugh Branch_____ Cut Bank, Montana
Cecil Hay _____ Marlin, Texas
Alfred Taube _____ Omaha, Nebraska
Patrick Bryne _____ Chicago, Illinois
Paul Nateswa _____ Seama, New Mexico
William Peterson_____ Lake Park, Iowa
Richard Scott _____ Helena, Montana
Gareth Reed_____ Walla Walla, Washington
Ray Wilson _____ Long Beach, Calif.
Deno Zucca _____ Pocahontas, Illinois
Neil Piovino_____ Chicago, Illinois
Edward Berry _____ Topango, Calif.
Dennis Rainwater _____ Paris, Arkansas
Max Greenburg_____ None Listed
Neil Jovina _____ None Listed
Glen Hagstrom _____ Spokane, Wash.
Richard Chapman_____ Guilford, Conn.
Quentine Devore_____ Wray, Colorado
Ted Easton _____ Venice, Calif.
Paul Gernandt_____ Davenport, Iowa
John Reiff _____ Glen Ullin, North Dakota
Frank Potyraj _____ Grand Rapids, Michigan
Fred Schumm_____ Staten Island, New York
Edward Seaman _____ Middleport, New York

Carl Stuard _____ Walthill, Nebraska
Roy Terry _____ Bakersfield, Calif.
Karl Tobey, _____ Fallon, Nevada
Rufus Turnbow _____ Konawa, Oklahoma
Albert Parker_____ Deming, New Mexico

Privates First Class

Lloyd Anderson_____ Everett, Washington
Richard Barnes_____ San Antonio, Texas
Louis Barry _____ Louisville, Kentucky
Eugene Clark _____ Lincoln, Nebraska
David Coull_____ Atlantic City, New Jersey
James Cowan_____ Fullerton,California
Howard Hall _____ Haleyville, Alabama
Allen Gutridge_____ Baker, Oregon
Sipriano Greigo_____ Albuquerque, New Mexico
John Gordon_____ Chicago, Illinois
Frank Franchini_____ Albuquerque, New Mexico
John Dugan _____ Springfield, Ohio
Lawrence Hall_____ Jellico, Tennessee
Joseph Henry _____ Kelso, Washington
Raymond Holland_____ Deland, Florida
Louis Macholl _____ Marcellus, New York
Robert Paco _____ Greenville, South Carolina
George Parrott _____ Bryan, Ohio
Don Robertson _____ Ardmore, Oklahoma
Roy Jones, Sr. _____ Visalia, Calif.
Samuel Korrocks _____ Oakland, Calif.
J. B. Miller_____ Brownwood, Texas
Pat Parker_____ Calium, Oklahoma
Carroll Sherman _____ Baton Rouge, La.
Field Reed, Sr. _____ Harrodsburg, Ky.
Ralph Rodrigues_____ Bernalilla, New Mexico
William Shults _____Corsecona, Texas
Field Reed, Sr._____Harrodsburg, Ky.
Ted Thomas_____Mangum, Oklahoma
Robert Unger _____ Berkley Springs, West Va.
John West_____ Rowell, New Mexico

Louis Zeliz_____	Chicago. Illinois
Dale Forrest _____	Richmond, Calif.
Jack Ostrom _____	Miles City, Mont.
Samuel Horrocks _____	Oakland, Calif.
Sjpriano Srugo _____	None Listed
Robert Strasters _____	Salt Lake City, Utah
Lester Vitek_____	Chelsea, Iowa
Peter Soppoknersky _____	None Listed
Lorne Cox_____	Medford, Oregon
Harold Amos_____	Afton. Iowa
Richard Beck _____	Atlanta., Georgia
Clarence Bower _____	Mt. Sterling, Ohio
Paul Browning_____	Princeton, New Jersey
Preston Bryant _____	Blue Springs, Nebraska
Benjamin Cabreiro _____	Hilo, Hawaii
Carl Carlson _____	Bronx, New York
Julius Cobb_____	Colorado Springs, Col
Sidney Coy _____	Louisville, Ky
Robert Decker_____	Omaha, Nebraska
Cecil Easiley _____	Houston, Texas
Claude Gibbons _____	Tracy, Calif.
Herbert Herzog_____	Akron, Ohio
Charles Jensen_____	Chicago, Illinois
Vernice Kauffman _____	Fayetteville, Pa.
Norman Lev _____	Chicago, Illinois
Sanford Locke_____	Suffolk, Va
George McHale_____	East St. Louis, Ill.
John Moores _____	Woodbine, Iowa
Winthrop Pinkham _____	Dover, New Hampshire
William Rieck _____	Utica, Michigan
William Seckinger_____	Lilly, Pa.
Ernesto Serrani_____	Coyote, New Mexico
Jeff Smith _____	McCrory, Arkansas
Donald Snyder _____	Pittsburgh, Pa.
Marshall Stoutenburgh _____	Kelly Corners, New York
Ira Taylor_____	Lexington, Texas
Joseph Thibeault_____	Lawrence, Mass.
Foch Tixtier _____	Albquerque, New Mexico

Charles Tupy_____ Waucoma, Iowa
Dale Vonlinger _____ Mansfield, Illinois
Grandison Vroman _____ Ithaca, New York
Eugene Watson _____ Tucson, Arizona
Ben Williams_____ Espnanola, New Mexico
Benjamin Williams _____ Crandall, Mississipi
Chester Easton_____ Englewood, Calif.
Fred Vinton _____ Jackson, Michigan
Herman Silk _____ Isable, South Dakota
Lawdell Yates _____ Collidge, Arizona
Thomas Wood _____ Detroit, Michigan
Frank Wilson_____ Salinas, Calif.

Privates

Herman Ancelet _____ Basco, Illinois
John Bailey _____ Chicago, Illinois
Lellon Barnes _____ Carrizoa, New Mexico
Archie Bellair, Jr._____ Port Neches, Texas
Merwyn Chenoweth _____ Grass Valley, California
Lawrence Courtney_____ Monroe, Wisconsin
Carno Elkins _____ Tuscaloosa, Oklahoma
Eugene Evers _____ Dyersville, Iowa
Travis Flowers_____ Scranton, North Carolina
Thomas Gorman, Jr._____ El Segundo, California
William Harrison _____ Bozeman, Montana
Dean Henderson_____ Gooding, Idaho
Charles Hickey _____ Portland, Oregon
James Hildebrand_____ Chicago, Illinois
Arthur Hilshorst_____ Mt. Washington, Ohio
John McCarthy _____ Dripping Springs, Texas
Vernon Jones _____ Alameda, California
Willie Jornogin _____ Peoria, Illinois
William Kirkpatrick _____ Eugene, Oregon
Walter Lawrence_____ Sioux City, Iowa
Clarence Mitchell _____ Huntsville, Texas
Lee Moore_____ St. Joseph, Missouri
James Ogg _____ Los Angeles, Calif.
Jack Peak _____ Leonard, Texas

Felix Peterek	Yuma, Arizona
Edgar Peters	Lake Park, Iowa
Robert Ross	Coffeyville, Kansas
Jesus Santos	Hebberville, Texas
Edward Searkey	Lynn, Mass.
George Sharpshire	Scottsville, Ky.
Carl Smith	Oakland City, Indiana
Ralph Spinelli	Sewickley, Pa.
Dale Gilbert	Ashton, Illinois
Virgil Greenaway	Old Hickory, Tenn.
Lloyd Jackson	Holcomb, Missouri
Troy Holt	Fayetteville, Arkansas
Farley Hall	Huntington, W. Virginia
Edward Johnson	Chicago, Illinois
Herman Kelier	Pineola, North Carolina
Richard Kellog	Salinas, Calif.
William Lash	Willioughly, Ohio
Julius Cob	Colorado Springs, Col.
Joseph Stanford	Pittsburgh, Pa.
George Steiner	Loomix, Calif.
Melvin Baxter	Mangum, Oklahoma
Joe Chavez	Belen, New Mexico
Bruce Choate	Little Rock, Arkansas
William Duncan	Troutville, Va.
Elbert Easterwood	Weatherford, Texas
John Elms	Shafter, Calif.
Alfred Farrell	East Rockaway, New York
Burnise Fay	Albuquerque, New Mexico
Nelson Fonseca	San Jose, Calif.
Gordon Fultz	Cresson, Pa.
Dale Gilbert	Ashton, Illinois
Virgil Greenaway	Wayne City, Indiana.

Privates

Ralph Spinelli	Sewickley, Pa.
Joseph Stanford	Pittsburgh, Pa.
George Steiner	Loomis, Calif.
Melvin Baxter	Nangum, Oklahoma

Joe Chavea_____ Belen, New Mexico
Bruce Choate _____ Little Rock, Ark.
William Duncan _____ Troutville, Va.
Elbert Easterwood _____ Weatherford, Texas
John Elms_____ Shafter, Calif
Alfred Farrell _____ East Rockaway, New York
Burnise Fay _____ Albuquerque, New Nexico
Nelson Fonseca _____ San Jose, Calif.
Gordon Fultz _____ Cresson, Pa.
Dale Gilbert_____ Ashton, Illinois
Virgil Greenaway_____ Wayne City, Indiana
Lloyd Jackson _____ Holcomb, Missouri
Troy Holt _____ Fayetteville, Ark.
Farley Hall _____ Huntington, W. Virginia
Edward Johnson   _____ Chicago, Illinois
Herman Kelier _____ Pineola, North Carolina
Richard Kellog _____ Salinas, Calif.
William Lash _____ Willoughly, Ohio
Gerome Leek _____ Marshall, Calif.
Vincent Lemely _____ Livingston, Montana
J.M. Lillard _____ Caddo, Oklahoma
Joseph Limbauch _____ Orosso, Michigan
Chester McGlosson _____ Latonia, Ky.
Peter Connacher _____ Portland, Oregon
Sam Sina _____ RoseadaNew Mexico
James Turner _____ Varnado, La.
Macario Villaloboz_____ Rapid City, South Dakota
William Warren _____ Wichita, Kansas
Buster Wilkerson _____ Deming, New Mexico
Lawrence Williams _____ Lendive, Montana
James York _____ Syracuse, New York
Edward Gordon_____ Jackson, Mississippi
James Newman _____ Forth Worth, Texas
Don Adams _____ Artesia, New Mexico
William Alhschwede _____ Thayer,Nebraska
John Alford _____ Pensacola, Fla.
Uriah Ash _____ Fairmount, West Virginia
William Baker _____ Oakland, Calif.

Lee Bennett _____ Mound City, Mo.
Russel Boatwright _____ Colorado Springs, Colorado
Robert Body _____ Detroit, Mich.
James Boyle _____ Joshua, Texas

Privates

John Braunberger_____ Portland. Oregon
Charles Buchanan _____ Vicksburgh, Miss.
Joe Burks _____ Dumas Texas
Ben Chavez _____ Soboyeto, New Mexico
Harold Memmler_____ Chicago, Ill.
Norman Meon _____ none listed
Roy Morris _____ Covington, Ky.
Henry Peontek _____ Springfield, Ill.
Breed Phillips _____ Tangipahoa, La.
Loren Pierce _____ Princeton, Minn.
Peter Prinat_____ Cleveland, Ohio
Ira Pitts _____ Shawnee, Kansas
Earl Quay _____ Springfield, Mo.
Frank Rawlinson_____ Philadelphia, Pa.
Lawrence Robinson _____ Wayland, Ky.
Marvel Ross _____ Syracuse, New York
Alfredo Sanchez _____ Clayton, New Mexico
Joe Schnieder_____ Los Angeles, Calif.
Lamar Wilkinson _____ Provo, Utah
Clarence Warton_____ Laredo, Texas
Oliver Wetzel_____ Spencer, Iowa
Joseph Wengronowitz_____ Chicago, Illinois
James Teel _____ Texarkana, Texas
William King, Sr. _____ Rey Bay, Alabama
Willia Vincent _____ Klamath Falls, Oregon
Philip Rohde _____ Hamden, Conn.

U.S. Navy Enlisted Men

P/C John Walker_____ Vandergrift,Pa.
LM I/C William Thompson_____ Garott, Kansas
CBM Walter Kain _____ Baltimore, Md.

C/R Ralph Ham_____ Zambales, Philippines
CTM Everett Dillard _____ Cavite, Philippines
F I/C Ralph Taylor _____ LaFollette, Tenn.
GM 3/C George Tarkanish _____ Youngstown, Ohio
M/M I/C Delbert Sparks_____ Louisville, Ky.
C/QM Martin Seliga _____ Fitchburg, Mass.
F 2/C Melvin Moritz _____ Sedro-Wooley, Wash
CMM Robert Monrow _____ Monterey, Calif.
CY Max McCoy_____ San Luis Obispo, Calif.
WT 2/C Orvin Kringler_____ WestEnd, Iowa
Bernard Holen_____ None Listed
CMM Fern Boaz _____ Glencoe, Ky.
S I/C Lynn Brotherson_____ None Listed
F 2/C Joseph Burke _____ San Francisco, Calif.
QM I/C Clovis McAlpin _____ Gilmer, Texas
Charles Kelly_____ Camarines Sur, Philippines
Joseph Herron _____ Preston, Iowa
CMM Robert Pitchford _____ Long Beach, Calif.
SK I/C John Burtz _____ Farrell, Pa.
F 2/C William Girard _____ Ashland Den, Ky.
CM I/C Clarence Hall _____ Grand Crossing, Fl.
Pay Clerk Paul Jackson _____ Long Beach, Calif.
B 2/C Paul Kelsey_____ Suffern, New York
CBM Thomas Kreiger _____ Spring City, Penn.
CY James McCarthy_____ New York City
I/C P O J.E.A. Morin _____ Danver, Mass.
CMM Ernest Richett _____ Shanghai, China
CBM Harry Stefl _____ Pasay, Philippines
EM 2/C Virgil Wemmer _____ Salinas, Calif.
CGM Harry Willis _____ Hamilton, Ohio
AC MM Carl Silverman_____ Wareham, Mass.
GM I/C Thomas Slater _____ Philadelphia, Penn.

U.S. Military - Rank or Branch Not Listed
Thomas Mason, Jr. _____ Elkland, Pa.
Otis Bills _____ Phoenix, Arizona
John Cook, Jr._____ San Marco, Texas
George Distel _____ Washington, D.C.

Kenneth Gorden _____ Merrifield, Minn.
Albert Hayes _____ Lawrenceburg, New Mexico
Olin Johnson _____ Clovis, New Mexico
Alfred Jolley _____ Safian, California
Ira Jeffries _____ Marlington, W. Va.
Jearuld Drown _____ San Diego, Calif.

U.S. Civilians
Edward Normandy Jr. _____ Manila
Osborne Jones _____ None Listed
Hugh Keays _____ Cleveland Heights, Ohio
George Weedon _____ Elberton, Wash.
Max Wait _____ North LIttle Rock, Arkansas
Theodore Rosenberg _____ Easton, Pa.
Raymond Osborne _____ Dayton, Texas
Leonard Menges _____ Manila
Frank Ellsworth _____ Long Beach, Calif.
William Fossoth _____ Pompanga, Philippines
Ray Fouts (or Fouth) _____ Manila
Hale Hutchins _____ Salt Lake City, Utah
Clyde Jenkins _____ Bellflower, Calif.
Jesse Light _____ Manila
Worden Clark _____ Wisconsin
Mason Blair _____ Onawa, Iowa
Robert Bary _____ Orlando, Florida
Dean Albee _____ Eureka, Montana
Joseph Embree _____ Silver Springs, Mo.
J. W. Georgenton _____ Los Angeles, Calif.
John Huntley _____ Manila (Hope, Ark.)
Elmer McNeilly _____ West Orange, New Jersey
John Spradlin _____ Pasay, Rizal, Philippines
Christopher Sullivan _____ Manila
John Thompson _____ Long Beach, Calif.
Dick Verkey _____ San Francisco, Calif.
Carl Stoops _____ Manila

British Military
Sgt. Robert Bell _____ Lancashire, England

Gnr. Stanely Dellar _____ Hitchchin Herts, England
Pvt. George Heeley _____ Birmingham, England
Cpl. Sidney Stevens _____ Lincolnshire, England
Gnr. Reginald Wyatt _____ Kent, England
Cp. George Laytol_____ Cambridgeshire, England
Sglman. Thomas Potter _____ Lavenshire, England
Sglman, Walter Riley _____ None Listed
Cpl. Sidney Stevens _____ Lincolnshire, England
Cnr. Reginald Wyatt _____ Kent, England
Cpl. George Laytol _____ Cambridgeshire, England
Sglman. Thomas Potter _____ Lavenshire, England
Sglman. Walter Riley _____ None Listed
PFC Dennis Keating_____ Essex, England
John Allan _____ London, England
Sgt. Lesley Palmer _____ Suffolk, England
L/Sgt. Herbert Markham _____ Nottingham, England
Driver George Barber _____ Nottingham, England
Pvt. John Cuncliffe _____ Manchester, Lanco, England
AC-I David Hallan_____ Chesterfield, Derby, England
Gilbert Maker _____ Morden, Surrey, England
L/Cpl J.C. Slaughter _____ Norfolke, England
Pvt. George Martin _____ Lancastershire
Sglman. Thomas Potter _____ Lancastershire
Sgt. George Shardlow _____ N. Leicester, England

British Civilians
Leslie McWilliams_____ Cheltenham, England

Dutch Military
Sgt. Dutch Klein _____ Buitenzorg, Java
Pvt. Gerard Van Diggelen_____ Malay, Java
St. Casper Muelman_____ Utrecht, Holland

Norwegian Civilians
Bgorne Leira_____ Aalesund, Norway
Aksel Svendsen _____ Frederecksted, Norway

BIBLIOGRAPHY

Books

Abraham, Abie, Ghost of Batan Speaks. New York: Vantage Press, 1971

Agoncillo, Teodoro A., The Fateful Years: Japan's Adventure in the Phillippines. Quezon City, Philippines: Garcia, 1965

Apple, Benjamin, We Were There At The Battle of Bataan. New York: Grosset & Dunlap, 1957.

Archer, Jules, The Philippines Fight For Freedom. London: Crowell-Colloer-Macmillan Ltd., 1970/

Asprey, Robert B. War In The Shadows. New York: Doubleday & Co., 1975.

Belote, J. H. and W. N. Belote, Corregidor: The Saga of a Fortress. New York: Harper & Row, 1967.

Calvocoressi, Peter ande Guy Wint, Total War. New York: Pantheon Books, 1972.

Conroy, Robert, The Battle of Bataan. London: Macmillan, 1969.

Falk, Stanley, Liberation of the Philippines. New York: Ballantine Books, 1971

Falk, Stanley, The March of Death. New York: W.W. Norton, 1962.

Hartendorp, A.V.H., : The Japanese Occupation of the Philippines. Manila: Bookmark, 1967

Hartendorp, A.V. H., The Santo Tomas Story. New York: McGraw-Hill, 1964.

Hersey, John, Men on Bataan. New York: Alfred A. Knopf, 1942.

Ind, Lt. Col. Allison, Bataan, The Judgment Seat. New York: Macmillan, 1944.

Keats, John, They Fought Alone. New York: J. B. Lippencott, 1963.

Kieth, Billy, Days of Anguish, Days of Hope, New York: Doubleday, 1972.

Krueger, General Walter, From Down Under to Nippon. Washington, C.C.: Combat Forces Press, 1953.

Poweleit, Major Alvin C., M.D. USAFFE, 1975

MacArthur, General Douglas, Reminiscences. New York; Van Nostrand-Reinhold, 1969.

Mellnik, General Steve, Philippine Diary, 1939-1945. New York: Van Nostrand-Reinhold, 1969.

Morton, Louis, The Fall of the Philippines, Washington, D.C.: U.S. Government Printing Office, 1953.

Redmond, Juanita, I Served on Bataan. Philadelphia: J. B. Lippencott, 1943.

Reyes, Pedrito and Mercedes, Grau-Santamaria, Pictorial History of the Philippines. Quezon City: Capitol Publishing House, 1953.

Romulo, Colonel Carlo s P. I Saw the Fall of the Philippines. New York: Doubleday-Daron, 1943.

Rutherford, Ward, Fall of the Philippines. New York: Ballantine Books, 1971.

Smith, Robert Ross, Triumph In The Philippines. Washington, D.C: U.S. Government Printing Office, 1963.

Stewart, Sidney, Give Us This Day. New York: W. W. Norton, 1957.

Taruc, Luis, He Who Rides The Tiger. New York: Fredrick A. Praeger, 1967.

Taylor, Vince, Cabanatuan, Waco, Texas, Texian Press, 1985.

Toland, John, But Not In Shame. New York: Random House, 1961.

Volckmann, Colonel R.W., We Remained. New York: W. W. Norton, 1954.

Wainwright, General Jonathan M., General Wainwright's Story. New York: Doubleday, 1946.

Weinstein, Alfred A., Barbed-Wire-Surgeon. New York: Macmillan, 1961.

White, W. L. They Were Expendable. New York; Harcourt, Brace and World, 1942.

Watari, Gasel, Philippine Expeditionary Force, Japan: Group Information Department, 1943.

Manuscripts, Documents, Official Papers and Military Studies

Hockstrasser, Lt. Lewis B., They Were First - The True Story of the Alamo Scouts, 1944.

"Exposure Under Fire - An Official History of Signal Corps Photography in the Luzon Operations", prepared by U.S. Army Signal Corps, Southwest Pacific Area, 1945.

"Narrative History, 547th Night Fighter Squadron", Albert F. Simpson Historical Research Center, USAF. Maxwell AFB, Alabama, USA.

"Ranger in Review":, Luzon, Philippines: 6th U.S. Army, 1945.

"War History #6", Defense Training Institute; The Japanese Defense Agency, War History Dept., Tokyo, Japan.

"Guide to Japanese Monographs", Office of the Chief of Military History, Dept. of U.S. Army, Washington, DC 1945-1960.

"Japanese Monograph #2 - Philippine 1941-42 Operations Record, Phase I", Office of the Chief of Military History, Dept. of U. S. Army, Washington, D.C.

"Japanese Studies in World War II, 14th Army Operations" Office of the Chief of Military History, Department of U.S. Army, Washington, D.C.

"Japanese Studies in World War II, 14th Army Operations" Office of the Chief of Military History, Dept. of U.S. Army, Washington, D.C.

"Ranger Mission at the Pangatian Prison Camp", Headquarters, 6th Ranger Infantry Battalion, AGO File. U.S. GTovernment Archives, Washington, DC 1945.

"The 6th Rangers - Narrative of the 6th Ranger Battalion from January 2, 145 to July I, 1956", U.S. Government Archives, Washington, D.C.

"The 6th U.S. Army Report of the Luzon Campaign, January 9, 1945 - June 30, 1945, U.S. Government Archives, Washington, D.C.

Wainwright, General Jonathan M. "Report of Operations, U.S. Army Forces, Far East and U.S. Forces in the Philippines; 1941-1942", U.S. Government Archives, Washington, D.C. August 10th, 1946.

Pajota, Major Juan, We Kept the Torch Burning, 1977.

Selected Articles

Bersola, Colonel Pedro C. "We Witnessed General King's Surrender", Philippine Free Press, April, 1972.

Hibbs, Ralph E. M.D., "Beriberi in Japanese Prison Camps", Annals of Internal Medicine, August, 1946.

Mucci, Henry A., Lt. Colonel, "Rescue at Cabanatuan", Infantry Journal, April, 1945.

Mucci, Henry A. Lt. Colonel, "We Swore We'd Die or Do IT!", The Saturday Evening Post, April, 1945.

Mydans, Carl, :"The Rescue at Cabanatuan", Life, Feb. 26, 1945.

St. George, Ozzie, Sgt., "Three Years on Luzon" Yank, March, 1945.

Stroupe, Ray M. Captain, "Rescue By the Rangers", Military Review, December, 1945.

GLOSSARY

1. Bamboo Telegraph - A name given by the GI's to the communication system employed by Filipinos. Effected by "runners" spreading verbal news from one village to the next.

2. Banzai ! - (Literally 10,000 years!) A shout used by Japanese to wish themselves or someone else good luck and long life. In World War II, usually associated with "Banzai Charge" because Imperial troops used it as a war cry when entering battle.

3. BAR - Browning Automatic Rifle. Used by the Sixth Rangers instead of machine guns because it can be carried and fired by one man.

4. Barrio - A small community villiage.

5. Bazooka - Offically "Rocket Launcher, Shoulder Type", also called a "stove pipe." A 2.46 inch rocket launcher with a smooth bore steel tube about five feet long, open at both ends. The Bazooka gained its name from its resemblance to the crude musical horn of the same name used by a radio comedian of the time, Mr. Bob Burns.

6. Bolo - A narrow blade knife 18 - 24" long with a handle made of wood or carabao horn. Used as both a tool and a weapon. Single edge with only a slight curve to the blade.

7. Buri Hat - A wide brim, round hat, handmade from straw.

8. Carabao - Filipino name for a water buffalo, a beast of burden used through out Asia.

311

9.Carabao Cart - A small wooden two wheel cart pulled by a carabao.

10. Constabulary - Similar to our "State Police."

11. DWAKS - A large amphibious tank commonly called, "Ducks!"

12.Ganap - Slang for the former "Sacdalista" headed by Benigno Ramos who took refuge in Japan before the war but continued to send instructions for his followers to cooperate with the Japanese Imperial Army. Collaborators.

13. HUKS - Hukbo Ng Boyan Labon Sa Hapon (Lit. Peoples Army to Fight The Japanese). Also , HUKBALAHAP. Socialist - communist group lead by Luis Taruc from 1938 to about 1955. Today, known as the NPA (New Peoples Army).

14. Leyte - A major island in the center of the Philippine Islands.

15. Ilocano - A "tribe" or group of people found mostly in the Northwestern or Central part of Luzon, the Philippines. The Ilocano language is different from Tagalog.

16. Kamikaze - (Literally "Divine Wind" or "Holy Wind") A name taken by the Imperial Air units whose pilots committed suicide by crashing their planes, loaded with explosives, into enemy targets.

17. Mabuhay ! - A Filipino word meaning, "long life." It is used as a greeting, goodby or, as a war cry.

18.Makapili - (Literally "For Philippines.") Slang for Filipinos who collaborated with the Japanese. The Makapili acted individually. The Ganaps were somewhat organized as a group.

19.Narra - Wood used from the Narra tree which is extremely hard. Often used in the Philippines for flooring, doors and "wood carvings."

20. NCO - Non Commissioned Office

21. Nipa - Grass and bamboo or bamboo strips hand woven together. A Nipa hut, for example, would be a small house made from these materials.

22.PT Boat - Patrol Torpedo Boat. High speed 60 - 100 foot boats were usually equipped with torpedoes, machine guns and "depth" charge explosives.

23. Small Arms - Military slang used to identify rifles, pistols, carbines, etc.

24. Sucking Chest Wound - A wound where the chest and lungs are punctured. The lungs continue to suck in air through the puncture wound.

25. Tagalog - One of over 85 Filipino languages. Now, the "official" language of the Philippines. Also used to identify a group of people whose language is Tagalog. Before World war II, the Tagalogs were located mostly around the Manila Bay area of Luzon, the Philippines

26. Tommy Gun - Thompson submachine gun which fires a .45 cal. bullet. The military model is fed from a magazine type clip rather than a drum.

27. USAFFE - United States Army Far East. The combined American and Filipino Army when the Filipinos were offically inducted into the U.S. Army in 1941. Under the command of General MacArthur.

28. Very Pistol - (Also, Verey). A pistol used to fire a colored signal flare into the air.